Digital Platforms and Transformation of Healthcare Organizations

COVID-19 accelerated healthcare's transition towards digital technology since it helped expand the capacity of healthcare organizations (HCOs) through extended patient access and isolation. In addition to HCOs, this transition was adopted by other participants in the healthcare ecosystem, such as independent digital health platform (DHP) vendors, self-insured employers, drug chains/pharmacy benefit managers, and insurance companies. It was not long before independent DHPs, payers, and self-insured employers realized the value of digital technology, so they increased their commitment towards this transition.

The goal of this book is to help HCOs understand, prepare, implement, and leverage digital transformation. The book opines that, to be successful, digital transformation must be led and supported by senior management. Equally important is the cultural transformation of HCOs towards successful change management, which requires an evolutionary approach to continuous process improvements of increasing scope and complexity. Next, HCOs must generate a comprehensive digital transformation roadmap that aligns with their strategic plan for enhancing clinical and related capabilities while improving patient engagement. To accomplish their digital transformation, HCO management and key stakeholders must comprehend and meet prerequisite requirements for: digital health platforms, advanced information technology, and work transformation methodologies. DHPs, and associated hardware and software complements, form the foundation of digital health technologies prevalent in modern-day healthcare and have gained increasing importance since COVID-19. Advanced information technology includes concepts vital to healthcare transformation such as EHRs, interoperability, big data, artificial intelligence, natural language processing, data security, and privacy. Lastly, work transformation methodologies address work redesign that incorporates different levels of process improvements and phases of digital transformation, lean/six sigma, agile methodologies, and human factors engineering to ensure well-designed interfaces for care providers and patients.

The overarching goal of this book is to provide a roadmap for US healthcare towards an organized digital transformation which will lead to improved outcomes, reduced costs, and improved patient satisfaction.

Digital Platforms and Transformation of Healthcare Organizations

Integrating Digital Platforms with Advanced IT Systems and Work Transformation

Rajiv Kapur

Routledge
Taylor & Francis Group

A PRODUCTIVITY PRESS BOOK

First published 2024
by Routledge
605 Third Avenue, New York, NY 10158

and by Routledge
4 Park Square, Milton Park, Abingdon, Oxon, OX14 4RN

Routledge is an imprint of the Taylor & Francis Group, an informa business

ISBN: 9781032432786 (hbk)
ISBN: 9781032432779 (pbk)
ISBN: 9781003366584 (ebk)

DOI: 10.4324/9781003366584

Typeset in Garamond
by Deanta Global Publishing Services, Chennai, India

This book is dedicated to my wife, Uma, who was my constant source of inspiration, encouragement, and counsel during the writing process. Her ability to listen patiently and ask insightful questions that addressed the heart of the matter never ceased to amaze me. They were instrumental in steering this effort.

Contents

Acknowledgment

I would like to offer special thanks to Rob Frieden for his support and consultation. His practical insight significantly contributed to shaping this book.

About the Author

 **Rajiv Kapur** has worked in the provider-based healthcare sector for over 35 years in different roles. He completed his PhD in Industrial Engineering in 1981 from the University of Texas at Arlington in conjunction with Wichita State University and the Cerebral Palsy Research Foundation of Kansas. The project, Available Motion Inventory (AMI), helped in the development of models that were utilized to modify workspaces and employ severely handicapped cerebral palsied individuals at Boeing Military Aircraft Company.

Kapur then joined Holy Cross Hospital, Silver Spring, Maryland, as a management engineer. He subsequently worked at Georgetown University Medical Center (GUMC) as Senior Management Engineer, Director of Management Systems, and Assistant Administrator, Systems (VP and CIO). At GUMC, he led the design and development of a first fourth-generation language (4GL) electronic health record named patient care information system (PCIS) which was implemented with the help of a grant from Sun Microsystems (now Oracle). Kapur presented his preliminary findings from PCIS at healthcare conferences across Germany, Austria, France, and England. Post GUMC, Kapur worked at SoftMed, a health information management company, as VP and COO, Adventist Healthcare, a mid-Atlantic based healthcare system, as Corporate VP and CIO, and at Doctors Community Healthcare Corporation (DCHC) as Senior VP and CIO.

In 2003 Kapur formed Cura Consulting Solutions, Inc. (Cura) that offered expertise in IT implementations, facilities management, and productivity improvement. He was invited to join Cavanaugh Consulting Group as Principal. Cura provided implementation, integration, and IT management support to several healthcare organizations across the US. Over this period, he regularly met with CEOs, CIOs, senior healthcare executives, HIT teams, and Board of Directors to establish direction, get input, and provide feedback.

Over the years, Kapur has taught undergraduate and graduate engineering and business courses at several universities. He taught as a full-time instructor at Wichita State University while conducting research associated with his PhD. Subsequently, he taught as an adjunct at Virginia Tech, George Washington University, University of Maryland, Georgetown University, and San Jose State University (SJSU). In 2016, he joined Santa Clara University's (SCU) Information Systems and Analytics (ISA) Department, School of Business, as an Academic Year Adjunct Lecturer, which included teaching undergraduate and graduate courses.

In 2021, Kapur decided to document his experience and expertise in optimizing healthcare through the effective design and implementation of HIT systems. This led to the development of this book which was enabled by his professional experience, the emergence of telehealth, and courses taught on software platforms, systems engineering, and information systems.

Over the years, Kapur has presented at several conferences and universities. Most presentations and papers have been related to AMI, PCIS, and methodologies for effectively designing and implementing HIT systems.

Common Acronyms

ACO	Accountable Care Organizations
ADT	Admission, Discharge, Transfer
AHA	American Hospital Association
AI	Artificial Intelligence
AMA	American Medical Association
AMC	Academic Medical Center
API	Application Programming Interface
APM	Alternative Payment Model
AWS	Amazon Web Services
B2B	Business to Business
B2C	Business to Consumer
BA	Business Associate
C-CDA®	Consolidated CDA
CBT	Cognitive Behavioral Therapy
CCD®	Continuity of Care Documents
CDA®	Clinical Document Architecture
CDC	Centers for Disease Control and Prevention
CDO	Chief Data Officer
CDS	Clinical Decision Support
CDTO	Chief Digital Transformation Officer/Chief Digital Officer
CE	Covered Entity
CIO	Chief Information Officer
CISA	Cybersecurity and Infrastructure Security Agency
CISO	Chief Information Security Officer
CL	Capability Level
CMIO	Chief Medical Information Officer
CMS	Center for Medicare and Medicaid Services
CNIO	Chief Nursing Informatics Officer

COPD	Chronic Obstructive Pulmonary Disease
CRM	Customer Relationship Management
CSA	Cloud Security Alliance
CSF	Critical Success Factor (represents goals and objectives of an organization)
DaaS	Desktop as a Service
DAX	Dragon Ambient eXperience
DHP	Digital Health Platform
DICOM	Digital Imaging and Communications in Medicine
DRS	Designated Record Set
DT	Digital Transformation
DTO	Digital Transformation Office
DTx	Digital Therapeutics
EDI	Electronic Data Exchange
EFT	Electronic Fund Transfer
EHI	Electronic Health Information
EHR	Electronic Health Record
EMPI	Enterprise Master Patient Index
EMR	Electronic Medical Record
ERP	Enterprise Resource Planning
FDA	Food and Drug Administration
FFS	Fee for Service
FHIR®	Fast Healthcare Interoperability Resources
FTP	File Transfer Protocol
GPO	Group Purchasing Organization
HaH	Hospital at Home
HCO	Healthcare Organization
HCP	Healthcare Professional
HFE	Human Factors Engineering
HHS	Health and Human Services
HIE	Health Information Exchange
HIMSS	Healthcare Information and Management Systems Society
HIN	Health Information Network
HIPAA	Health Insurance Portability and Accountability Act
HISP	Health Information Service Providers
HIT	Health Information Technology
HITRUST	Health Information Trust Alliance
IaaS	Infrastructure as a Service
IB	Information Blocking

ICD	International Classification of Diseases
IDS	Intrusion Detection System
IHE	Integrating the Healthcare Enterprise
iOS	iPhone OS
IoT	Internet of Things
IP	Internet Protocol
ISO	International Standards Organization
ISV	Independent Software Vendor
KPI	Key Performance Indicator
LLM	Large Language Model
LSS	Lean Six Sigma
M&A	Merger and Acquisition
MDR	Managed Detection Response
MFA	Multi-Factor Authentication
ML	Machine Learning
MRN	Medical Record Number
MSK	Musculoskeletal
MSSP	Medicare Shared Savings Program
NHIN	National Health Information Network
NIST	National Institutes of Standards and Technology
NLP	Natural Language Processing
OCR	Office of Civil Rights
OIG	Office of Inspector General
ONC	Office of National Coordinator of Health Information Technology
OS	Operating System
OSI	Open Systems Interconnection
PaaS	Platform as a Service
PACS	Picture Archiving and Communication System
PCI-DSS	Payment Card Industry Data Security Standards
PCMH	Patient-Centered Medical Home
PERT	Program Evaluation and Review Technique
PGHD	Patient-Generated Health Data
PHE	Public Health Emergency
PHI	Protected Health Information
PHM	Population Health Management
PHR	Personal Health Record
PI	Process Improvement
PII	Personally Identifiable Information

PKE	Personal Key Encryption
PKI	Personal Key Infrastructure
PMO	Project Management Office
QHIN	Qualified Health Information Network
RDS	Remote Desktop Services
RFID	Radio Frequency Identification
RIS	Radiology Information System
RLS	Record Locator Service
RPM	Remote Patient Monitoring
RTLS	Real-Time Location Services
SaaS	Software as a Service
SCM	Supply Chain Management
SDK	Software Development Kit
SDLC	System Development Life Cycle
SDOH	Social Determinants of Health
SIEM	Security Information and Event management
SLA	Service Level Agreement
SMART®	Substitutable Medical Applications and Reusable Technologies
TAT	Turnaround Time
TCP/IP	Transmission Control Protocol/Internet Protocol
TEFCA	Trusted Exchange Framework and Common Agreement
TPO	Treatment, Payment, and Operations
UI	User Interface
USCDI	United States Core Data for Interoperability
UX	User Experience
VDI	Virtual Desktop Infrastructure
VHA	Virtual Health Assistant
VPN	Virtual Private Network

Chapter 1

Introduction

According to the Centers for Medicare & Medicaid Services (CMS), national health spending in the US is projected to grow at an average annual rate of 5.4% for 2019–2028 and to reach $6.2 trillion by 2028. In addition to unsustainable spending levels, the current healthcare system does not adequately consider patient needs such as convenient access to healthcare services.

Digital Platforms

Over the past decade digital platforms have played a key role in disrupting several industries, notably, media, hotel, transportation, publishing, and retail. These platforms are successful in disrupting industries that are information intensive, fragmented, and encumbered by roadblocks and regulatory controls. Platform-intensive industries discovered that well-managed platforms can continually expand producers and consumers, grow market share, redefine markets, and disrupt other industries. For example, iPhone is a misnomer. With the core objective of providing mobile voice services, it has disrupted several industries including email, text messages, personal computers, gaming devices, applications, cameras, navigational systems, and video conferencing. Apple and iPhone are fast becoming key enablers of healthcare's platform for patient engagement.

DOI: 10.4324/9781003366584-1

Adoption of Digital Platforms by Healthcare

Prior to the pandemic, traditional healthcare organizations had been slow to adopt telehealth platforms. However, COVID-19 incentivized the use of telehealth and complements to meet influx of patients and isolation requirements. This adoption was further enabled by the public health emergency (PHE) which eased federal and state restrictions for provider licensure requirements and telehealth payments. The telehealth care model demonstrated the power of digital solutions and the convenience of home healthcare.

In contrast to traditional healthcare organizations, nontraditional providers such as independent platforms, payers, employers, and retailers have increasingly adopted telehealth solutions. These providers initially focused on primary care and specialties such as behavioral health. Over time, they have transitioned to chronic disease management through home care solutions that utilize remote patient monitoring and other AI-enabled technologies for continuous monitoring. Digital services are either acquired, licensed, or developed in-house and are staffed by care providers.

Digital primary care models enable payers and employers to form alliances with traditional healthcare organizations for services across the care continuum. The transition to primary care and the emergence of value-based care by nontraditional providers are explained in a Bain & Company study reported in a 2022 press release. According to the study, 30% of the primary care market could be captured by retailers, payers, and independent startups by 2030. The report authors state that the shift from fee-for-service (FFS) to value-based reimbursement models will accelerate the transition of primary care to nontraditional providers. This is because payers are incentivizing population health management with full capitation arrangements. Besides lowering costs, nontraditional providers of care are demonstrating better clinical outcomes.

Adoption of Digital Health by Healthcare Organizations (HCOs)

Leading healthcare systems have long recognized the power of digital platforms. Besides increasing patient access, these platforms enable innovative care solutions by combining AI technologies with care models. Patient outcomes, along with cost reductions, resulting from these care models are encouraging.

The pandemic required healthcare organizations to use telehealth solutions. Since the height of the pandemic, patient and provider surveys have documented satisfaction with synchronous and asynchronous access to telehealth and AI-enabled care services. However, a majority of HCOs remain reluctant to transition to digital health. This can be attributed to several factors, namely FFS insurance plans, inability to take risks, high capital requirements, lack of a digital health vision, provider resistance, lack of IT capability, and lack of organizational acceptance of digital disruption. This is counter to the direction of value-based reimbursement models favored by nontraditional providers of care which require HCOs to digitally transform their patient services to participate in risk-based arrangements.

The Book

The goal of this book is to help HCOs understand the requirements of digital health solutions including platforms and advanced technologies, and work transformation methods as enablers of innovative care models. The book recommends that successful digital transformation efforts be led and supported by senior management. In addition, HCOs should cultivate a change management culture to effectively transition to functional and process disruptions that result from digital transformation efforts. Prior to initiating digital transformation efforts, HCOs should develop a digital health plan that supports their business objectives and incorporates advanced digital systems to generate care models.

Organization

The premise of the book is that successful digital transformation requires a confluence of digital health platforms (DHPs), advanced information technology, and work transformation methods. In this confluence, the role of work transformation is to enable HCOs to develop innovative care models utilizing advanced digital technologies and IT systems.

The book has been divided into three sections representing digital health platforms, information technology, and work transformation methods. Each section consists of chapters that are linked to the section topic and digital transformation. The organization of the three sections is important in that readers can familiarize themselves with the fundamentals of DHPs including telehealth solutions in Section I prior to reviewing advanced IT systems in Section II followed by work transformation in Section III that includes a framework to help HCOs assess their readiness for digital transformation. Since topics in every chapter include references to additional information in other chapters, readers may read these chapters in a manner that best meets their needs and interests.

Philosophy

The book is an amalgamation of principles, adaptations, case examples, and practical methodologies designed to help HCOs in their digital health journey. Whenever possible, provider-driven healthcare examples have been included to help readers understand the principles and their applications. The book offers guidance for digital transformation efforts of different structures, scope, and complexity of service offerings. The Assessment Framework presented towards the end of the book can be used to assess HCO readiness for digital transformation. It can be customized to meet HCO business goals and digital transformation objectives. Completing the framework results in a gap matrix that can be used as the basis for a remediation plan to improve organizational readiness. The remediation process can increase organizational understanding of the requirements for digital transformation.

Description

Section I focuses on digital health platforms. It includes Chapters 2–6 that address different aspects of digital platforms, including developing a digital health vision. The goal of the first section is to familiarize readers with digital platforms, including telehealth and AI-enabled platforms used in the delivery of healthcare. As HCOs increase adoption of digital health models, they will uncover innovative ways to use digital technologies to improve patient outcomes and satisfaction. To accommodate these innovations, it is important to understand the foundations of digital health platforms. This section discusses factors that influence the emergence of telehealth and other DHPs. It is designed to help HCOs understand ways to select digital health solutions that can meet their current and future digital health needs.

Chapter 2 briefly explains the principles associated with digital platforms, including reasons for their popularity and growth. This chapter includes the drivers of e-commerce platforms along with examples of provider-based healthcare. The goal of this chapter is to introduce readers to the foundations of digital platforms including architecture and classification. Understanding these foundations is key to understanding telehealth systems and complementary DHPs.

Chapter 3 discusses DHPs including telehealth systems which include several communication channels such as video conferencing, phone, secure email, and text messaging. This chapter discusses design and operational similarities and differences between e-commerce and healthcare platforms. The analysis is designed to help users further their understanding of factors that influence the design of DHPs. The chapter includes a classification of digital health platforms that accommodates health information exchanges, data analytics and functional complements. It explains the concepts of application programming interfaces (APIs) and their role in DHP innovation. While HCOs and vendors have adopted FHIR APIs for data exchange, aggregation, and analytics, most have not adopted APIs to encourage third parties to develop complements for their platforms. This can be a source of significant revenue generation, as evidenced by e-commerce platforms such as Salesforce, Twilio, and Amazon. Third-party enhancements on DHPs can be helpful in meeting HCO functional and workflow requirements.

Chapter 4 explains the different configurations that can be used by DHPs, including telehealth solutions. By understanding potential DHP configurations and associated case scenarios, and mapping them to their digital health vision, HCOs can understand the platform configuration that can meet that vision. In addition to telehealth systems, this chapter also discusses configurations for specialty platforms such as SCM, speech recognition, EHRs, and PACS/RIS.

Chapter 5 offers a methodology for developing a digital health strategy and criteria for selecting DHPs. This includes platform architecture, categories, configuration, and governance philosophies. While most HCOs participate as buyers of products and services on DHPs, a few may consider ownership and management partnerships to influence platform direction. In that context, this chapter offers management strategies for owning and managing DHPs.

Chapter 6 discusses different types of platforms accompanied by examples. This chapter is designed to help HCOs understand different DHP types in order to operationalize their digital health vision.

The goal of Section II is to introduce readers to IT systems that can effectively support DHPs and work transformation efforts of different levels of complexity. The field of information technology is too broad and complex to be covered in these chapters, but an attempt has been made to cover

IT systems that are required for digital transformation efforts. This section covers a range of topics including management and usability of EHRs and IT systems, data interoperability, AI models, security, privacy, and technical considerations. These topics have been covered in four chapters.

Chapter 7 explores the value of IT to organizational business strategy, IT governance philosophy that supports central leadership augmented with decentralized project prioritization and ownership, IT management strategies, and project management methodologies that engage functional users to ensure that desired project outcomes are met. This chapter is critical since support of senior management is the principal driver of successful digital transformation efforts.

Chapter 8 discusses issues and recommendations associated with the usability of EHRs, AI systems, and DHPs. These systems are designed for use by physicians, nurses, ancillaries, allied health professionals, and patients. This chapter addresses factors that influence the usability of EHR and other IT systems. These are important for designing digital healthcare models that satisfy care provider and patient requirements. The chapter concludes with human factors engineering techniques that utilize user interface design principles and design thinking methods to develop information systems that optimize user experience.

Chapter 9 introduces readers to interoperability, digital data sets, and AI systems. Due to the fragmented healthcare model, data interoperability is key to generating the patient longitudinal health record that includes data from intelligent devices, public agencies, and HIEs. It concludes its discussion on interoperability by providing information on various HIEs including ONC's TEFCA, a key enabler for nationwide interoperability of patient information.

Since digital health generates large data sets, it is important to leverage big data through AI-supported analytics that recognize trends and patterns and can be used as major clinical decision support and image recognition. This chapter discusses key considerations related to AI-enabled systems, including AI bias, clinical applicability, FDA guidelines, security, privacy, and workflow integration. The goal of this chapter is to guide reader understanding of patient data exchange and analytics in digital transformation efforts.

Chapter 10 discusses cybersecurity and ways to reduce the threat of cyberattacks and compromises to patient privacy. It considers security and privacy frameworks and also offers tools and techniques for HCO consideration. It recommends that HCOs must obtain cyber-insurance which offers the added benefit of gap analysis and remediation based on insurer cybersecurity requirements. Lastly, this chapter includes technical consider-ations related to cloud computing, client devices, and network configuration that improve cybersecurity while also adapting to digital health require-ments. Lack of adequate security and privacy will impact the ability of HCOs to transition to digital health models.

The third section discusses work transformation methods, tools, design principles, and an assessment framework to assist HCOs with their digital transformation efforts. While the design principles and assessment frame-work chapters are a culmination of principles, requirements, and findings stated in prior chapters, work transformation is essential to successful imple-mentation of digital transformation projects.

Chapter 11 divides work transformation efforts into process improvement levels and digital transformation phases of increasing scope and complex-ity. It recommends that HCOs establish a change management culture prior to digital transformation and recommends a methodology for establishing the culture. In addition, this chapter includes examples of several HCOs that leverage virtual systems to innovate the care process. Chapter 12 presents tools and techniques that support process improvement and digital transfor-mation efforts in HCOs.

Chapter 13 offers a compendium of design principles from previous chapters. These principles are presented in a table and each principle is linked by a reference to the chapter from which it is derived. HCOs should review these principles prior to reviewing the Framework presented in Chapter 14. The Assessment Framework is designed to assess HCO readiness for digital transformation (DT). Since the Framework assesses diverse top-ics, it is recommended that HCOs form a DT steering committee including functional experts who can assess topics included in the Framework. The steering committee will be responsible for understanding and customizing the Framework prior to assessing each objective and generating gaps to be remediated prior to DT efforts.

This book includes underlying principles, methodologies, and tools that are supported by practical solutions and case examples to enable digital transformation efforts. It is designed to serve as a guide for HCOs and a ref-erence source for educators and startups interested in digital healthcare.

DIGITAL HEALTH PLATFORMS (DHPS)

The goal of Section I is to introduce readers to the fundamentals of digital health platforms and criteria for selecting DHPs, including telehealth platforms, that best meet their digital health strategy. Chapters in this section include discussion on principles that drive digital platforms; technological considerations, including architecture, categories, and configuration; and examples of different types of DHPs, including telehealth and intelligent complements. In addition, Chapter 5 introduces a guide for developing digital health strategy, techniques for digital health management, HCO participation levels on DHPs, and governance protocols for DHPs. This section includes the following five chapters: Digital Platforms – A Primer, Introduction to DHPs, DHP Configurations, DHP Strategies, and DHP Types.

After reading Section I readers understand that operationalizing a digital health vision may consider using several DHPs, including telehealth platforms. HCOs embarking on their digital health journey should consider telehealth systems that can support flexible configurations and are architected to encourage alliances with other platforms, partners and third-party innovators, integration for improved workflows, and compliance with future advancements.

DOI: 10.4324/9781003366584-2

Chapter 2

Primer: Digital Platforms

Introduction

Marketplaces have enabled the sale of goods and services as long as humans have engaged in trade. They evolved into physical malls to enable storeowners and consumers to congregate in a defined area. However, the reach of malls, in terms of the number of shops they can accommodate and the area from which they can draw consumers, is limited. These limitations were further exposed with the commercialization of the internet where shopping in e-marketplaces was only limited by the buyer's ability to access the internet. Therefore, from the outset, the internet has been a disruptive tool to the traditional ways of doing business.

The use of the internet as a disrupter of traditional businesses further evolved when digital platforms began leveraging it as an infrastructure and coordination mechanism. For example, instead of using the internet for sales of "physical" newspapers, the publishing industry was transformed by digitizing news and making it available over the internet, eliminating the traditional paper medium and its logistical complexities. In the world of digital platforms, the digital and physical worlds began to converge.

The fundamental requirements of disruption via digital platforms are to leverage advanced technologies with disruptive workflows, and a redefined scope, to alter the value structure while extending market share.

Example 1: Amazon was founded as an e-commerce company to sell books over the internet. It subsequently expanded operations by including goods and services including an e-marketplace to aggregate third-party

DOI: 10.4324/9781003366584-3

sellers. This was enabled by a highly automated logistics management system. Amazon also disrupted the computing industry through Amazon Web Services (AWS) by providing cloud computing services to help businesses store and process application systems and big data. Amazon continues to disrupt different industries, notably the publishing industry through the development of digital readers, digital books, and disintermediation of traditional publishers.

Example 2: Apple transitioned from a traditional product company to iTunes – connecting people on their iPods to music on iTunes acquired through publishers. They subsequently made available application programming interfaces (APIs) and software development kits (SDKs) for iOS (iPhone OS) to third-party developers. Submitted applications undergo review and approval by Apple developers prior to acceptance in the App Store. This empowers external developers to contribute to the platform by developing quality games, education, and other software which enhances the value of the platform.

Several Silicon Valley companies such as Facebook (publishing market), Airbnb (hotel/lodging industry), Uber (taxi market), and Google (informing equalizer) were started on the foundations of digital platforms by creating value through interactions between external producers and consumers. As of January 31, 2023, the market capitalization of these companies was as follows: Facebook – $394.77 billion, Airbnb – $70.38 billion, Uber – $62.03 billion, and Google – $1.28 trillion. Other technological giants, Apple, Microsoft, and Amazon, leveraged their traditional portfolios to develop digital platforms and operate in hybrid mode – traditional and platform. As of January 31, 2023, the market capitalization of these companies was as follows: Apple – $2.26 trillion, Microsoft – $1.85 trillion, and Amazon – $1.05 trillion. These examples illustrate how US companies have leveraged digital platforms for growth.

The following primer discusses the principles on which e-commerce, social media, and other digital platforms have been developed. While digital platforms operate under the same foundational principles, they are customized to meet the requirements of different industries. Once we have discussed principles for digital platforms, we will transition to digital health platforms in Chapter 3.

Explaining Platforms

Traditional Organizations

Traditional businesses control all aspects of production and generate a finished product from raw materials (see Figure 2.1). Their operations follow a

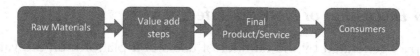

Figure 2.1 Traditional organizations.

pipeline configuration since they sequentially add value to raw materials, to generate the finished product/service. Traditional businesses focus on lowering production cost by increasing supply. This enables them to sell their products at lower prices and improve market share. They operate under supply economies of scale.

Digital Platforms

Digital platforms use advanced technologies to manage the generation of value for their ecosystem. A basic configuration of digital platforms is included in Figure 2.2. As the figure indicates, digital platforms support functionality that enables interactions between producers, developers, suppliers, and consumers.

Digital platforms focus on increasing demand through improved value for platform participants – producers and consumers. They operate under demand economies of scale, a term used by two experts largely responsible for popularizing the concept of network effects, Hal Varian, Chief Economist of Google, and UC Berkeley Haas Business School Professor Carl Shapiro. Demand economies of scale are fueled by increasing value experienced by platform users with an increase in the number of users. They are the principal drivers of value for digital platforms.

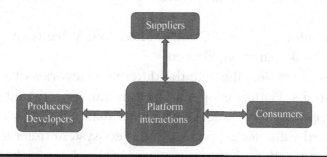

Figure 2.2 Basic configuration of digital platforms.

A Brief Discussion of Network Effects

The impact generated by the number of users of a platform on the value created for each platform user is termed network effects. In well-managed platforms this process builds on its own success; increased value attracts additional users to the platform which further increases value for platform users generating a virtuous cycle. The impact of positive network effects can alter markets for products and services. However, platforms that introduce friction can reduce value for platform users as the number of users on the platform increases. This phenomenon is termed negative network effects and can be detrimental to the platform. Successful platforms minimize negative network effects while optimizing positive network effects. Since well-managed platforms can redefine and expand markets, their valuations are higher than comparable traditional businesses.

Classification of Digital Platforms

In broad terms digital platforms can be classified as *transaction* platforms, which provide value to participants through online marketplaces, and *innovation* platforms, which provide value to participants through third-party innovation on their platform. Most modern-day digital platforms operate as *integration* platforms, a combination of *innovation* platforms and online marketplaces. *Integration* platforms operate marketplaces for third-party complements – hardware, software, and services – that further enhance the value of *innovation* platforms for participants.

Examples:

Transaction Platforms: Apple App Store, Google Play Store, Airbnb, Uber, Amazon Marketplace, Facebook social network, Salesforce Exchange

Innovation Platforms: Apple iOS, Google Android, Facebook for developers, IBM Watson, Microsoft Azure, Amazon Web Services, Airbnb development platform

Integration Platforms: Apple, Google, Microsoft, Valve (game developer), Salesforce, Facebook, Amazon, Tencent

The previous examples illustrate the different categories of platform-based organizations. Platforms operate best in multi-sided configurations which, when appropriately designed, generate maximum network effects through improved value for all parties in the ecosystem (refer to Figure 2.2, for example). *Transaction* platforms are marketplaces for exchange of goods, services, or information. They capture a fee from sales or through advertisements (Cusumano, Yoffie and Gawer 2020). *Innovation* platforms provide value to participants through third-party innovations such as data aggregation, software, hardware, and service to continuously enhance their platform. These innovations enhance value to ecosystem participants through network effects and subsequent increase in market size. These platforms generate revenues through direct consumer sales.

Digital platforms manage their ecosystem by analyzing data available on the platform. They use the resultant analytics to reduce friction and generate optimal matches between buyers and sellers, improve curation, and invite external complements (*innovation* platforms). This strategy can continuously improve the state of digital platforms and user experience and provides several revenue sources. For example, innovation social media platforms can generate revenues by aggregating and analyzing user data for advertisement revenues and third-party sales.

Platform Design

The design of a platform begins with defining the key interaction desired on the platform. This key interaction is called "core interaction." A core interaction is the value exchange that attracts users to the platform. Platform designers understand core interactions in traditional industries and roadblocks that impact the efficiency and effectiveness of these interactions. They then design platforms that support workflows to circumvent or eliminate roadblocks while disrupting the industry. Federal regulators continue to implement laws to regulate platforms that continuously charter new territories in their "disruption" journey.

Digital platforms that have generated strong network effects focus on the platform design by considering the following: platform participants including different types of sellers and buyers, platform-supported products or services, efficiently and effectively matching buyers with sellers. In this discussion, *sellers* and *buyers* can be interpreted as *creators* and *consumers*. For example, Facebook has creators or sellers who post updates and friends who consume it. When friends respond to the updates, they become creators and the recipients become consumers. This cycle continues to generate network effects. Since owners and operators develop platforms for use by the ecosystem of developers and users, their design is focused on making their platform offerings attractive to the ecosystem and making it easy for consumers to find the products and services they are looking for on the platform.

A key requirement for digital platform startups is to attract users to the platform. They must start with producers and sellers to attract consumers and buyers. This "equation" between balancing producers and consumers tilts to consumers once there are enough producers to attract them to the platform. The question is how to initially attract producers and sellers to the platform. This can be done through incentives, and demand aggregation benefits for smaller producers and sellers to get visibility through the platform. In conjunction with "seeding" the platform with product/service offerings, it must attract consumers and buyers. This can be done by advertisements or by attracting users to the platform to use product/service offerings. While advertisements can bring users to the platform, only active participation keeps users coming back to the platform and contributes to increased network effects.

The assumption for designing digital platforms is that consumers will pay for platform-related products and services. Therefore, designers focus on making the platform convenient and easy for consumer access, navigation, and locating desired products/services. This attracts more buyers and sellers to the platform. On the other hand, most payments for healthcare services and products are invoiced to public and private payers. Private payers manage insurance plans on behalf of employers. This impacts platform design, which is discussed in Chapters 3–5.

Platform Architecture

As mentioned, platforms should be architected for easy (*frictionless*) access, navigation, and location of products/services offered on the platform. A key design feature for successful interactions is platform *openness* to users, developers, and other actors in the ecosystem. Digital platforms that are not open to users will likely drive them away, while those that do not offer tools and techniques for third-party developers will eliminate a potential source of revenue while reducing platform innovation and value to users.

Platforms with multiple owners and operators are likely to be more "open" in order to consider the goals and objectives of different owners/ operators. While this impact is real, it cannot be controlled by changes to platform architecture. Therefore, in this section, we will discuss platform openness criteria in relation to platform users and producers/developers that

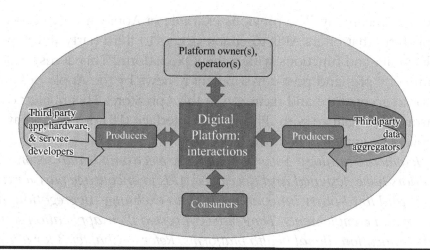

Figure 2.3   Platform design considerations: users and third-party developers.

are managed by platform designers. Platform design considerations related to users and producers are represented in Figure 2.3 and discussed below.

A. **Openness to users:** A key driver of digital platforms is user participation. When user participation involves creation of value units, then platform architecture must allow "frictionless" seeding of content. However, too much openness introduces poor-quality content which leads to negative network effects. Therefore, to maintain content quality and resultant network effects, platforms must enable curation tools/mechanisms for screening and feedback, along with governance policies that promote quality content. A challenge faced by social media and other content platforms is to maintain a balance between the right to free speech and content quality.

   Healthcare analogy: "Openness" of patient-protected health information is covered under HIPAA privacy and security regulations that permit the use of patient information for treatment, payment, and operations. Therefore, user access to patient information must conform to HIPAA requirements in digital health platforms. Refer to Chapter 3 for additional information.

B. **Openness to third-party developers of software, hardware, and services complements:** Platform architecture that offers different types of APIs to third-party developers and data aggregators transitions to openness. Salesforce, Amazon, Apple, Facebook, and Google have used public APIs to generate significant revenues while enhancing their value to users. Managing digital platforms implies understanding the power of the "API" economy. The previous example of Apple and iOS describes a platform that offers APIs to enable access to third-party developers to select data and functions within the iOS platform. This access is accompanied by pre- and post-development reviews by the Apple design team prior to acceptance and inclusion in the App Store. This quality control ensures compliance with iPhone user interface (UI) design and avoids duplicate complements in the App Store.

Healthcare analogy: Several healthcare electronic health record (EHR) vendors have designed and developed APIs to encourage partner extensions and third-party innovations in data exchange, aggregation, and functional complements. They have converted their application software into innovation digital health platforms. Refer to Chapter 3 for additional information on the categories of innovation platforms in healthcare.

Disruption Strategies Used by Digital Platforms

While industries in the past have been transformed through automation and work redesign, platform-based transformations have disrupted multiple industries. As previously mentioned, digital platforms utilize advanced digital technologies to enable users to connect, network, and gain value. A goal of successful digital platforms is to provide excess value – more value than that expected by users. For example, shopping on Amazon provides users access to difficult-to-find products and services at aggressive pricing while saving time to travel and search for products and services. In addition, *recommendation engines* direct users to purchase products and services they were not originally looking for. So, while users are purchasing products and services, they are also getting added value through recommendation engines, access to a vast variety of products and services from across the world, excellent supply chain, and competitive pricing. This keeps consumers coming back to the platform. In turn, sellers get access to a vast array of worldwide consumers.

Since digital platforms incentivize external resources, management must "look" to the ecosystem for production and sales. As a result, well-established digital platforms with strong network effects are difficult to compete against. Examples are Amazon, Walmart.com, Microsoft Office, Salesforce, eBay, Expedia.com, and Facebook.

There are several ways by which digital platforms disrupt organizations. The following five strategies are noteworthy.

1. **Creating new forms of value:** platforms are designed to enable self-service for producers and consumers. They accomplish this by lowering participation barriers for platform producers which attracts value to the platform. This in turn attracts consumers to consume the value. For example, platforms such as YouTube, Twitter, Quora, and Facebook have become authoritative sources of consumer-generated media, information, and communication.

   Healthcare analogy: Smart wearables, devices, and health apps are enabling self-help care for patients by monitoring and managing their health. In addition, apps such as Apple Health can aggregate, format, and upload patient health information from these devices linked to the iPhone for patient and provider use.

2. **Restructuring consumption of products and services:** people renting their homes (Airbnb), people using their vehicles as taxi service (Lyft, Uber), people using services to deliver meals and groceries (Amazon Prime, Door dash, Uber Eats), elderly using services for transportation to and from their medical appointments (Uber, Lyft).

   Healthcare analogy: providing at-home care, instead of traditional onsite care, for chronically ill patients. For example, intelligent monitors and care protocols can enable hospital-at-home models that provide acute-level care at home through hybrid care models.

3. **Resource sharing:** can be accomplished by separating asset from value. This strategy is effective for reducing business capital expenditures while increasing revenues. For example, businesses can share expensive assets such as manufacturing plants.

   Healthcare analogy: Cohealo allows expensive equipment (MRIs, CT scan) to be shared between hospitals lowering capital expenses for involved hospitals.

4. **Eliminate or automate intermediaries:** traditional publishing houses continue to be replaced by the Amazon publishing platform where consumers decide the fate of published materials instead of publishers; advertising agencies are being replaced by Google AdWords, Twitter, Facebook, and other social media platforms.

   Healthcare analogy: eliminate "friction" in the patient care process. For example, instead of patients calling provider offices to schedule and modify appointments for onsite visits, providing online access to schedule and modify appointments is convenient and leads to improved patient satisfaction. Patient engagement is further increased if providers offer

*multiple modalities, such as text, secure emails, phone calls, and video
visits, for more immediate consultation.*

5. **Aggregation:** provide a central market to serve widely dispersed individuals and organizations. Amazon marketplace is an example of market aggregation.

   *Healthcare analogy: a transaction platform to enable an ecosystem of
   behavioral healthcare providers to connect with patients. This benefits
   patients and providers.*

Business Participation on Digital Platforms

We have previously discussed business platforms that cater to consumers, partners, and businesses such as developers of applications, hardware, and services. While consumers and businesses can purchase and sell products and services on digital platforms, businesses can also participate on digital platforms through ownership and operation which are two separate and distinct functions. For example, platform owners may choose to contract with other business(es) to operate the platform which requires establishing platform governance policies, configuration decisions regarding platform openness, and architecture. Platform operators must also understand ways to engage ecosystem participants to generate network effects. Options for business participation on platforms are presented in Figure 2.4.

Option A: Businesses buy and sell products and services on platforms. Most platforms operate marketplaces to handle third-party sales. The demand by platform buyers drives value for each platform participant through increased sales, improved service, and lower costs. Businesses participate on platforms to buy and sell supply chain services, electronic data interchange (EDI), electronic fund transfer (EFT), software, hardware, and services. They benefit from demand aggregation on platforms. Examples: Amazon, Microsoft, Apple, and Google.

Option B: In this option, platforms are owned and operated by the same business(es). Depending on its architecture, third-party vendors can buy, build, and sell on the platform. This model affords control over platform architecture, including revenue capture, since platform operators (managers) own the platform. Both Apple iOS and Facebook platforms were closed to outside developers at the outset but subsequently supported APIs to

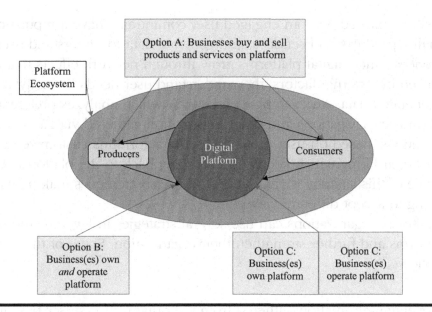

Figure 2.4   Options for business participation on digital platforms.

accommodate third-party innovations which spurred growth. Examples: Apple iOS, Salesforce, Amazon, and Facebook.

Option C: In this option, platforms are owned by a business(es) and operated by another business(es). Businesses with similar interests may own a platform that is operated by another business to compete with other platforms. For example, Orbitz was formed by several airlines to compete against Travelocity. The other option is where the owner of a platform encourages multiple operators to accelerate platform growth. For example, Google purchased Android OS to compete with iOS and decided to open its architecture and allow device makers (operators) to customize and sell mobile phones using Android, for example, Samsung, LG, Huawei, Nokia, Sony, and Motorola (Parker, Van Alstyne and Choudary 2016).

Healthcare platforms: Healthcare organizations (HCOs) principally utilize Option A by participating on digital health platforms (DHPs) to utilize products and services. In contrast, nontraditional providers of care such as employers, payers, and retailers principally own/operate DHPs (Options B and C).

Transitioning Traditional Businesses to Platforms

As traditional technology companies have demonstrated, it is a good business strategy to transition their product offerings to platforms provided they are well established with an engaged user community, have a reputation for quality products and services, and generate data to understand user preferences. Since digital platforms grow through network effects that are influenced by external factors, they understand user needs by analyzing user-generated data. An example is Facebook which analyzes preferences based on user navigations and other information gathered via Facebook conversations. Based on user preferences, the algorithms customize news feeds to their liking which keeps users coming back to the platform. A consequence of this strategy is "hardening" of user preferences making users unwilling to accept different viewpoints.

Traditional organizations can use several strategies to leverage the power of platforms and further strengthen their organization. Some of these strategies follow:

1. Leverage information gathered from the organization's user base to design platforms that supplement the organization's existing products and services. This strategy is widely used since it assumes low risk yet can increase sales for the organization. For example, Walmart.com complements traditional brick-and-mortar stores and provides APIs for third-party development.
2. Convert a product line into a platform. Apple used this strategy when it developed iTunes to supplement sales of iPods. It contracted with music producers to sell directly on iPods. This moved iPods from a product to a music platform with Apple controlling the marketplace for music. Another example is application vendors who convert their application systems into a platform by offering software as a service (SaaS) configuration. Since many of these application vendors continue to design and manage traditional application systems, they operate as hybrid organizations.
3. Convert the entire traditional organization to platform configuration. This is the riskiest of all strategies and should be executed with care since it also requires management restructuring and training.

HCOs transition from traditional to platform operations by utilizing the first two strategies. For example, most HCOs are using digital platforms such as telehealth and digital complements, to supplement service offerings which can be classified as the first strategy. On the other hand, select health systems have created, or are in the process of creating, virtual care centers that work with traditional brick-and-mortar care to extend service offerings. In this instance virtual care centers can be classified under the second strategy.

Key Takeaways

1. Digital platforms have been used to disrupt organizations throughout the US, Europe, and China.
2. Market capitalization of platform-oriented organizations is significantly higher than comparable traditional organizations.
3. Traditional organizations operate in a supply-side economy of scale whereas platforms operate under demand economies of scale which can shift the demand curve to increase market size.
4. Network effects is the impact number of platform users have on the value created for each user on the platform.
5. There are two types of platforms – *marketplace* and *innovation*. *Marketplace* platforms facilitate transactions between buyers and sellers whereas *innovation* platforms encourage partner and third-party innovations to improve user value on the platform. Both types of platforms can be integrated to operate as *integration* platforms.
6. Platform architecture can be open or closed and is dependent on ownership/management, level of user access, and APIs.
7. Platforms can disrupt traditional businesses in several ways, including creating new forms of value, restructuring consumption of products and services, resource sharing, eliminating or reducing user "friction," and demand aggregation.
8. Platform ecosystem for businesses consists of buyers, sellers, owners, and managers (operators). Businesses can also leverage platforms through partnerships with other businesses.
9. Managing platforms requires a rethinking of techniques by focusing attention on the ecosystem as opposed to internal operations.

References

Cusumano, Michael A., David B. Yoffie, and Annabelle Gawer. 2020. "The Future of Platforms." *MIT Sloan Management Review*. February 11. https://sloanreview.mit.edu/article/the-future-of-platforms/.

Parker, Geoffrey G., Marshall W. Van Alstyne, and Sangeet Paul Choudary. 2016. *Platform Revolution*. New York/London: W.W. Norton & Company.

Recommended Readings

Cusumano, Michael A., David B. Yoffie, and Annabelle Gawer. 2020. "The Future of Platforms." *MIT Sloan Management Review*. February 11. https://sloanreview .mit.edu/article/the-future-of-platforms/.

Evans, David S., Andrei Hagiu, and Richard Schmalensee. 2008. *Invisible Engines*. Cambridge, MA: The MIT Press.

Parker, Geoffrey G., Marshall W. Van Alstyne, and Sangeet Paul Choudary. 2016. *Platform Revolution*. New York/London: W.W. Norton & Company.

Shapiro, Carl, and Hal R. Varian. 1998. *Information Rules:A Strategic Guide to the Network Economy*. Brighton, MA: Harvard Business School Press.

Tiwana, Amrit. 2014. *Platform Ecosystems*. Waltham, MA: Morgan Kaufmann.

Van Alstyne, Marshall W., Geoffrey G. Parker, and Sangeet Paul Choudary. 2016. "Pipelines, Platforms, and the New Rules of Strategy." *Harvard Business Review*. April. https://hbr.org/2016/04/pipelines-platforms-and-the-new-rules-of -strategy.

Zhu, Feng, and Nathan Furr. 2016. "Products to Platforms: Making the Leap." *Harvard Business Review*. April. https://hbr.org/2016/04/products-to-platforms -making-the-leap.

Chapter 3

Introduction to Digital Health Platforms (DHPs)

Introduction

The pandemic highlighted telehealth platforms as key enablers of patient care by simplifying patient access while meeting isolation requirements. Telehealth platforms support multiple communication modalities such as secure email, SMS/text messaging, voice calls, and video calls that make it convenient for patients to engage with care providers. These modalities are enabled by patient portals that offer a digital front door.

The adoption of telehealth platforms by HCOs was assisted by the congressional passage of public health emergency (PHE) which relaxed federal and cross-state provider licensing requirements and enabled CMS and private payers to compensate care provision via telehealth modalities. This care process also simplified provider workflow and increased satisfaction with telehealth systems.

In addition to accommodating patient care requirements introduced by the pandemic, virtual care models have demonstrated the ability to improve patient outcomes through population health management (PHM) and value-based care. According to a McKinsey & Company analysis telehealth encounters have the potential to save $250 billion in healthcare expenditures annually across covered populations (Siwicki 2022).

The following discussion focuses on factors that influence the design of DHPs, design and operational similarities and differences between

DOI: 10.4324/9781003366584-4

e-commerce and healthcare platforms, current state of DHPs, key stakeholders of DHPs, platform architecture, and platform classification.

Factors That Influence Design of Healthcare Platforms

Chapter 2 discussed the disruptive potential of nonhealthcare platforms, including e-commerce marketplaces and innovations. These platforms disrupt industries by removing roadblocks and reducing governmental regulations. While telehealth and other digital platforms have demonstrated their disruptive potential, they operate under regulatory controls that cannot (and should not) be disrupted. These controls are designed to enable longitudinal patient records, protecting healthcare providers and patients from unregulated intelligent platforms and, most importantly, protecting the security and privacy of EHI. DHPs are mandated to abide by HIPAA security and privacy rules, which are associated with stiff non-compliance penalties.

In addition to regulatory controls, healthcare reimbursement systems continue to influence the delivery of care. For example, telehealth platforms cannot be designed to principally attract consumers since they are not the primary payer for platform-offered services. Instead, these platforms must form alliances with businesses such as HCOs, payers, and employers to attract members and patients. Fortunately, the transition towards value-based reimbursement is aligning the design of telehealth platforms towards consumerism. While the reasons for designing platforms to attract consumers to healthcare and e-commerce platforms are different, healthcare platforms are moving towards service offerings to increase patient engagement.

Similarities: Healthcare and E-commerce (Nonhealthcare) Platforms

Regardless of healthcare environmental factors, there are design and operational similarities between e-commerce and healthcare platforms. Both platform categories rely on large sets of information, partnerships, third-party contributions, and M&As and contribute to innovative hybrid workflows.

Information

- E-commerce platforms manage the ecosystem by analyzing data generated on the platforms. Without this analysis e-commerce platforms cannot curate functional offerings to expand the ecosystem of their users.

■ Healthcare platforms analyze healthcare data generated through intelligent devices and digital platforms to improve patient care. However, that does not necessarily expand the ecosystem.

Alliances

■ E-commerce platforms improve their value to ecosystems through partnerships and alliances to enhance their functional offerings.
■ Healthcare platforms participate in partially or fully capitated reimbursement alliances with traditional and nontraditional providers of care.

External Contributors

■ E-commerce platforms rely on third parties to improve their ecosystem. These enhancements generate a significant revenue model while enhancing value for platform users.
■ Healthcare platforms rely on partners and third-party software, hardware, and service contributors to enhance the value of their platforms, for example, CDS and intelligent devices.

M&As

■ E-commerce platforms rely on mergers and acquisitions to expand functionality.
■ Healthcare platforms continue their trend towards mergers and acquisitions to support a broader spectrum of the care continuum.

Hybrid Workflows

■ E-commerce platforms combine virtual, brick-and-mortar, AI, and intelligent machines to generate desired workflows.
■ Healthcare platforms realize their digital health vision through workflows that combine multiple modalities such as onsite, virtual, intelligent devices, and home health to generate hybrid care models.

Differences: Healthcare and E-commerce Platforms

The following categories outline design and operational differences between e-commerce and healthcare platforms.

Design

- E-commerce platforms are driven by network effects, the value derived by platform users due to the number of platform users. As users experience value, the platform attracts new users, which in turn increases value for all platform participants. These platforms increase active users by reducing "friction." This continuously increasing cycle of active consumers and producers shifts the demand curve. Implicit in this growth is the assumption that producers and consumers act based on their best interests through platform participation.

- Healthcare platform design and operation is impacted by payers and regulatory controls. Consumers who use DHPs for care provision are generally not the reimbursors of services. Their participation is the result of employer sponsored insurance plans and reimbursement criteria. Therefore, these platforms cannot grow through consumer demand, rather they grow through contractual arrangements with HCOs, employers, and payers. With the advent of value-based care, DHP designs are also becoming consumer oriented. While this design re-orientation can shift the demand curve through increased patient engagement, it will likely not result in increased reimbursement due to capitation models.

Core Offerings

- E-commerce platforms operate as multi-sided platforms that include sellers, buyers, developers, and service providers. These platforms grow quickly through powerful network effects.

- Healthcare platforms generally operate in a one-sided mode by offering a comprehensive array of services that integrate technology, applications, protocols, and care providers. This inhibits network effects and ecosystem growth.

Management

- E-commerce platforms grow by managing the external ecosystem of users.

- Healthcare platforms use traditional alliances, partnerships, and contracts to increase platform participation.

Disruption

- E-commerce platforms disrupt governmental regulations, intermediaries, and other controls, to reduce "friction" for users and generate network effects.
- Healthcare platforms cannot disrupt regulatory controls or payer mandates which prevents them from generating network effects.

Analysis: Healthcare and E-commerce Platforms

The analysis of differences between e-commerce and healthcare platforms indicates that it is difficult for healthcare platforms to generate strong network effects due to regulatory controls, insurance plans, and one-sided platform configurations. Given these constraints, it is difficult, not impossible, for the emergence of a predominant healthcare platform.

However, similarities between these platform types indicate that healthcare platforms generally operate as e-commerce platforms. For example, healthcare platforms must also analyze patient information, be efficient and effective for care providers and patients, form alliances and partnerships, encourage third-party contributions, and offer flexible configurations to accommodate innovative workflows.

Lastly, healthcare platforms should provide patients easy access to their health information to enable increased patient engagement.

Digital Healthcare: Digital healthcare organizations continue to disrupt existing care models within their ecosystem by improving care efficiency and effectiveness. Continued transition to capitated payment models will increase the use of DHPs to improve outcomes and lower costs. In healthcare, this level of "disruption" will be welcome.

Current State of DHPs

Since the start of COVID-19, the number of DHPs has grown around a few themes: primary care, urgent care, behavioral health (includes a broad range of acuity), benefits navigation, physical therapy (PT)/musculoskeletal (MSK) care companies, and chronic disease management. This growth has been fueled by significant investments by venture capitalists in DHPs which has resulted in fragmented patient care.

Digital healthcare continues to shift towards virtual and in-person offerings by traditional and nontraditional providers of care. Traditional providers include HCOs whereas nontraditional providers include independent digital health platforms (DHPs), payers, and employers. Most payers and employers own and operate telehealth platforms and service offerings. On the other hand, HCOs participate as buyers of products and services on telehealth and other DHPs. Regardless of platform ownership and participation, digital health models rely on care coordination through multi-disciplinary teams that utilize advanced digital technologies and AI systems to develop innovative care models.

In order to extend their services across the care continuum, nontraditional providers supplement virtual telehealth care with home healthcare provider visits (Amazon) and in-store clinics (Walgreens). In addition to extending their range of services, nontraditional providers form alliances and contracts with HCOs to generate hybrid care models that use combinations of in-person care, telehealth, home health, and intelligent devices. These hybrid models are further enabled by contracts between traditional and nontraditional providers to support value-based reimbursement models.

According to the 2021 Amwell/HIMSS Analytics survey providers are using different telehealth modalities, namely video, phone, patient portal, and text, to support chronic condition management, prescription refills, surgical or inpatient follow-up, primary care, urgent care, acute care/specialty consults, musculoskeletal care, behavioral health, and other outpatient visits. Patients prefer video modalities; however, they use phone and patient portal to order prescription refills. This same survey indicated that "roughly 1 in 6 integrated delivery networks and 1 in 5 academic medical centers reported using eight or more platforms for digital care" (Amwell 2021).

The survey documents an increase in the use of platforms by both providers and patients. Large HCOs, such as multi-entity health systems and academic medical centers (AMCs), use several platforms to support virtual services. This has been largely fueled by the imperative to combat the pandemic, an increasing recognition of the value of digital health, and focus of healthcare platforms on select service offerings. Multiple platforms can introduce lack of provider familiarization and ineffective workflows, patient difficulties in accessing electronic health information (EHI) and services, and increased security and privacy risks.

DHP consolidations are on track to provide patient diagnosis and treatments for the most prevalent health problems in the US. For example, (a) Teladoc, primary care provider, acquired Livongo Health that specializes in comprehensive diabetes management; (b) Carbon Health which combines in-person clinics with virtual primary care has acquired Steady Health, an integrated diabetes care platform; (c) One Medical, a membership-based primary care provider, is launching Impact, a homegrown solution to support digital chronic care management.

The pace of DHP mergers and acquisitions (M&As) accelerated in 2021 due to their financial viability but has slowed down in 2022. Rock Health computed the following digital health M&As over three years: 146 in 2020, 273 in 2021, and 144 for the first three quarters of 2022. These M&As reflect the desire of DHPs that offer select services (such as primary care and mental health) to add new services while increasing the depth and scope of their existing offerings. The 2022 Q1–Q3 statistics reflect inflationary concerns, economic contraction, and global factors (Nagappan, et al. 2022).

Key Stakeholders of DHPs

The healthcare ecosystem comprises a variety of stakeholders namely HCOs, members/patients, employers, payers, vendors, standards and regulatory organizations, health information exchanges (HIEs), pharmaceuticals, researchers, and suppliers. Vendors include makers of medical devices, instruments, IT systems, and third-party complements. HIEs can be configured as local, state, regional, and national organizations to support interoperability and offer value-added services.

As mentioned, care provision is transitioning to virtual models supported by HCOs, independent DHPs, payers, and employers. These stakeholders configure and utilize DHPs in different ways to make healthcare accessible to members, consumers, and patients while reducing costs and improving outcomes.

1. Nontraditional providers of care – Independent DHPs: Independent DHP owners and operators offer a range of services to meet the needs of patients, traditional and nontraditional providers of care. Several independent DHPs have transitioned to hybrid care models that combine virtual care with home health and in-person care. These services can be used directly by patients or through referrals from HCOs, payers, and employers.

2. Nontraditional providers of care – Payers and Employers: Payers/Employers who have transitioned to provide patient care services, primarily own, and operate DHPs. Several have transitioned to hybrid care models that combine virtual care with home health and in-person care. These platforms are designed for use by members and employees.

NOTE: The configuration of the platforms discussed in 1 and 2 above centers around a telehealth platform that comprises electronic information systems (specialty application systems and EHRs) and telecommunication technologies (videoconferencing, streaming media, store-and-forward imaging, internet, and wireless communications). These platforms are staffed by physicians and other care providers (employed or affiliated)

3. HCOs: HCOs primarily adopt virtual and at-home care models by participating as buyers on vendor DHPs. The healthcare landscape comprises telehealth and DHPs that use a variety of configurations to support a broad range of services. Leading HCOs have developed software applications, including AI models, to support their clinical requirements. These applications can be offered for sale on a marketplace to other providers. Select HCOs also participate as owners and managers of DHPs to meet their digital health requirements. HCO ownership and management of DHPs can be accomplished individually or in conjunction with partners including HCOs and independent DHPs.

HCO participation levels on DHPs, including ownership and management, are discussed in Chapter 5.

DHPs: Openness and Intelligence

As stated in Chapter 2, the platform architecture defines its "openness" to impact platform users and third-party developers. The degree of "openness" is also influenced by the number of owners and operators of the platform since several owners/operators can require platform architecture to accommodate different philosophies to achieve platform goals. Changes to platform architecture due to multiple owners/operators are influenced by their goals and therefore cannot be redesigned. The following discussion addresses the impact of platform architecture on users and third-party developers.

DHP Openness to Users

HIPAA security and privacy requirements control the "openness" of DHPs to users. This implies that access to protected health information is strictly regulated and controlled by DHPs. Therefore, it is not possible to design DHPs to provide users access to information other than that allowed by HIPAA for treatment, payment, and operations. For example, healthcare platforms offer proxy access to patient family members and caregivers to limit access to patient protected health information.

DHP Openness to Third-Party Developers

In order to enhance platform functionality through external developer contributions, DHPs can be architected to support data and functional APIs. Data APIs support interoperability and AI analytics namely clinical decision support (CDS) and PHM. Functional APIs support application, hardware, and service systems. DHPs that provide well-designed and developed APIs to partners and third-party vendors attract complements for increased platform "intelligence" and value. In fact, e-commerce platforms consider APIs as key product offerings to attract quality extensions and complements. The following discussion details the different types of APIs and how they can be used by DHPs.

APIs are interfaces that allow external software programs to interact with core functionality in digital platforms. They provide specifications for use by third-party developers to leverage platform functionality and data sets. The design of platform APIs influences the flexibility in acquiring partners and platform growth. They can be used by third parties to develop AI models, applications, analytics, and software/hardware complements.

APIs can be configured as public or private/partner. Public APIs are open and available to other organizations for innovation and use. Platforms that provide public APIs are restricted in the assets they share, have a vision of third-party innovations they wish to attract, and are carefully designed for security. In addition, third-party innovations on platforms, continue to add value for platform users. Public APIs have been used by platforms to generate significant revenues, for example, Google Maps, Facebook, Twitter, Salesforce, Amazon, and Twilio.

Private APIs are used by internal platform developers and are less restrictive in terms of shared assets. These APIs are more commonly used as compared to public APIs. Private APIs are customized for partners that enter into formal relationships with a platform. For example, DHPs that enter into contractual relationships with extension developers provide increased access to shared assets while imposing quality control requirements to improve the quality of third-party extensions on the platform.

APIs can support access to functional routines as well as data on digital platforms. Platform complements through APIs have long been encouraged by progressive platform vendors such as SAP, Salesforce, Airbnb, Amazon, Apple iOS, and Google Android. For example, Twilio shares its functionality, such as text messages, phone calls, SMS shortcodes, VOIP, two-factor authentication, and more through APIs to customers; Google shares its Google Maps functionality through APIs that can be embedded in automobile navigation systems; Salesforce offers APIs to share information with customer systems. It also offers partner apps on its platform marketplace.

EHR vendors such as Athenahealth, Allscripts, and Epic have recognized that besides core platform offerings they must work with third-party vendors to enhance platform functionality while accommodating HCO workflow requirements. This concept is further extended through marketplaces that offer healthcare services.

EHRs and DHPs utilize FHIR® APIs to enable data interoperability, a federal mandate documented in ONC's 21st Century Cures Act designed to give patients access to their EHI. This Rule requires healthcare to utilize standard APIs to enable secure access to patient EHI. API data exchange via FHIR (the federal government standard) allows mobile applications to request data elements needed for the product's functions which is useful as healthcare operations transition towards smartphones. For example, SMART on FHIR is an ONC-sponsored standard used by Apple Health to extract data from EHRs and incorporate relevant patient-generated data into the EHR.

In general, healthcare vendors have been slow to adopt APIs as a significant component of their functional enhancement and revenue generation strategy.

Classification of DHPs

DHPs are classified based on their architecture and value offerings to the ecosystem. E-commerce platforms are generally classified as *transaction* (or marketplace) and *innovation*. In this definition, *transaction platforms* provide value to platform participants through completed transactions between buyers and sellers and *innovation platforms* provide value to platform participants through third-party data aggregators, functional complementors, and extension developers. Most modern-day platforms accommodate third-party innovations in a marketplace (for example, an app store). These platforms are architected as *integration platforms* which include innovation and transaction capabilities.

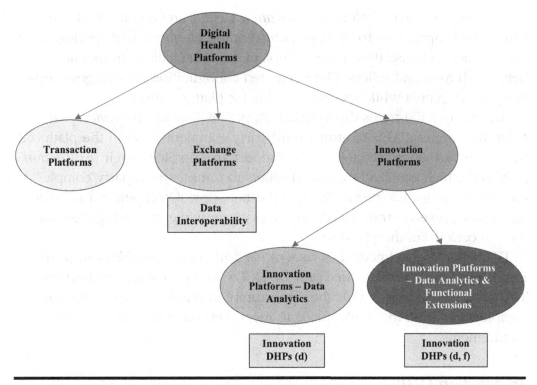

Figure 3.1   Classification of digital health platforms (DHPs).

To accommodate healthcare operations, DHPs have been classified into three categories (refer to Figure 3.1): *transaction* (marketplace) *platforms*, *exchange platforms*, and *innovation platforms*. The category of *exchange platforms* reflects the importance of data interoperability in the evolution of digital health. In addition, *innovation platforms* have been subdivided based on their ability to support data, and functional complements from third parties who are independent developers or partners.

Innovation DHPs are subdivided into *Innovation DHPs (data)* that support third-party data analytics, for example, analytics, CDS, PHM, and image AI models, and *Innovation DHPs (data, function)* that support data analytics and functional extensions/complements. Based on this classification, DHPs that support third-party data and functional innovations offer flexibility in meeting HCO digital health needs.

As stated, *innovation DHP (d)* and *innovation DHP (d, f)* define different levels of third-party innovations on the platform. Subsequent references to DHPs that promote innovations will be classified as *innovation* DHPs. If necessary, the classification will specify whether the *innovation* DHP supports data and/or functional complements.

As in e-commerce platforms, *innovation* DHPs can be combined with *transaction* capabilities to operate as *integration platforms* that support a marketplace to house third-party complements and facilitate transactions between buyers and sellers. The integrated configuration encourages third-party development while increasing value for platform users.

An example illustrates this concept. Apple's iOS is an *integration platform* that supports APIs to attract third-party complementors to the platform. Apple has further architected iOS to support an App Store, their *transaction platform*, which enables buyers and sellers to transact third-party complements such as games, productivity, and other apps. iOS captures a percentage of each revenue transaction on the platform while increasing the value users receive from the platform.

DHPs that are architected as *integration platforms to enable third-party innovation and a marketplace* provide HCOs with customization options. This architecture gives HCOs the opportunity to purchase and implement complements from the marketplace to meet their functional and workflow requirements.

Transaction DHPs

Figure 3.2 offers a representation of the ecosystem for healthcare transaction or marketplace platforms. These platforms are digital health marketplaces that generate value by connecting ecosystem participants and promoting sales of supplies, access to staffing services, and access to patient care services. The platform architecture minimizes friction and curation to connect buyers and sellers quickly and accurately. It captures transactions that occur on the platform for tracking and revenue generation. Transaction platforms leverage data gathered on its platform to attract more consumers and producers. The following features serve as examples:

- Offer tools to attract users to the platform and implement rules for platform participation and attractiveness.
- Leverage demand aggregation, by providing a marketplace of different providers and suppliers. This helps provide visibility to different types of providers and suppliers and in turn gives consumers access to a broad variety of providers and suppliers.
- Generate analytics to improve curation and offer improved matches between consumer requirements and sellers.

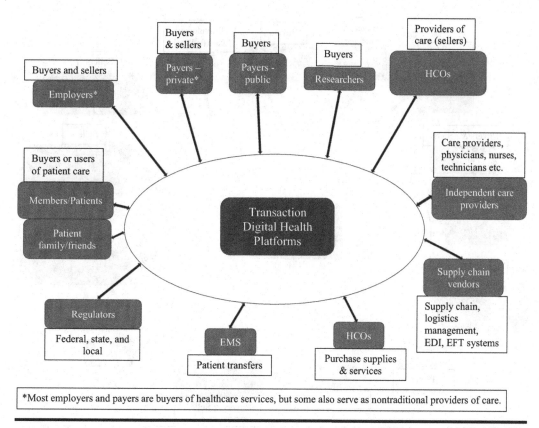

Figure 3.2   A representation of digital health platforms (transaction mode) and their ecosystem.

Exchange DHPs

Figure 3.3 offers a representation of the ecosystem for healthcare *exchange* and *innovation platforms*. As the figure indicates ecosystem of these platforms can include participants that can be buyers and sellers. For example, United Health is an insurance provider – buyer of patient services and seller of patient services (staffed by their team of providers and telehealth solutions). Also, HCOs can be buyers of supplies and sellers of services on these platforms.

Exchange platforms enable data interoperability between different participants of the healthcare ecosystem and are commonly referred to as health information exchanges (HIEs) or health information networks (HINs). In addition to operating as mechanisms for data exchange, several HIEs store patient data to enable state quality reporting and other requirements. Use cases offered by HIE platforms that store patient data have been discussed in Chapter 9.

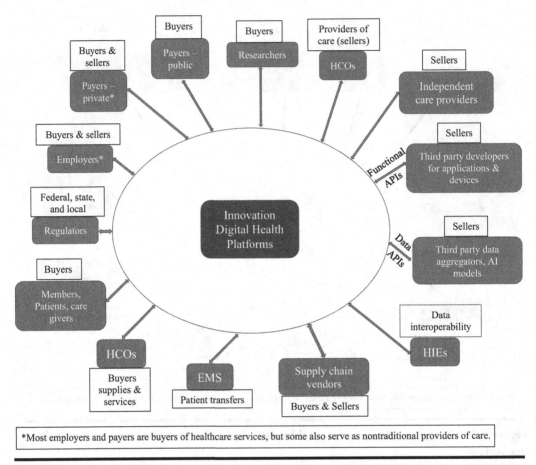

Figure 3.3 A representation of digital health platforms (innovation mode) and their ecosystem.

- HIEs are implemented at the local, state, regional, and national levels to facilitate patient data interoperability.
- These platforms serve a major function within the US healthcare system and operate under governance protocols that reduce risk to the security and privacy of patient data.

Innovation DHPs

Innovation DHPs can be configured to offer data and/or functional APIs to help HCOs meet their functional requirements. These platforms offer APIs that can be used by external developers or partners to provide functional extensions and complements which can be in the form of software, hardware, and service enhancements. Healthcare entities participating on innovation DHPs gain value through core functional offerings of the platform enhanced by third-party applications, devices, and integration services and analytics including PHM, risk assessment, AI models for CDS, and image AI algorithms.

- ■ *Innovation* DHPs provide APIs to data and function complementors to leverage their products and services directly and enhance platform value.
- ■ *Innovation* DHPs generate data and gather data from devices, HCO-EHRs, and other sources within its ecosystem. It is important for the platform and participants to validate AI algorithms for bias prior to use.
- ■ *Innovation* DHPs that wish to offer a marketplace to third-party developers can be architected as *integration platforms*.

As a result of extensions and complements, *innovation platforms* can employ additional revenue generation strategies through licensing and support services.

Post Pandemic Adoption of DHPs by HCOs

Since the end of the COVID pandemic, several HCOs have significantly reduced or eliminated their use of telehealth systems. This is due to a reduction in patient volume, telehealth expenses, uncertainty of permanent legislation around federal licensure requirements, and telehealth payments. Most of all, the use of telehealth systems has been reduced or eliminated by HCOs that are unable or unwilling to digitally transform their operations to generate a digital health strategy.

On the other hand, telehealth's potential has been evident to independently owned and operated DHPs, payers, retailers, and employers who have become the new wave of *nontraditional patient care providers*. These *providers* have been expanding their offerings for members and patients across the care continuum by (a) consolidating services and technologies through M&As, (b) supplementing virtual care with home healthcare, and (c) implementing in-person care models in retail stores and other areas.

Leading health systems have integrated telehealth and advanced clinical decision support models in their care models to be at the forefront of digital health. They are well positioned to expand their patient care options, participate in value-based arrangements, and partner with *nontraditional providers*.

In order to select telehealth and other DHPs to meet their digital requirements, Chapters 4 and 5 discuss DHP configurations, service offerings, and governance protocols. In addition, Chapter 5 discusses strength, weakness, opportunities, and threats (SWOT) analysis to develop a digital health vision and participation levels on DHPs that include ownership and management.

Key Takeaways

1. DHPs include asynchronous and synchronous telehealth modalities such as video conferencing, phone, patient portal, secure email, and text.
2. The COVID-19 pandemic resulted in the funding and development of DHPs that provide similar services. This platform sprawl has led to a disjointed approach to virtual care.
3. According to a McKinsey & Company analysis telehealth encounters have the potential to save $250 billion in healthcare expenditures annually across covered populations.
4. Since the onset of COVID-19, the number and type of service offerings from DHPs have expanded to include primary care, urgent care, behavioral health (to support a range of acuities), benefits navigation, PT/MSK companies, and chronic disease management.
5. Key stakeholders, own and operate DHPs in different ways to make healthcare more accessible to members, consumers, and patients while reducing costs and improving outcomes. These stakeholders are DHPs, payers, self-insured employers, and HCOs.
6. Payers and employers who own DHPs direct their employees to these platforms. They enter into contracts with other employers, independent DHPs, and payers and, whenever possible, form risk alliances with HCOs to generate accountable care organizations (ACOs) & value-based reimbursement models.
7. HCOs enter into contracts with other HCOs, independent DHPs, employers, and payers and, whenever possible, form risk alliances to generate ACOs.
8. HCOs can leverage DHPs as buyers, sellers, owners, and operators. HCO use of DHPs depends on their clinical requirements.

9. DHP architecture should support APIs to allow innovation from partners and third parties. The design and quality of APIs dictate the quality of complements available on the DHP.
10. DHPs can be architected to operate under the following categories: transactions, data exchange, data innovation, and data/functional innovation. Integration platforms are architected to support marketplaces within innovation platforms. HCOs should select telehealth platforms and DHPs that meet their strategic needs.
11. The analysis of differences between e-commerce and healthcare platforms indicates that it is difficult for healthcare platforms to generate strong network effects due to regulatory controls, insurance plans, and one-sided platform configurations. Given these constraints it is difficult, not impossible, for the emergence of a predominant healthcare platform.
12. Similarities between these platform types indicate that healthcare platforms must analyze patient information, be efficient and effective for care providers and patients, form alliances and partnerships, encourage third-party contributions, and offer flexible configurations to accommodate innovative workflows.
13. Digital healthcare organizations continue to disrupt existing care models within their ecosystem by improving care efficiency and effectiveness. Continued transition to capitated payment models will increase the use of platforms to improve outcomes and lower costs. In healthcare, this level of "disruption" will be a welcome relief.

References

Amwell. 2021. "Building the Future of Virtual Care: Streamlined, Scalable, Sustainable. Insights from Amwell's 2021 Survey of Health Plans, Hospitals and Health Systems, and Clinicians." *Connected with Care.* September 28. https://connectwithcare.org/building-the-future-of-virtual-care-streamlined-scalable-sustainable-insights-from-amwells-2021-survey-of-health-plans-hospitals-and-health-systems-and-clinicians/.

Nagappan, Ashwini, Josh Moscato, Jackie Palermo, and Uday Suresh. 2022. "It Takes Two: Exploring 2022 Digital Health M&A Trends." *Rockhealth.* November 7. https://rockhealth.com/insights/it-takes-two-exploring-2022-digital-health-ma-trends/.

Siwicki, Bill. 2022. "Cleveland Clinic Leader: Telehealth Now a 'Permanent Mode' of Care Delivery." *Healthcare IT News*. February 1. https://www.healthcareit-news.com/news/cleveland-clinic-leader-telehealth-now-permanent-mode-care-delivery.

Recommended Readings

Bennett, Jessica. 2022. "What is an API, and How Does it Work?" *Salesforce*. Accessed October 2022. https://www.salesforce.com/products/integration/resources/what-is-an-api/.

Hoffman, Chris. 2021. "What is an API, and How do Developers Use Them?" *How to Geek*. August 12. https://www.howtogeek.com/343877/what-is-an-api/.

Lauret, Arnaud. 2015. "Should Every Company consider Providing an API?" *Nordic APIS*. June 9. https://nordicapis.com/should-every-company-consider-providing-an-api/.

Walker, Alyssa. 2022. "What is API? Full Form, Meaning, Definition, Types & Example." *Guru99*. October 22. https://www.guru99.com/what-is-api.html.

Wilde, Erik. 2020. "Designing Private, Partner, and Public APIs: What's the Difference?" *Axway Blog*. August 19. https://blog.axway.com/learning-center/apis/api-management/private-partner-public-apis-whats-the-difference.

Chapter 4

Digital Healthcare Platform Configurations

Introduction

Chapter 3 introduced digital health platforms (DHPs), differences with e-commerce (nonhealthcare) platforms, DHP architecture, and categories. It surmised that due to similarity in requirements, the design for DHPs is similar to e-commerce platforms; however, the growth of healthcare platforms is controlled due to regulatory and payer requirements.

Most discussion on DHPs centers around the use of telehealth to provide patient services of different levels and complexity which can be classified as key interactions. Patient services and associated interactions are disrupted through DHPs based on their configuration and services provided. In this chapter we will introduce DHP configurations for telehealth systems and complementary platforms that enable digital care models. Each DHP/telehealth configuration includes patient care scenarios to help HCOs select the most appropriate solution for their digital health requirements.

Platforms are configured to offer services to their ecosystem. Chapter 4 discusses DHP configurations that can serve HCOs of different sizes, scope, and complexity. Telehealth platform configurations include a telehealth system which supports voice, video, SMS/text, and secure email communication, EHR applications, specialty modules that assess and support the workflow of diseases, data interoperability, workflow integration support, and care providers that operate the platform.

DOI: 10.4324/9781003366584-5

Vendor-developed telehealth platforms are configured in a variety of ways to accommodate a broad range of care models – from providers who want to extend virtual primary care for their patients to HCOs that intend to digitally transform their care models using a variety of DHPs. For example, configuration requirements for telehealth platforms that support at-home care such as hospital-at-home and chronic disease management using biometric monitors and digital therapeutics must be driven by clinical protocols and complementary DHPs that together form the telehealth system.

DHP Architectural Considerations

Since APIs are key enablers of ongoing innovation on DHPs, it is important to reiterate the power of APIs to form alliances and partnerships with other businesses and customers. APIs allow HCOs, partners, and third-party developers to access information or software functional capabilities from platforms. According to Mulesoft, "Today's APIs have become so valuable that they comprise a large part of many business revenues. For example, on average, 35% of organizations' revenue is now generated by APIs and related implementations. These companies are contributing to a marketplace of thousands of APIs, otherwise referred to as the API economy" (Frye n.d.).

It is important for DHPs to distinguish themselves by the variety and quality of their API offerings. Each DHP develops and maintains core platform functionality and relies on APIs to attract data and functional enhancements. Therefore, as part of their due diligence, HCOs must explore the variety and quality of third-party enhancements, to meet their desired functionality and workflows. HCOs should remember that well-configured and well-managed DHPs continue to offer innovative APIs to increase value for participating HCOs.

M&A activities can impact the architecture of DHPs depending on integration strategy. This can result in slow responding platform apps, malfunctioning telehealth equipment, and a disparate collection of functional systems. The challenge faced by HCOs is to understand existing DHP functional offerings and architectural homogeneity to generate seamless care models.

Definitions: Telehealth and Digital Health

Telehealth

The Health Resources Service Administration (HRSA) describes telehealth "as the use of electronic information and telecommunications technologies to support long-distance clinical health care, patient, and professional health-related education, public health, and health administration. Technologies include videoconferencing, the internet, store-and-forward imaging, streaming media, and terrestrial and wireless communications" (HRSA 2019).

Since "electronic information" in the HRSA description broadly refers to patient's electronic health record, this chapter includes software systems such as EHRs and specialized application modules responsible for the generation and storage of electronic information. These systems work in conjunction with telecommunication technologies to form a comprehensive telehealth solution.

Digital Health

According to the FDA "the broad scope of digital health includes categories such as mobile health (mHealth), health information technology (IT), wearable devices, telehealth and telemedicine, and personalized medicine" (FDA 2020).

Another digital health perspective from Zdnet "digital health can cover everything from wearable gadgets to ingestible sensors, from mobile health apps to artificial intelligence, from robotic carers to electronic records. Really, it's about applying digital transformation, through disruptive technologies and culture change, to the healthcare sector" (Best 2019).

Telehealth Configurations

Tables 4.1–4.5 illustrate five telehealth configurations used by DHP vendors depending on their service offerings, target market, and stage of evolution. Each configuration is designed to support different scopes and complexity of offerings designed to meet HCO telehealth requirements. DHP configurations are also dictated by vendor offerings, prevalence, variety, and quality of APIs, third-party alliances, and complements.

Telehealth (A) – turnkey configuration: offer turnkey solutions including telehealth platforms (telecommunication technologies, specialty applications, and EHR), providers, data exchange, and *third-party data complements*. In this configuration, patient data is exchanged with HCO EHR, and patients are cared for by the DHP providers. DHPs that primarily offer turnkey configurations operate as one-sided marketplaces of services.

Telehealth (B) – flexible configuration: Like telehealth (A) this configuration offers a turnkey solution including telehealth system, providers, data exchange, and *third-party data complements*. However, this configuration can support HCO-EHRs and HCO providers. This flexibility can accommodate HCO workflows that require in-house providers to leverage DHP service offerings.

Telehealth (C) – configuration supports a broad range of services: this configuration offers a range of services and system options including turnkey services, data exchange, and *third-party data and functional complements*. This configuration can accommodate HCOs that prefer to use in-house EHR and specialty applications to better accommodate HCO workflows and in-house providers. It is the most flexible configuration both in terms of service offerings and accommodating third-party innovations.

Telehealth (D) – telecommunication technologies: this configuration offers telecommunication technologies, data exchange, and third-party data complements. It can be embedded in HCO EHR, specialty applications, and support HCO providers. The effectiveness of this configuration is contingent upon workflow integration with EHR applications.

DHP (E) – digital marketplace: this solution offers a digital marketplace for patient care, purchasing supplies, renting equipment, staffing, etc. These platforms offer turnkey solutions that connect HCOs with consumers, providers, suppliers, and HCOs.

DHP configurations A, B, C, and D center around telehealth platforms. Following these discussions, we will explore specialty applications using examples of supply chain management (SCM), medical speech recognition, and EHR platforms.

Note: HCOs that are in the process of evaluating telehealth and other DHPs for their digital health needs should review vendor platform governance philosophies presented in Chapter 5.

Telehealth (A) – Turnkey Configuration (Refer to Table 4.1)

Telehealth configuration A comprises a turnkey solution in which the vendor owns and operates the telehealth system comprising telecommunications technologies, software complements, EHR, and application systems. This solution includes care providers that are employed or affiliated with the telehealth vendor.

This configuration can support a variety of telehealth solutions depending on their service offerings. A lack of system flexibility can inhibit the platform's ability to support HCO workflow requirements. These platforms can be architected to encourage third-party data analytics and algorithmic developers to enhance their functional offerings. HCOs should therefore determine whether platform-offered services and analytics can meet their current and future needs and whether third-party solutions can help.

Table 4.1   DHP Configuration A: Turnkey System, Third-Party Data Complements

Functions	Offering Organization
Telecommunications technologies	DHP owned & operated
Application modules to support patient care	DHP owned/licensed
EHR	DHP owned/licensed
Care providers: physicians, nurses, allied professionals	DHP employed or affiliated
HCO workflow customization	Limited
Data interoperability with HCO	DHP supported API
Optional Configuration	
Data analytics and AI models	Partners & third-party vendors – dependent on DHP architecture

Telehealth Scenario 1

A rural hospital wishes to extend service hours for primary care, behavioral health, and care coordination services for its patients using a digital solution that includes providers.

■ **Proposed Telehealth Configuration:** Since the hospital wishes to extend service hours while providing remote primary care, behavioral health, and care coordination services, it should consider a vendor-developed telehealth platform that offers turnkey services (Configuration A). The hospital should confirm that the selected platform offers desired services and can interface patient data back to their EHR. It should also assess DHP governance philosophies (refer Chapter 5) that impact the security and privacy of patient data as well as the quality of third-party extensions that can further enhance patient experience.

Telehealth Scenario 2

A hospital would like to offer *on-demand* and *scheduled* primary care e-visits by utilizing platform-affiliated providers. Hospital providers will continue to provide in-person patient visits. The hospital would like patients to schedule virtual or in-person appointments through the hospital-sponsored patient portal depending on physician availability.

- ■ **Proposed Telehealth Configuration:** The hospital should consider telehealth configuration A since on-demand and scheduled primary care provides patients access to both hospital-based care providers using the hospital EHR or telehealth-based EHR and care providers. Patients can access available providers through their portal. HCO and vendor EHR systems can exchange data via an HIE platform.

Telehealth (B) – Flexible Configuration (Refer to Table 4.2)

Telehealth configuration B comprises a turnkey solution in which the DHP vendor owns and operates the telehealth system comprising telecommunications technologies, software complements, EHR, and specialty application systems. This solution includes care providers that are DHP employed or affiliated. The flexibility of this configuration allows it to be used by HCO-affiliated providers and EHRs.

Depending on the services offered by the telehealth platform, configuration B can accommodate HCO workflow requirements for a variety of telehealth solutions including chronic diseases and remote acute care management. In this configuration, telehealth vendors encourage third-party data analytics and algorithmic developers as part of their offerings. These platforms can be architected to accommodate a marketplace to house third-party data analytics and AI models which can complement HCO workflows. HCOs should therefore determine whether platform-offered services and analytics can meet their current and future needs and whether third-party solutions can help their functional workflow requirements.

Table 4.2 DHP Configuration B: EHR Flexibility, Third-Party Data Complements

Functions	Offering Organization
Telecommunications technologies	DHP owned & operated
Application modules to support patient care	DHP owned/licensed
EHR	DHP or HCO owned/licensed
Care providers: physicians, nurses, allied professionals	DHP or HCO employed or affiliated
HCO workflow customization	Broad. Enabled by the flexibility in sharing subsystems between DHP and HCO
Data interoperability with HCO	DHP supported API
Data analytics and AI models	Partners and third-party vendors
Optional Configuration	
AI models available on DHP marketplace	DHP can be architected to offer partner & third-party complements via e-marketplace

Telehealth Scenario 3

A hospital has developed a three-year strategic plan to transition care models to digital health. It would like to implement its telehealth system in phases – starting from primary care and extending their virtual care offerings to at-home management of chronic heart diseases and diabetes.

- ■ **Proposed Telehealth Configuration:** Depending on services offered by telehealth platforms configured as B and in-house operational requirements, the hospital can consider configuration B platforms. For example, if the hospital is satisfied with core platform functional offerings that include specialty applications in its telehealth solution, digital therapeutics, and biometric monitors to manage at-home heart health and chronic diabetes, it should consider configuration B. This configuration also gives the hospital the option to utilize its EHR which should be integrated with the telehealth solution.

Telehealth (C) – Configuration Supports a Broad Range of Services (Refer to Table 4.3)

Telehealth configuration C offers the maximum flexibility and innovation since it can support a turnkey solution for a broad range of services or a combination of HCO and vendor resources depending on HCO functional capabilities and workflow requirements.

The services and flexibility offered in Configuration C are further enabled by DHPs innovation architecture and third-party marketplaces (optional). Functional and data innovations developed for these telehealth platforms can accommodate a variety of HCO functional and workflow requirements. These platforms can support different levels of scope and complexity of chronic diseases and acute care through hospital at home.

Table 4.3 DHP Configuration C: Application/EHR Flexibility, Third-Party Data & Functional Complements Available on E-marketplace

Functions	Offering Organization
Telecommunications technologies	DHP owned & operated
Application modules to support patient care	DHP or HCO owned/licensed
EHR	DHP or HCO owned/licensed
Care providers: physicians, nurses, allied professionals	DHP or HCO employed or affiliated
HCO workflow customization	Broad. Enabled by the flexibility in sharing subsystems between DHP and HCO
Data interoperability with HCO	DHP supported API
Data analytics and AI models	Partner and third-party vendors
Functional extensions	Extension developers
Optional Configurations	
AI models available on e-marketplace	DHP includes e-marketplace
Functional extensions available on e-marketplace	DHP includes e-marketplace

Telehealth Scenario 4

A health system has developed a five-year strategic plan to transition from volume care to value care. The system wishes to transition to value-based care models to support partial and full capitation. In this context they wish to reduce costs by supporting chronic diseases such as diabetes, COPD, cancer care, and heart health from the patient's home. In addition, the hospital system wishes to implement a hospital-at-home program that supports post-surgery patient recovery.

■ **Proposed Telehealth Configuration:** While HCOs should pursue their telehealth and remote home care goals through a singular telehealth solution that supports all their services, workflows, and technology requirements, this is an example where the present state of telehealth offerings may require multiple platforms. Since the health system wishes to transition to value-based care models during its five-year plan, it should select platform configuration C that offers services desired to support the health system's phased implementation. This includes remote patient management for diabetes, COPD, cancer care, heart health, and a hospital-at-home program for risk-based alternative payment models (APMs). The HCO should also confirm whether the platform can support integration with other telehealth platforms.

Telehealth (D) – Telecommunication Technologies (Refer to Table 4.4)

In configuration D, platform vendors own and operate the telecommunication technologies including cloud storage. HCOs embed these platforms in in-house purchased/licensed EHR, patient portals, and application systems. The resultant platform is operated by HCO-based care providers (affiliated or employed).

This configuration is limited to the applications owned and operated by HCOs, or in the platform marketplace, to support hybrid care models. This configuration can accommodate third-party data aggregation and analytics.

Table 4.4 DHP Configuration D: Telehealth System Only

Functions	Offering Organization
Telecommunications technologies	DHP owned & operated
Application modules to support patient care	HCO owned/licensed
EHR	HCO owned/licensed
Care providers: physicians, nurses, allied professionals	DHP or HCO employed or affiliated
HCO workflow customization	Limited by the capabilities of the videoconferencing system which must be integrated with HCO application systems
Data interoperability with HCO	DHP supported API
Data analytics and AI models	Partners and third-party vendors

Telehealth Scenario 5

A provider clinic wishes to add telehealth capabilities to its practice management offerings. The clinic would like to provide remote patient care using synchronous (video and voice) and asynchronous (email and text) modalities.

■ **Proposed Telehealth Configuration:** This provider clinic is a candidate for configuration D that offers telecommunication technologies including cloud storage. The clinic should search for telehealth systems that offer online scheduling and patient waiting areas that can interoperate with the clinic's existing EHR and application systems. The clinic should assess core functional platform offerings and third-party complements to enhance their patient-provider experience.

DHP (E) – Digital Marketplace (Refer to Table 4.5)

In this configuration the digital platform is a marketplace that connects buyers and sellers. The following use cases describe ways in which these platforms are used.

a) HCOs and suppliers. HCO purchasing history on platforms can be analyzed using business intelligence tools to match with suppliers that best meet their requirements, for example, timeliness, cost, and returns.

b) HCOs/recruiters with patient care applicants such as RNs, and other allied professionals.

c) Provider clinics and HCOs/consumers. Usage data generated on these platforms can improve matches on the platform. For example, provider specialties could match with patient requirements increasing platform network effects.

d) Depending on their functional offerings and configuration, digital marketplaces can support ACOs, MSSPs, and other value-based reimbursement models by collaborating with payers and inviting provider participation on the platform.

Table 4.5   DHP Configuration E: E-marketplace

Functions	Offering Organization
Telecommunications technologies	DHP owned & operated
Application modules – suppliers and patient care	DHP owned & operated
EHR – as needed	DHP owned & operated
E-marketplace for supplies	HCOs and suppliers
E-marketplace for patient care	Independent, HCO employed or affiliated care providers including physicians, nurses, and allied professionals as required
HCO workflow customization	Limited. HCOs can use these platforms to supplement in-house care systems. Data generated is used to improve filtering and matching functions of these platforms
Data interoperability with HCO	N/A

DHP Scenario 6

A radiology imaging center wishes to purchase imaging algorithms to aid its busy radiologists with diagnosing images of different modalities. The center is unsure of the best way to accomplish its goals.

■ **Proposed DHP Configuration**: Image AI marketplaces (configuration E) link buyers with third-party algorithm developers. These marketplaces also include a feedback channel between developers and radiologists to improve their workflows. For example, Nuance's AI marketplace for diagnostic imaging offers image AI developers an API to connect their algorithms with radiologists utilizing Nuance PowerShare Network to exchange and share medical imaging.

Specialty Platform Configurations

HCOs use select applications that have transitioned to digital platforms. For example, supply chain management (SCM) systems have transitioned from marketplaces that facilitate supply purchases to platforms that use AI innovations to ensure cost-effective, reliable, and timely acquisition, payment, and delivery of supplies. Similarly, medical speech recognition platforms have evolved as digital platforms where not only can they be "embedded" into EHRs and other application systems but accommodate third-party AI models. Finally, EHR solutions have transformed into platforms by encouraging partners and third-party developers to implement AI solutions which can convert them into intelligent clinical assistants.

The following discussion, along with DHP configurations, helps to better understand systems that are integral to patient care.

1. **Healthcare Supply Chain Management:** for this example, SCM systems include group purchasing organization (GPO), electronic data interchange (EDI), accounts payable (AP) automation, contracting, data pooling (Global Data Synchronization Network), and clinical data mining.
2. **Medical Speech Recognition Systems:** these platforms are "embeddable" since they operate best when integrated into different systems to enhance user productivity and effectiveness. Medical speech recognition systems have been enhanced to incorporate ambient clinical solutions. Since these platforms are embedded in provider EHR workflows, they are well equipped to offer APIs to accommodate AI systems, e.g., image AI models.
3. **EHRs Platforms:** these platforms can support intelligent clinical assistants from partners and third-party AI developers in their existing systems. For example, CDS models are designed to proactively detect diseases and help compliance with treatment protocols. Appropriately configured and certified CDS are increasingly playing a role in improving the state of healthcare. These can be integrated into appropriately architected EHRs platforms.

Healthcare SCM Platforms

In order to support healthcare's evolving supply needs, SCM platforms include GPO, EDI, AP automation, contracting, data pooling (Global Data Synchronization Network), clinical data mining (data from FDA UDI, Device Recalls, MAUDE reports, Orthopedic Network News classifications, and pairs them with market pricing details for value-driven product outcomes), supply chain visibility to help HCOs locate medical supplies by generating a risk score of potential disruptions based on geographic, quality, or sustainability practices. These platforms can be co-owned and/or co-managed by HCOs.

Modern SCM platforms help precision tracking and management of healthcare supplies, including ORs, ERs, pharmaceuticals, and patient units. They automate the supply chain from procurement to payment, utilize AI analytics to enable medical supply management by patient condition including sourcing them cost-effectively, and provide supply chain visibility to avoid disruptions.

Table 4.6 proposes a platform configuration to support healthcare SCM. This configuration includes options that reflect whether the platform principally relies on its internal development team to develop, maintain, and enhance core functional offerings or third-party developers. For example, if the core functionality offered by the supply chain platform does not include advanced functionality such as AI analytics, tracking/management of supplies, and supply chain visibility, the platform can offer appropriate APIs to encourage partner organizations and third parties to develop functional extensions and data analytics.

SCM platforms can offer both data and functional APIs depending on their configuration. The API ecosystem enables them to support interoperability, AI analytics, including predictive modeling, and extension developers

Table 4.6   Configuration: Healthcare SCM Platforms

Functions	Offering Organization
Telecommunications technologies	DHP owned & operated
AI analytics, tracking/management supplies, supply chain visibility	Incorporated in core DHP functionality
Data integration with HCOs	DHP & HCO
Data aggregators and AI models	Partners and third-party vendors – contingent on DHP API offerings
Functional enhancements	Extension developers – contingent on DHP API offerings

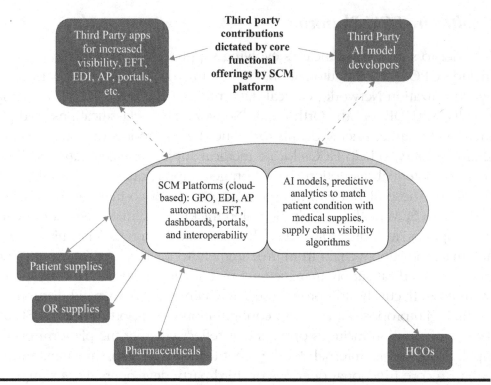

Figure 4.1 Supply chain management platform ecosystem (a representation).

such as EFT, EDI, AP automation, dashboards, and portals that extend the value of core platform offerings.

The goal of modern SCM platforms is to transition from standard marketplaces to innovation platforms that support HCOs through predictive modeling, risk management, and productivity enhancement tools, via in-house efforts or third-party complements. Platforms configured to enhance core offerings through third parties tend to better support evolving HCO supply needs.

Figure 4.1 represents major participants in SCM platforms operating in innovation mode. It includes the technical infrastructure required to support smart SCM platforms such as a public or private cloud, GPO, EDI, AP automation, EFT, dashboards, portals, and interoperability. As the figure indicates third-party contributions towards the technical infrastructure for predictive analytics, increased supply chain visibility, EFT, and EDI are a function of platform functional offerings, type, and quality of APIs.

Medical Speech Recognition Platforms

Medical speech recognition platforms capture and create a detailed clinical note from multi-party conversations during on-site and virtual encounters with patients. These platforms improve patient throughput, reduce clinical documentation time, and improve provider satisfaction scores for clinical documentation. Since speech recognition apps work with a variety of documentation systems, they are designed as embeddable platforms with appropriate APIs and software development kits (SDKs) to embed in different healthcare apps and clinical documentation systems associated with EHRs.

Nuance Dragon Ambient eXperience (DAX) was bought by Microsoft in April 2021 and is hosted on the Microsoft Azure cloud platform. It uses natural language processing (NLP) and AI models to capture physician-patient conversation and create a clinical document. For example, Microsoft has integrated Nuance DAX with Microsoft Teams to synthesize physician-patient conversation captured during telehealth visits. It incorporates patient data with contextual information from the EHR to auto-populate a clinical note in the patient's medical record ready for physician review and approval (Nuance 2022).

DAX is a HITRUST-CSF-certified (refer to Chapter 10 for additional information on HITRUST CSF) cloud-based solution. Outcomes from healthcare systems that use Nuance DAX are (a) 50% reduction in documentation time; (b) 70% reduction in feelings of fatigue and burnout; (c) 79% of physicians said DAX improves the quality of documentation; (d) 83% of patients report their physician is more personable and conversational (Nuance, n.d.).

To work effectively, speech recognition platforms must accommodate a variety of provider workflows which requires an open configuration that supports data and functional innovation. Table 4.7 proposes a configuration for medical speech recognition platforms that accommodates customized workflows by facilitating integration with different EHRs, third-party developers, PACS/RIS, clinical documentation systems, and telehealth platforms.

Figure 4.2 represents the major participants in speech recognition platforms operating in *integration mode*. Since these platforms can be embedded in a variety of documentation and telehealth systems, their architecture includes APIs that promote data exchange, data, and functional complements from partners and third parties.

EHR Platforms

This section proposes configurations for EHR digital platforms. Prior to the adoption of EHRs, these systems were developed and implemented as applications; however, the generation and aggregation of structured and unstructured patient data led to the development of AI models for clinical decision

Table 4.7 Configuration: Medical Speech Recognition Platforms

Functions	Offering Organization
Speech recognition, AI algorithms, interoperability, cloud-based	DHP owned & operated
Clinical applications, patient portal, PACS/RIS	HCO owned/licensed
Telecommunications technologies	Third parties
EHRs	HCO owned/licensed
HCO workflow integration	DHP & HCO
Care providers – salaried or affiliated	HCO
Data analytics and AI models	Partners and third-party developers
• AI models available on DHP marketplace	• DHP platforms support third-party image AI models
Functional complements	Complement developers
• Functional complements available on DHP marketplace	• DHP platforms support third-party software and hardware functional complements

Note: DHP configuration can accommodate HCO-EHRs, other application vendors, telehealth platforms, PACS/RIS, and third-party app developers. DHP supports data exchange, third-party analytics, and functional complements that can be offered via e-marketplaces to enable HCO workflow customization.

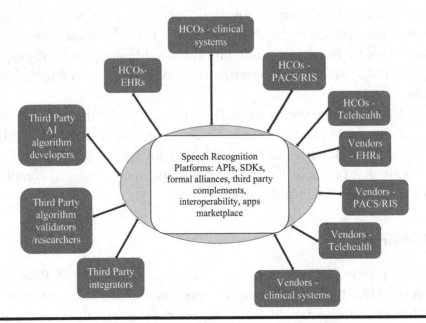

Figure 4.2 Speech recognition platform ecosystem (a representation).

support. This has incentivized EHR vendors to transition to digital platforms to accommodate partners and third-party developers for AI clinical decision support models, data analytics, and functional models.

EHR vendors have traditionally developed clinical decision rules that provide alerts such as drug-drug, lab-drug, and food-drug interactions. These alerts are triggered when the rules indicate an interaction between clinical codes and patient information (such as allergies). However, advances in data storage and analytics, combined with the availability of big data, have transitioned vendors to develop AI algorithms that support clinical decisions. These systems provide physicians with disease alerts and follow-up treatment reminders using evidence-based protocols.

Several EHR vendors and partners have developed CDS to provide prompt alerts and clinical guidelines for physicians. However, a majority of AI innovation has been spearheaded by third-party experts with knowledge and experience in modeling unstructured patient data using machine language (ML), NLP, and deep learning techniques. EHR platforms offer APIs that can be used to implement partner or third-party developed CDS. EHRs and AI systems are further integrated with telecommunications technologies, specialty applications, and communication devices such as cell phones and pagers to promptly alert care providers and assist with compliance. (Refer to Chapter 9 for a discussion on AI systems and integration engines.)

HCOs interested in incorporating AI models to assist provider decision process must understand the assumptions and training data used to construct and train AI models and ensure absence of bias. Finally, EHR vendors that are architected as *integration* platforms support a marketplace for third-party AI models which can be evaluated and integrated in HCO-licensed platforms depending on their patient population and provider workflow requirements.

Table 4.8 proposes a configuration for EHR platforms that accommodate a variety of CDS AI models.

AI models can be co-owned and/or co-managed by health systems, hospitals, and physician groups for providing clinical expertise in evaluating algorithms for universal applicability using data from their patient population. It is important these algorithms are analyzed for absence of bias prior to adoption.

Figure 4.3 represents major participants in EHR platforms that support third-party data innovation. EHR platforms that accommodate a variety of complements should offer data and functions APIs to extend their analytical and functional capabilities. The ecosystem for EHR platforms includes FDA, data owners, patients, HCOs, providers, and third-party developers – AI

Table 4.8   Configuration: EHR Platforms

Functions	Offering Organization
EHRs and speech recognition	HCO licensed (DHP owned/operated)
Interoperability, cloud operation, and data aggregation	HCO licensed (DHP owned/operated)
Validation of AI models including bias	DHPs & HCOs
Workflow integration of AI models in HCOs	DHPs & HCOs
Telecommunications technologies	DHPs
Physicians – independent, salaried, or affiliated	HCOs, independent providers, physician groups
Analytics and AI models	Third-party vendors
• AI models available on DHP marketplace	• DHPs architected as *integration platforms* operate as innovation marketplaces for third-party AI models

Note: DHP configuration can accommodate application vendors, telehealth platforms, speech recognition, and third-party developers.

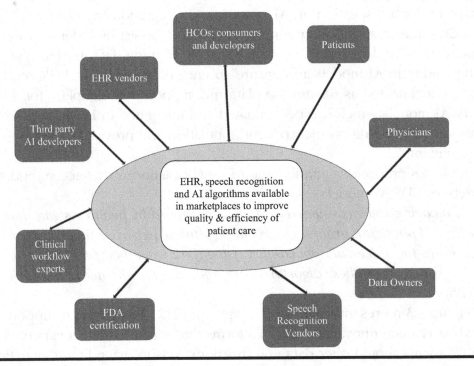

Figure 4.3   EHRs platform ecosystem (a representation).

models and others, vendors, clinical workflow experts, and speech recognition vendors.

Key Takeaways

1. DHPs can be designed and architected to support different aspects of the ecosystem: as *marketplaces* for buyers and sellers, *exchange* platforms, and *innovation* platforms that provide added value through ecosystem contributions.
2. Telehealth platforms consist of care providers and the telehealth system. The telehealth system comprises telecommunications technologies (videoconferencing, the internet, store-and-forward imaging, streaming media, and wireless communications), specialty applications, and EHRs.
3. This chapter defines five configurations for telehealth platforms.
   - Telehealth (A) – turnkey configuration offers turnkey solutions including telehealth systems (telecommunication technologies, specialty applications, and EHR), care providers, data exchange, and third-party data complements.
   - Telehealth (B) – like telehealth (A), this configuration offers a turnkey solution including telehealth system, providers, data exchange, and third-party data complements. *It can, however, be integrated with HCO EHR and support HCO providers.*
   - Telehealth (C) – this configuration offers a range of services and system options including turnkey solutions, data exchange, and third-party data and functional complements. *It can also be integrated with HCO EHR and specialty applications and support HCO providers.*
   - Telehealth (D) – telecommunication technologies: this configuration offers telecommunication technologies, data exchange, and third-party data complements. It can be embedded in HCO EHR, specialty applications, and support HCO providers.
   - DHP (E) – digital marketplace: this solution offers a digital marketplace for patient care, purchasing supplies, renting equipment, staffing, etc. These platforms offer turnkey solutions that connect HCOs with consumers, providers, suppliers, and HCOs.
4. Six scenarios, representing key functionalities in healthcare organizations, have been included with proposed configuration/design options. HCOs can use these as guides for selecting platforms that can accommodate current and future needs.

5. HCOs should assess platforms based on their architecture and configurations and platform governance protocols.
6. Configurations for select specialty DHPs include examples of SCM, Medical Speech Recognition, and EHR platforms.

References

Best, Jo. 2019. "What is Digital Health? Everything You Need to Know About the Future of Healthcare." *ZDNET.* February 1. https://www.zdnet.com/google-amp/article/what-is-digital-health/.

FDA. 2020. "What is Digital Health?" *US Food & Drug Administration.* September 9. https://www.fda.gov/medical-devices/digital-health-center-excellence/what-digital-health.

Frye, Ma-Keba. n.d. "What is an API?" *Mulesoft.* Accessed November 2022. https://www.mulesoft.com/resources/api/what-is-an-api/.

HRSA. 2019. "HealthIT.gov." *ONC.* October 17. https://www.healthit.gov/faq/what-telehealth-how-telehealth-different-telemedicine.

Nuance. n.d. *Automatically Document Care with the Dragon Ambient eXperience.* Accessed November 2022. https://www.nuance.com/healthcare/ambient-clinical-intelligence.html.

Nuance. 2022. *Datasheet/Automatically Document Care with the Dragon Ambient eXperience.* September. https://www.nuance.com/asset/en_us/collateral/healthcare/data-sheet/ds-ambient-clinical-intelligence-en-us.pdf.

Chapter 5

Digital Health Platform Strategies

Introduction

Post-pandemic healthcare continues to demonstrate the power of digital care models in supporting value-based care models and patient engagement. While uncertainties remain regarding the status of licensure and telehealth payments, virtual care continues to be adopted by nontraditional providers, such as independent DHPs, payers, employers, and retailers, to meet their digital health needs. Even though leading HCOs have long recognized the value of virtual care and its role in extended services and innovation models, the trend towards digital health is primarily fueled by nontraditional providers of care.

Most businesses find it difficult to transition from traditional to platform configuration. This process is challenging for brick-and-mortar hospitals, health systems, and physician clinics that lack a comprehensive digital health strategy, in-house IT capability, and understanding of DHPs. All this is compounded by lack of capital funding and reimbursement incentives.

According to a survey conducted by Amwell and HIMSS Analytics asking senior executives at hospitals, health systems, and health plans around the country about their post-pandemic strategy, the following trends emerged: (1) Despite consumer enthusiasm and advantages of telehealth in many situations, clinical resistance and reimbursement uncertainty remain; (2) technology challenges faced by hospitals and health systems center around lack of integration and interoperability and platform "sprawl"; (3) while stakeholders

DOI: 10.4324/9781003366584-6

lack a cohesive vision for future state, they agree on a streamlined experience for patients and providers, interoperability between HIS and platforms, and a single telehealth platform to support future growth (Amwell 2021).

This chapter explores strategies for HCOs, including developing a digital health vision, selecting DHPs, and considering DHP governance philosophy and participation strategies.

Digital Health and DHPs

It is important to develop a digital health vision prior to initiating digital transformation initiatives. While a digital health strategy may appear daunting, HCO executives well understand that most strategies are five-year plans that should be implemented in phases that reflect short-, medium-, and long-term business objectives. Virtual care models can impact patient care across the HCO due to their reach and convenience. An example of virtual care models that utilize multi-disciplinary teams to improve patient care is illustrated in the following statement from Frank McGillin, CEO of The Clinic by Cleveland Clinic:

> Pairing patients with virtual support from a multidisciplinary team of experts reduces the risk of suboptimal treatment plans. Just as important: virtual multidisciplinary visits eliminate long travel times and exposure to COVID-19 for vulnerable patients. For employers and health plans, the right diagnosis and treatment equates to better member outcomes and reduced costs of care. Similarly, intelligent remote monitoring that alerts clinicians to the need for intervention in real time is a vital tool.
>
> **(Siwicki 2022)**

A comprehensive digital transformation plan must ensure that patient data generated on third-party digital platforms – telehealth, assistive, or remote complements – is integrated with the patient's data stored in the HCOs EHR. To the extent possible this data should be shared at the semantic level (refer to Chapter 9) to ensure workflow compatibility and post-aggregation analytics.

Digital health comprises telehealth, extensions, hardware, and software complements such as advanced IT systems and analytics such as CDS. For effective digital transformation, these advanced technologies must blend into HCO clinical care models using work transformation methods (refer Chapter 11).

Establishing a Digital Health Vision

Prior to developing a digital health strategy, it is helpful for HCOs to contact health systems with experience in virtual care models to understand their journey and benefits. For example, Kaiser Permanente and Mercy Virtual have been deploying virtual care models prior to the pandemic (refer Chapter 11). It is informative to learn about ongoing innovations in digital care models being implemented in health systems.

To develop a comprehensive digital health strategy HCOs should understand their strengths, weaknesses, opportunities, and threats. This can be accomplished through a SWOT analysis. Since the goal is to determine the key requirements of their digital health strategy, this analysis must assess organizational strengths and weaknesses as they relate to formulating a digital health strategy, and opportunities and threats as they relate to the external healthcare market.

The following factors can be considered during a SWOT analysis.

HCO Strengths: identify strengths associated with competitive advantage in the existing healthcare environment, including centers of excellence, reputation for quality care, cost advantage, innovation, medical specialties, care provider satisfaction, patient satisfaction, and value-based partnerships.

HCO Weaknesses: identify areas of weakness that require attention. These areas can relate to a lack of desired strengths, lawsuits, lack of care provider satisfaction, lack of patient satisfaction, weak IT systems, and inability to take risks.

Opportunities for HCOs: identify new market possibilities, utilizing technological advancements such as telehealth solutions, DHP complements, AI models, and partnerships with HCOs, employers, and payers, to support value-based care and at-home care models.

Threats for HCOs: identify threats facing the organization, including regulatory changes, nontraditional providers such as independent DHPs, employers, and payers, turnover of physicians, nurses, pharmacists, and allied personnel, and a shift from fee-for-service (FFS) to value-based reimbursement models.

A digital health vision for HCOs should consider the following:

1. Redefine markets to take advantage of DHPs:

   As part of developing their digital health vision, HCOs should consider new market opportunities to leverage their clinical and technical expertise and specializations because of virtualization.

2. Patient engagement:

   The HCO digital health vision must improve patient outreach and engagement. A *digital front door* can support patient services, export, and import patient information for improved care management, and virtual communication modalities that offer efficient provider access. In addition, wellness information, digital assistants that help compliance with therapies, and seamless integration with brick-and-mortar care create an omnichannel patient experience which increases patient engagement.

3. Care provider support:

   Digital health results in large data sets comprising device-generated patient data supplemented by genomics, home health, nursing homes, and social agencies. A digital health vision should consider these data sets and the best ways to aggregate, analyze, and use these to improve patient care. In addition, the vision should include physician support through intelligent EHRs and digital clinical assistants.

4. Alliances and partnerships with traditional and nontraditional providers of digital care models:

   HCOs establishing a digital health vision should consider extending service capabilities through alliances and partnerships with traditional and nontraditional providers of care. Digital alliances and partnerships increase service abilities and market share.

5. Value-based contracts with HCOs and nontraditional providers:

   HCOs establishing a digital health vision should consider entering into value-based reimbursement contracts with other HCOs, independent DHPs, payers, and employers. These partnerships require population risk management and encourage wellness care and early detection and treatment of diseases.

6. Information technology supports organizational and external alliances and partnerships:

   The role of HCO-based IT should evolve to support alliances within and outside the organization. Digital transformation efforts within HCOs require IT alliances with experts in digital transformation, innovative technologies, privacy, and security. External to HCOs, IT should form alliances with telehealth, DHP vendors, and HCOs that have designed innovative care models.

7. Desired outcomes:

A central component of the digital health vision is desired outcomes from digital transformation. During planning stages, these outcomes can be defined through critical success factors (CSFs) to reflect organizational goals and objectives and key performance indicators (KPIs) that support measures to monitor progress towards CSFs. Chapter 11 discusses CSFs and KPIs and their importance in healthcare transformation efforts.

Once HCOs establish a digital health vision, they can develop *current* and *proposed* workflows to reflect the impact of technology and types of care provider roles. While *current* user workflows incorporate existing technologies, *proposed* workflows include advanced technologies to help achieve their digital vision. It will be helpful for HCOs to understand the types of telehealth platforms and complements prior to initiating workflows (refer to Chapter 6).

While advancements in digital technologies, and ongoing use cases, will evolve care models, *proposed* workflows, during the planning stage, can provide the foundation to operationalize HCO digital health strategy. The technological requirements identified through *proposed* workflows can also provide direction for platform architecture, configuration, and service offerings.

Selecting DHPs

Once workflows have been developed and bottlenecks and gaps identified, HCOs should investigate and evaluate configurations, services offered, and governance philosophy of DHPs to help accomplish their digital health vision. Figure 5.1 illustrates the phases and criteria for selecting telehealth and other DHPs. The phases relate to developing digital health vision, whereas the guidelines help HCOs understand the criteria for selecting telehealth and other DHPs. The following guidelines can assist with that effort:

■ DHP vendor growth strategy and stability are important considerations. Platform growth through M&As can lead to convoluted architectures that lack the flexibility to seamlessly support HCO digital health

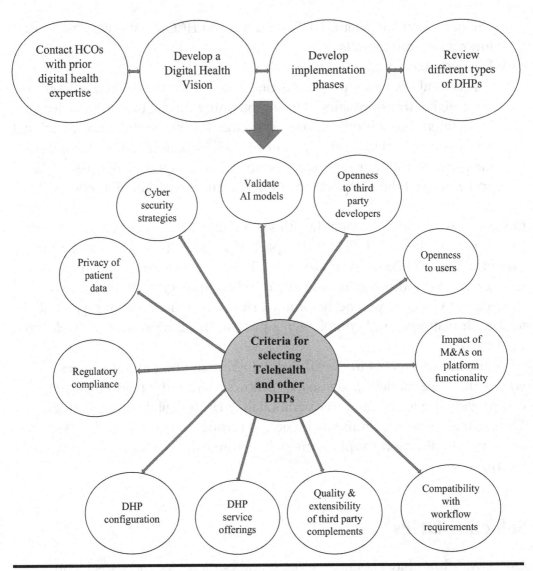

Figure 5.1 Selecting telehealth and other digital health platforms (DHPs).

strategies. DHP vendor stability should also be assessed to ensure long-term viability.

■ DHP governance philosophies must be assessed to determine compatibility with HCO business requirements and value systems. Platform governance includes information on prior M&As and their impact on core platform functional offerings, "openness" of DHPs to users and developers, cybersecurity practices, privacy of patient data, validating AI models for absence of bias, and regulatory compliance. The following section discusses DHP governance related factors in additional detail.

■ Understand configuration flexibility to support services, modular integration, patient care excellence, revenue generation models, ownership structure (to understand future goals and objectives), and existing clientele.

HCOs select DHPs based on their size, clinical needs, and ability to support clinical and technical requirements. For example, HCOs may select DHPs ranging from turnkey solutions that include DHP-affiliated providers to flexible configurations ranging from a combination of telehealth platforms, specialty application systems, and providers (refer to Chapter 4). Regardless, patient data exchange between HCOs and DHPs must support provider and patient preferred workflows. In addition, DHP functional offerings must achieve desired workflows, clinical protocols, and revised policies and procedures prior to implementation.

HCOs that utilize multiple DHPs to accomplish their digital health vision assume responsibility for managing the integrated digital health solution, including compliance with security and privacy of patient data.

Chapter 6 offers different types of DHPs, including vendor examples, to assist with the selection process. DHPs include telehealth systems, DHP complements (biometric monitors, RPMs, smart wearables, and digital therapeutics), EHRs and AI models, SCM, and e-marketplaces. While several ambulatory EHR vendors have integrated telehealth services in their offerings, Chapter 6 considers EHRs distinct from telehealth platforms since major EHR vendors are increasingly re-architecting their systems to encourage participation from partners, independent software vendors (ISVs), and third-party hardware complement developers.

DHP Governance

Platform governance reflects the philosophy and ethics of DHP management. It is important for HCOs to understand platform governance to determine compatibility with organizational ethics and digital health strategy. The following DHP governance factors can be considered for evaluation (see Figure 5.1).

1. **Mergers and Acquisitions:**
   a. Has DHP been a part of M&As? Reasons?
   b. Has DHP M&A activity impacted its core functional offerings?

2. **Openness:** The core architecture of innovation DHPs includes a variety of APIs, the quality of which dictates third-party extensions. These extensions generate additional value for DHP users. To understand these extensions, HCOs should ask the following questions.
   a. Is the platform open to third-party innovation and user access?
   b. What is the level of control exercised by DHP owners/managers? Open platforms encourage innovation and growth while increasing data scatter and increased security and privacy risks. Chapter 3 section on *DHPs: Openness and Intelligence* addresses this topic.
   c. Which third-party vendors have contributed to DHP? What data and functional complements have been developed?
   d. How are third-party complements used by other ecosystem participants?
3. **Cyber-risks:** How are risks of cyberattacks mitigated by the DHP? The following examples offer guidance to determine risk mitigation strategies against cyberattacks. Does the DHP
   a. Utilize public APIs that have been designed to be secure from cyberattacks?
   b. Utilize a cybersecurity framework (NIST or HITRUST) to assess and certify the cybersecurity of the platform, including their cloud vendor. Refer to Chapter 10 for additional information on security frameworks?
   c. Ensure cybersecurity of third-party medical devices through vendor contracts?
   d. Assess data security and privacy practices of third parties and their offerings on DHPs?
4. **Privacy of patient data (refer to Chapter 10 for additional information on privacy of patient data):**
   a. Does patient data stored in HCO-EHRs, which interoperates with DHPs, become a part of the DHP?
   b. How is privacy of patient data protected on the DHP?
   c. Does DHP use patient data as a part of its revenue generation strategies?
   d. Is patient data stored indefinitely? Why? Where?
5. **Validation of AI models:** what methodology is used to validate absence of bias in AI models that are part of the DHP offering?
6. **Regulatory Compliance:** what strategies are used for compliance with federal and state regulations?

HCO Participation Levels on DHPs

HCOs can participate as buyers, sellers, owners, and managers (operators) of DHPs. A digital health strategy in hospitals, health systems, and academic medical centers (AMCs) will likely comprise multiple DHPs with participation levels designed to achieve organizational objectives. HCO participation levels on DHPs differ from *nontraditional* providers such as payers and employers who mostly own and operate telehealth platforms and complements for their service offerings.

HCOs predominantly participate as buyers (and sellers) of products and services on DHPs. Over time, however, their needs may evolve to increase their participation to management, and ownership. In several situations, HCOs and DHPs benefit from co-managing and/or co-owning DHPs. For example, while HCOs increase their ability to support in-house clinical models, DHP vendors get access to specialty guidance and enhanced clinical protocols.

HCO: Buyers and Sellers on DHPs

1. Marketplace platforms

   HCOs participate as buyers of products and services on *marketplace platforms* which offer the benefit of aggregating different sellers and reduced costs. HCO participation as sellers on e-marketplace platforms generates revenue.

   The following examples of marketplace platforms are discussed in Chapter 6.
   - Medley: healthcare jobs platform.
   - Cohealo: biomed device sharing platform.
   - RealSelf: connects cosmetic surgery patients and providers.

2. Exchange platforms

   HCOs can participate as "buyers" and "sellers" to exchange patient data on HIEs. While patient data is neither bought nor sold, it is sent and received between participating entities via exchange platforms. Data exchange platforms operate at the local, state, regional, and national levels. Local and regional platforms often aggregate and analyze patient data for participating HCOs, including contracts with states to provide patient quality reports.

   Examples of exchange platforms that have been further discussed in Chapter 9 are

- Local, state, vendor-owned, and regional HIEs generally store patient data that moves through their exchange. Examples of regional HIEs/ HINs are Chesapeake Regional Information System for our Patients (CRISP) that serve HCOs in the state of Maryland and D.C., and Cynchealth that serves HCOs in the states of Iowa and Nebraska.
- National HIEs (also known as health information networks) focus on EHI interoperability across participants that operate across the nation. Examples of nationwide HIEs are eHealth Exchange, CommonWell Health Alliance, Carequality, DirectTrust, Civitas, and TEFCA/QHINs.

3. Innovation platforms

HCOs generally participate as buyers of products and services on *innovation DHPs* to architect their digital health solution. *Innovation DHPs* comprise telehealth, DTx, RPMs, smart wearables, EHRs, CRM, and SCM.

The following examples of DHPs and telehealth can be classified as *innovation* platforms based on the descriptions in Chapter 4. These are elaborated in Chapter 6.

- Hinge Health: manages musculoskeletal (MSK) care from every stage ranging from prevention to post-surgery.
- Sword Health: AI-powered physical therapist for real-time biofeedback and therapists to remotely monitor patient progress.
- Kaia Health: uses computer vision to help patients track their exercises through a smartphone.
- Propeller Health: sensor attaches to an inhaler, linked to an app on a patient's phone, used by an asthma or COPD sufferer.
- WELT Smart Belt: associated algorithms calculate fall risk from abnormal gait patterns.
- Withings Scan Watches: health monitoring such as ECG measurements, sleep tracking, SpO2 monitoring, and proactive atrial fibrillation notifications.
- iRhythm (Zio): monitors different types of irregular heart rhythms.
- GHX: supports EDI, AP, supply data, and patient records into predictions such as cost-effective medical supplies for patient conditions and cost-effective sourcing.
- Curvo: enables HCOs to search over 1.2 million unique products and view cost and safety information.
- Premier: GPO that has alliances with AI-powered platforms to monitor suppliers and inventory levels.

- Included Health: uses data science to match an employee to the correct doctor or specialist in their network and tracks medical spending.
- Quartet Health: flags patients with comorbidities or who have not been treated for behavioral health issues.
- Papa: provides seniors assistance and patient health management such as virtual primary care, urgent care, and chronic care management.
- Zoom Healthcare: tele-video platform.
- Athenahealth: comprehensive telehealth solution provider.
- Amwell: comprehensive telehealth solution provider.

HCOs that develop AI clinical decision support (CDS), imaging AI models, products, or services may elect to participate as sellers on innovation DHPs. These products or services serve as complements to platform offerings.

HCO: Owners and Managers (Operators) of DHPs

1. Marketplace platforms

   HCOs that are co-owners of a group purchasing organization do not generally take on the role of platform management since that is an intensive, risk-based endeavor. HCOs that have ownership stake in separate DHP entities are likely to indirectly own and operate these platforms. Organizations can exert influence on platform strategies through management and ownership.

2. Exchange platforms

   HCOs are unlikely to own HIEs and HINs. This situation can occur in locally run HIEs that are co-owned by participating HCOs. However, co-ownership of HIEs is unlikely to impact HCO DT efforts.

3. Innovation platforms

   While there can be several reasons for HCOs to own and manage *innovation* DHPs, there are a few standout reasons:

   a. DHP managers require HCO clinical expertise to design and implement their digital solution. In these situations, the level of HCO participation can increase to co-owning and/or co-managing the platform.

   b. Increased engagement and reliance on DHPs can increase HCO participation level from purchasers to managers and owners. These transitions occur over time and require investment and expertise. It is not uncommon to see HCOs collaborate to co-own and co-manage DHPs.

c. HCOs with the requisite clinical and technical expertise and investment may elect to design, develop, staff, and implement customized telehealth solution by integrating software and hardware components from third parties. In these situations, HCOs should form a separate business entity to operate the platform.

HCOs that move into ownership and/or management of DHPs should understand the principles of platform management, especially those related to *inverting* firm operations. In order to understand the principles of e-commerce platform management, including network effects, readers are advised to review the recommended reading included at the end of this chapter.

Chapter 3 addresses similarities and differences between healthcare and e-commerce (nonhealthcare) platforms. Based on this analysis, it arrives at select management strategies for DHPs. We offer the following commentary on platform management for information technology, management, and human resources.

■ Information technology. In addition to designing and implementing DHPs that accommodate provider and patient requirements, IT should design and develop APIs that attract partners and third-party developers to enhance platform value. In effect, in addition to designing interfaces for internal developers, IT needs to invert its thinking to design APIs for outside developers. Prior to developing APIs, HCO-IT should understand enhancement requirements of DHP users.

■ DHP management should focus on alliances and partnerships to enhance functional offerings and improve value for users.

■ DHP management can consider mergers and acquisitions to expand their service and functional offerings.

■ HR should develop platform governance policies regarding degrees of "openness," quality, privacy, and ethical use.

Examples of HCOs participating as co-owners or co-managers on *innovation* platforms are:

■ HCOs as co-managers: Epic, Cerner, and Meditech sublicense their EHR platform to health systems to operate and support IT implementations of smaller community hospitals. Health systems that undertake the management of IT systems for other hospitals economically benefit from creating a mini-HIT ecosystem while aggregating and analyzing patient data on this platform for care coordination and other joint efforts.

■ HCOs as investors: Mayo Clinic and Kaiser Permanente have made significant strategic investments in Medically Home Group to encourage adoption by health systems and care providers. The goal is to increase capacity to address regulatory and legislative barriers and allow more patients across the US to receive high-quality acute and restorative care in their homes. "Medically Home's platform enables providers to address a significant range of clinical conditions at the higher end of the clinical acuity spectrum that is typically treated in traditional hospital settings, safely in a patient's home" (PR Newswire 2021).

Final Considerations

■ DHPs are positioned to grow past the COVID-19 pandemic. While the future of these platforms is still being written, it is evident that the trajectory of healthcare is on improving access to patients, lowering costs, and improving outcomes.

■ DHPs are configured to provide different levels and types of services based on their target audience. These platforms generally grow their services through acquisition and in-house development. The resultant DHPs either remain independent or are acquired by nontraditional providers of care such as employers, payers, and retail store owners.

Key Takeaways

■ It is important for HCOs to generate a digital health strategy and workflow prior to selecting DHPs.

■ A consideration for HCOs prior to generating a digital health strategy is to contact health systems with experience in virtual care models.

■ Digital health strategy can be developed using SWOT analysis and include the following considerations.
  – Redefine markets.
  – Patient engagement.
  – Increase attractiveness for care providers.

- Alliances and partnerships with traditional and nontraditional providers of care.
- Value-based contracts with HCOs and nontraditional providers of care.
- Refocus IT to support internal and external alliances and partnerships.
- Desired outcomes.

■ As part of selecting DHPs to meet their digital health vision, HCOs must consider several factors. These have been enumerated in the section on *Selecting DHPs* and outlined in Figure 5.1.

■ DHP Governance is an important consideration in the selection of DHPs.

■ HCO participation levels in DHPs is a function of their requirements and the phase of digital transformation.

■ HCOs that are interested in platform management can review the principles included in this chapter.

References

Amwell. 2021. "Building the Future of Virtual Care: Streamlined, Scalable, Sustainable." *Connected with Care.* September 28. https://connectwithcare.org /building-the-future-of-virtual-care-streamlined-scalable-sustainable-insights -from-amwells-2021-survey-of-health-plans-hospitals-and-health-systems-and -clinicians/.

PR Newswire. 2021. "Mayo Clinic, Kaiser Permanente Announce Strategic Investment in Medically Home to Expand Access to Serious or Complex Care at Home." *Cision PR Newswire.* May 13. https://www.prnewswire.com/ news-releases/mayo-clinic-kaiser-permanente-announce-strategic-investment -in-medically-home-to-expand-access-to-serious-or-complex-care-at-home -301290446.html.

Siwicki, Bill. 2022. "Cleveland Clinic Leader: Telehealth Now a 'Permanent Mode' of Care Delivery." *Healthcare IT News.* February 1. https://www.healthcareit-news.com/news/cleveland-clinic-leader-telehealth-now-permanent-mode-care -delivery.

Recommended Reading

Parker, Geoffrey G., Marshall W. Van Alstyne, and Sangeet Paul Choudary. 2016. *Platform Revolution.* New York/London: W.W. Norton & Company.

Chapter 6

DHP Types and Examples

Introduction

Digital platforms dominate the landscape. Social media, e-commerce, supply chain management, videoconferencing, and cloud computing platforms are ubiquitous. In fact, it is difficult to identify industries that have not yet been impacted by digital business models.

Most digital business models utilize several platforms – of different types and configurations. For example, the ease of use and simplicity of Zoom has made the name synonymous with video conferencing. However, Zoom and other video conferencing platforms are supported through AI systems and cloud computing platforms.

Another example illustrates the use of multiple platforms in accomplishing a complex e-commerce vision. The Amazon marketplace offers search tools to connect buyers and sellers. It supports the marketplace through a recommendation engine that incentivizes consumers to purchase products and services. An order triggers a series of backend operations to pick and package items through AI-enabled materials management platforms comprising self-learning robots. This process is efficient, accurate, and timely. Completed orders are transported via state-of-the-art logistics management systems that comprise a variety of delivery vehicles, including drones for select urban areas, to successfully navigate the last mile. Transactions and analytics are supported through Amazon's Web Services (AWS) and their cloud offerings which form the foundation for Amazon's digital e-commerce platform.

DOI: 10.4324/9781003366584-7

As a result of their customer-facing marketplace platform supplemented by business-facing innovation platforms, Amazon has captured a significant share of the US e-commerce market. Their supply chain management (SCM) platform has attracted sellers of different products and services to their marketplace, reducing the threat of substitute products and services. The resultant Amazon competitive advantage transcends into brick-and-mortar commerce markets.

The Amazon digital business model controls the business-to-consumer (B2C) and business-to-business (B2B) experience through comprehensive workflows that link consumer and business-facing platforms and systems. It illustrates the use of different modalities – physical, virtual, automation, and human-powered systems – to accomplish a business mission efficiently and effectively.

HCO digital health strategies follow the pattern of e-commerce platforms that utilize multiple types and modalities of platforms to accomplish their mission. However, HCOs predominantly utilize DHPs owned and operated by independent parties to accommodate the scope, complexity, and workflow requirements for their digital health vision. While e-commerce platforms integrate data across their different platforms, patient care requires data interoperability between different entities engaged in patient care.

Brick-and-mortar HCOs embarking on digital health will utilize different types of DHPs and modalities. The goal of digital transformation of HCOs is to integrate platforms to realize their digital health vision. This inevitably results in innovative care models that enable patient outreach and timely access to providers.

Enablers of Digital Integration

Different types of digital platforms integrate with one another through APIs. Platform configuration is strongly influenced by platform categories which are derived from its architecture. Platform architecture has been discussed in Chapter 3.

In healthcare, where functional controls are critical to ensure regulatory compliance, telehealth and EHR vendors are reluctant to place trust on third-party developers through public APIs. Therefore, telehealth and EHR vendors predominantly extend their APIs through partnerships and alliances.

DHP vendors can offer a combination of public and partner APIs depending on the type of complements they wish to attract.

Types of DHPs

This chapter discusses different types of DHPs such as telehealth systems, EHRs, digital therapeutics, RPMs, smart wearables, AI algorithms (CDS and image recognition), SCM, and others. Implicit in these examples are foundational platforms such as cloud computing. The discussion on each DHP type will include examples of systems and a brief description of their functions. DHPs that support specialty diseases should support third-party enhancements to stay updated with ongoing technological advances.

DHPs have been divided into telehealth systems, DHP complements for telehealth, EHRs and their complements, SCM, and e-marketplaces. In addition, we mention hybrid care models employed by HCOs. KP and Mercy Health are examples of HCOs that have implemented comprehensive digital health strategies. These are described in Chapter 11.

A. Telehealth systems are subdivided into four categories that support the following services:
   A1 Telecommunication infrastructure to support primary care
   A2 Primary care and specialty disease management
   A3 Comprehensive services across the care continuum
   A4 Complex chronic disease management
B. DHPs such as IoT-based remote patient monitors, DTx, intelligent wearables, support telehealth platforms.
C. EHRs/Patient Portals and Complementary Solutions
D. SCM Platforms
E. E-marketplace platforms offer functional capability to implement desired interaction for buyers and sellers.

A1. Telehealth Systems: Telemedicine Infrastructure to Support Primary Care

Telehealth platforms offer telemedicine infrastructure: these platforms are designed for use by HCOs with their own EHR, specialty apps, and access to care providers that can support primary care, urgent care, and related specialties.

These platforms provide virtual access to patients and providers through video and audio conferencing, secure email, and text systems. They may include functionality such as scheduling and notifications and are integrated in HCO EHRs for a seamless provider workflow.

Zoom Healthcare (zoom.us): The Zoom Developer Platform offers solutions that enable third-party developers and service providers including independent software vendors (ISVs) and partners to build applications and integrations on Zoom's industry-leading video-first unified communications platform. The Platform offers APIs, webhooks, and software development kits (SDKs) to

a) Build public apps.
b) Build private custom applications & innovative tools.
c) Enrich Zoom experiences & interactions.
d) Extend the value of the Zoom platform.

Case Examples

■ *Epic* EHR integrates with Zoom Health to facilitate the following: (a) launch a video visit directly from the Epic applications' telehealth work-flows, (b) collaborate with other doctors and specialists by annotating directly on the shared screen so that notations are visible to all attend-ees, (c) place patients in a waiting room to allow different providers to meet individually with the patient during a session, (d) provide secure connections between care providers, patient, and care providers.

■ *Cerner* EHR integrates with Zoom Health to facilitate the following (Jercich 2021): (a) in-chart notifications when a patient has entered the waiting room, (b) share test results and complete documentation while on Zoom, (c) send invite link to additional participants – family mem-bers, interpreters, and other care providers – to join the session.

A2. Telehealth Systems: Specialty Disease Management

Telehealth systems that focus on managing specialty diseases offer infrastruc-ture including videoconferencing links, EHR capabilities, diagnostic tools, specialty apps, and RPMs. They utilize evidence-based clinical protocols and are used by DHP-affiliated specialty providers through multi-disciplinary teams. These telehealth systems can be integrated with HCO EHRs and used by HCO affiliated and independent providers.

Chronic Disease: Behavioral Health Platforms

Introduction

Behavioral health has experienced an unprecedented global increase due to the COVID-19 pandemic. According to the 2023 "The State of Mental Health of America" report published by Mental Health America, "55% of adults with mental illness receive no treatment and 60% of youth with major depression do not receive mental health treatment."

Online mental health helps close this gap. It's a better fit for some people, depending on their personality, processing style, and financial situation. And there have been notable M&As: Headspace, a meditation and mindfulness app, and Ginger, telehealth services, merged in the fourth quarter of 2021(headspacehealth.com). This trend will continue until select platforms dominate the mental health ecosystem.

There are three levels of services offered by behavioral health platforms: (a) platforms with a principal focus on online meditation & mindfulness; (b) platforms that support online mental health services; (c) platforms that support services for a wide range of mental health through multiple treatment modalities, including medication management, therapy, and digital therapeutics.

These independent DHPs face competition from providers of virtual specialty disease management services such as Teladoc, Amwell, and MeMD (online provider of primary care and behavioral health services acquired by Walmart).

Case Examples

- **Meditation and Mindfulness Platforms:** As of early 2021 over 2000 meditation apps were available to consumers. Two digital platforms – Headspace and Calm – control roughly 70% (Borbely 2021) of this market through well-designed and packaged instructional techniques with intelligent elements such as allowing users to connect with friends to compare performances, leverage social media and partnerships with influencers, major airlines, and social media.
- **Mental Health Platforms:** are constantly evaluated by mental health experts for efficacy and effectiveness which incentivizes these DHPs to vet all coaches and therapists and combine that with evidence-based treatments such as online cognitive behavioral therapy (CBT). Mental health platforms generally provide some, or all, of the following services – preventive care, mental health coaching, therapy, and medication (excluding controlled medications).

There are several platforms that fall within this category: *Ginger* provides a range of mental healthcare that includes self-guided care resources, real-time text-based behavioral health coaching, video sessions, and psychiatry help. *BetterUp* provides virtual employee coaching and mental health assistance. *Talkspace* provides mental health therapy, assessment, healthy living support, and self-help tools. It offers psychiatry services for mental health and prescription management. *Lyra* offers evidence-based treatments like CBT, for mild or temporary mental health concerns by certified coaches. Treatments are offered via tele video or onsite. *Cerebral* provides mental health assessments, telehealth appointments with psychiatrists, and medication management.

■ **Mental Health Marketplace Platforms:** these platforms link a curated collection of mental health solutions. For example, Solera Health (soleranetwork.com), a mental and behavioral health marketplace has developed algorithms to link patients with programs that best meet their needs including a network of community organizations and digital therapeutics providers. It hosts Ginger, eMindful, and Headspace. Since Solera Health utilizes value-based care agreements with employers and plans, it supports high-acuity and medium-acuity patients with clinically validated mental health platforms. Solera is HITRUST certified.

Another variety of mental health marketplace platform is Quartet (quartethealth.com) which works with insurances to analyze claims and flag patients with potential mental health issues. It matches patients with mental healthcare providers (in-house and external) based on their preferences, clinical needs, and insurance. It staffs behavioral health clinics where treatment is provided by multi-disciplinary teams led by board-certified psychiatrists and composed of psychiatric nurse practitioners, licensed clinical social workers, nurse care managers, and patient care coordinators staffs. These clinics coordinate care with primary care physicians and community resources for patients with moderate to severe mental illness.

Chronic Disease: Joint Pain Platforms

Introduction

Musculoskeletal (MSK) spending has been growing primarily due to overuse of surgeries. In fact, this is an employer's highest medical claim expense. In the past decade, MSK claims have doubled in the US, "however, the number of people with MSK conditions has remained relatively constant. Rising claims costs have been driven by more expensive treatments, such as spinal fusions and expensive implants, overuse of MRIs, and the rise of outpatient 'spine centers' that have become lucrative businesses for owners," according to Hinge Health's State of MSK Report of 2022.

Most virtual physical therapy platforms contract with businesses and health plans for monetization. The virtual physical therapy platform space is undergoing M&As, and alliances with the goal of coordinating care with primary care providers, specialists, surgeons, and onsite physical therapists.

Case Examples

- **Hinge Health** (hingehealth.com) helps individuals manage MSK care from every stage ranging from prevention to post-surgery. Hinge Health reduces MSK pain, opioid use, and surgeries by pairing digital therapeutics with a clinical team including physicians, physical therapists, and board-certified health coaches. It uses Enso, an FDA-cleared device to electrically stimulate nerves for pain relief. Hinge Health has partnered with Carrum Health's digital Centers of Excellence (COE) platform to offer employers an affordable and comprehensive surgery-benefits program which uses top providers under bundled payment models. Provider incentives are aligned with quality performance for improved patient outcomes. Carrum Health's digital COE has independently validated 45% cost savings per procedure as published in a peer-reviewed study by RAND Corporation (Carrum Health 2021).
- **Sword Health** (swordhealth.com): offers Digital Therapist that enables patients to access physical therapists who connect them to wearable motion sensors that use a personalized AI-powered exercise program to get real-time biofeedback. In addition, physical therapists monitor patient progress. The solution also delivers video content, educational materials, daily recommendations, and clinical insights. Sword Health has acquired Vigilant Technologies (VIT), which offers wearables such as a shirt collar device that provides haptic feedback to the wearer to correct posture and prevent injuries. According to Sword Health, combined with educational modules tailored to specific job types, VIT reduces MSK injuries by 33% and unsafe behaviors by 47%.
- **Kaia Health** (kaiahealth.com) is a digital therapeutics company that creates evidence-based treatments for a range of conditions, including MSK pain and COPD. It uses care pathways that comprise live human coaching, tele-consultations with physical therapists, and computer vision technology to help patients track their exercises through a smartphone.

It has partnered with Luna to offer in-person PT services which brings MSK care to patients' homes. Luna claims to have more than 2,500 licensed physical therapists. Kaia Health also works closely with primary care physicians and specialists surrounding physical therapy.

DHPs for Critical Care Services

DHPs that offer critical care services enable HCOs to better utilize their intensivists as well support rural hospitals and critical access hospitals (CAHs). They can be configured as turnkey offerings by DHP vendors or support custom solutions to better meet the needs of HCOs.

- **Hicuity Health** (hicuityhealth.com) provides technology-enabled critical care services, including tele-ICU care and remote cardiac monitoring. It uses proprietary technology and a comprehensive clinical team (intensivists, advanced practice providers, nurses, respiratory therapists, and telemetry technicians) to deliver over a million high-acuity care interventions annually. Remote cardiac monitoring ensures that at-risk cardiac patients throughout the hospital are continuously monitored for arrhythmias.
- **Houston Methodist** has implemented a virtual ICU to support the significant increase during the COVID-19 pandemic. According to Roberta Schwartz, executive vice president and chief innovation officer at the health system, the care team that designed the platform used Caregility for their cameras and Medical Informatics Corp.'s Sickbay platform for their AI tools. Their intensivists were employed through Equum Medical (Jercich 2022).

A3. Telehealth Systems: Comprehensive Services across the Care Continuum

Telehealth platforms that offer comprehensive telehealth services including video links, EHR capabilities, diagnostic tools, staffed 24/7/365 by care providers and specialty apps to support primary care, urgent care, behavioral health, and chronic disease management. Most platform owners also operate in-person services such as clinics or home health visits by care providers.

HCOs can support their digital health strategies by partnering with these telehealth platforms and leveraging their services. Depending on configuration, HCOs can use the telehealth infrastructure offered by these platforms.

Case Examples

- **Bright.md** can diagnose and treat common conditions using asynchronous care delivery for a hybrid patient care experience. Bright.md uses 29 different online symptom assessment interviews to gather patient information for over 130 treatable diagnoses. The system uses this information to treat low-acuity conditions using evidence-based clinical decision support. Since Bright.md is integrated with HCO EHRs, it automates documentation for care providers and provides in-depth analytics. Bright.md maintains security compliance with certifications such as SOC2 Type 2, HIPAA, HITECH, and more.

- **CPSI** (cpsi.com) has expanded its EHR offerings for rural and community hospitals and clinics through acquisition of several companies. Notable among these is *Get Real Health* which offers patient engagement and empowerment solutions to public and private HCOs. These solutions include a care management program and a patient portal that promotes collaboration between patients and providers. *Get Real Health* launched TalkWithYourDoc.com, a telehealth solution which enables virtual medical visits between patients and providers for patient monitoring and diagnosis. TalkWithYourDoc.com connects patient's EHR, medical devices, health journals, surveys, and checklists through portals for patients and care providers, and is available as an Apple iOS or Android app.

- **eClinicalWorks** (eclinicalworks.com) offers a private cloud-based ambulatory EHR solution for provider offices. As part of their portfolio, they offer a telehealth platform which helps tele-visits for primary and specialty providers. The telehealth platform can be used with any EHR. However, users of eClinicalWorks can offer telehealth through a smartphone or iPad. eClinicalWorks has added an interoperability feature that generates a longitudinal view of a patient's health by gathering patient information from different sources such as specialists, clinics, urgent care centers, and hospitals that participate in the Carequality and CommonWell Health Alliance HIEs. eClinicalWorks also supports a virtual assistant which responds to provider requests for patient information such as progress notes and flowsheets and helps them conduct common tasks such as scheduling appointments.

- **Athenahealth** (athenahealth.com): provides a cloud-based suite of services including practice management solutions for primary care, gastroenterology, OB/GYN, orthopedics, and others. It includes a telehealth system that supports secure video, voice, email, and text messages, between patients and providers, and group video conferencing to accommodate consultants and family members in patient care sessions. In addition, Athenahealth includes a patient portal, patient scheduling, and bill payment which is facilitated through a cloud-based revenue cycle and practice management service that includes over 40 million billing rules by combining data from insurance carriers with that from physician practices. It offers analytics in terms of aggregating treatment information, including dosing and contraindications, to provide clinical support during computerized provider order entry.

■ **Amwell** (business.amwell.com): supports telehealth solutions through a suite of offerings including its EHR, affiliated physicians, and the Converge platform for EHRs. Amwell has developed standardized interfaces for several EHR providers, claims clearinghouse, and Surescripts. It follows FHIR standards and is HITRUST certified.

Amwell's Converge telehealth platform supports management of primary care and chronic diseases such as diabetes, birth control methods, hypertension, COPD and asthma, depression, headaches, tachycardia (rapid heart rate), insomnia, and dermatology issues. The Converge platform offers data and function APIs and SDKs to encourage software and hardware innovations by third parties and partners. For example, (a) Converge supports AI tools offered by the Google Cloud which can be used by external parties, (b) partners with TytoCare to enable its handheld exam kit featuring built-in visual guidance technology, (c) enables virtual second opinions with the Cleveland Clinic, (d) supports wearable remote patient monitoring through Biobeat, (e) supports a platform marketplace to allow third-party innovation such as AI models, and specialty apps to be available for purchase and integration for their workflow requirements.

In addition, clinical coverage is available 24/7/365 through Amwell's telehealth medical group.

■ **Teladoc Health** (teladoc.com) has announced a fully integrated virtual telehealth platform that supports primary care, mental health, and chronic disease management through a single portal. This also supports documenting social determinants of health (SDOH) so they can be considered in patient diagnosis and treatment. Teladoc Health's telehealth platform comprises video, audio, and asynchronous telemedicine services and provides 24/7 access to US-licensed doctors. In a study conducted by Teladoc Health, 60% of consumers preferred virtual access to all their care due to frustrations around care coordination. So, while Teladoc Health centers patient health management around virtual care, patients can access care coordination capabilities to in-person providers as needed.

Teladoc has acquired and implemented several platforms to support chronic and specialty care – notably *Livongo Health*. The *Livongo Health* platform operates Teladoc's virtual chronic disease management. It uses a mix of blood-glucose measuring technology and an application linked with certified diabetes educators to give advice when they see an out-of-range value. The app can be linked to smartphones of caregivers, family, and friends to update them of any out-of-range readings.

Livongo has used the diabetes management framework for other chronic disease applications such as hypertension, prediabetes, weight management, and behavioral health. In addition, Teladoc Health has acquired and implemented the following solutions:

a) *InTouch Technologies*, a virtual care platform that offers enterprise telehealth solutions for hospitals.

b) *Advanced Medical*, a telemedicine platform that helps connect patients with physicians for medical assistance.

c) *Best Doctor*, a medical consultation company that allows individuals to connect with doctors to review their diagnosis and treatment plans.

d) *myStrength Complete*, an integrated mental health service that provides targeted and personalized care.

■ **Included Health** (includedhealth.com): Grand Rounds and Doctor on Demand merged in May 2021 to form Included Health. This DHP uses data science to match an employee to the correct doctor or specialist in their network and tracks medical spending. Included Health also delivers All-Included Care using a nationwide practice of dedicated clinicians and an innovative platform. It includes primary care, behavioral health, urgent care, chronic condition management and prevention, 24/7 triage, navigation, and ongoing care coordination to ensure patients get the right care at the right time. Included Health combines virtual and in-person care with guidance and advocacy.

The Included Health care model is predicated on their research which indicates "50 percent of members have difficulty understanding their healthcare insurance coverage, 98 million individuals live in areas with primary care shortages," and "more than 60 percent of all counties in the U.S. do not have a single psychiatrist" (Included Health 2022).

Included Health utilizes a multi-disciplinary care team under the guidance of a member's primary care provider. It also provides population health support for all members ranging from healthy to high risk.

■ **MDLIVE** (mdlive.com) is a HITRUST-certified telehealth platform that provides 24/7/365 coverage throughout the 50 states and Puerto Rico. It provides virtual and in-person access to primary care, urgent care, dermatology, behavioral health, and employee assistance programs. It engages in value-based care arrangements which result in preventive care, in-network referrals, and on-formulary prescribing. The results are improved health outcomes and reduced total cost of care for patients, employer groups, and health plans.

■ **Carbon Health** (carbonhealth.com) is a virtual and in-person provider of primary care, urgent care, women's health, chronic disease management, LGBTQ+ health, mental health, and onsite imaging and labs. It operates several brick-and-mortar clinic locations and other unique in-person care models such as vans, mobile units, and mini health clinics, tents. Carbon Health has launched a metabolic assessment program that uses continuous glucose monitors (CGMs) to identify patients at high risk for diabetes. Through acquisitions of *Steady Health,* a virtual diabetes management company, and *Alertive Healthcare*, a developer of remote patient monitoring tools for at-home chronic disease management, Carbon Health is on track to offering comprehensive telehealth services – from primary to acute care at home.

■ **Aledade** (aledade.com) works with independent practices, health centers, and clinics to build and participate in primary care–based ACOs. Aledade empowers physicians to stay independent, focus on their patients, and thrive financially by keeping patients healthy. Aledade offers data analytics, user-friendly guided workflows, regulatory expertise, payer relationships, and hands-on support from experts. This platform leverages added functional workflow from independent EHRs in addition to data derived from the Aledade practice management system.

Senior Care: Services across the Care Continuum

Senior care platforms provide companionship to seniors to address the growing social isolation problem for 13.8 million older adults in the US (Source:

*Administration for Community Living's Administration on Aging). Many
platforms start with providing college students to prevent social isolation and
loneliness of seniors. Subsequently, these platforms increase their offerings
through remote monitoring tools/services along with virtual primary care,
mental health, and chronic care services. These platforms form alliances with
self-insured employers and insurance plans to monetize their services.*

Case Examples

- **Papa** (papa.com) is a leader in the senior care digital platform market. The platform pairs older adults and families with college students,
  Papa Pals, for companionship and assistance with everyday tasks such
  as grocery shopping, laundry, meal prep, companionship, and driving
  to doctor's appointments. Papa Pals help set up smartphones, tablets,
  and remote monitoring devices to measure BP, blood glucose, blood
  oxygen, pulse, and weight. They also provide support for Papa's virtual
  visit through Papa Health that consists of Papa Docs, a board-certified
  clinical team including physicians, nurse practitioners, and behavioral
  health specialists, to provide primary care, urgent care, and chronic
  care services.

  Papa has partnered with Milliman HealthIO, a digital health-tracking
  platform that allows users to record and share data and provides alerts
  if trends indicate a potential health problem. This collaboration allows
  companies to manage chronic conditions for Medicare Advantage plan
  members and other organizations.

- **Honor Technology** (honorcare.com) is a home and senior care platform that helps clients find and schedule caregivers, through Care Pros
  (Honor staff) or through partnership with home care agencies that
  manage caregiver operations. It has acquired *Home Instead*, a franchise
  business, that provides a large network of senior care at-home services
  such as household chores, hospice care, stroke rehabilitation, cancer
  care, Parkinson's care, memory care needs, and more.

A4. Telehealth Systems: Complex Disease Management – Hospital at Home (HaH)

*Telehealth platforms that fall under this category offer services that accom-
modate remote care models such as at-home care to facilitate chronic disease
management, remote ICU care (through intensivists), and Hospital at Home*

acute care using sophisticated remote monitoring devices. These platforms are staffed with care providers 24/7 who coordinate with HCO-based care providers. Since remote chronic care management is analogous to HaH models, we introduce readers to the HaH model, associated regulatory constraints, and vendor offerings.

Introduction to HaH Care Model

The HaH care model provides hospital-level care to acute older adults in their homes. In November 2020, CMS launched its *Acute Hospital Care at Home program*, which allowed hospitals to receive Medicare reimbursement for at-home care services provided to patients for more than 60 conditions. According to a HIMSS white paper "82 health systems and 186 hospitals across 33 states have been cleared for Medicare's Acute Care at Home Program" (Lovett 2022). The Advanced Care at Home Coalition, made up of major health systems such as Mayo Clinic, Kaiser Permanente, and Johns Hopkins, is advocating for CMS to make the *waiver program* permanent.

A key requirement for the HaH care model is remote monitoring of a patient's heart and breathing rate, weight changes, and activity levels. This is promising for patients in rural areas but requires broadband access to providers. The 2021 *infrastructure bill* signed into law by President Biden provides for expanding broadband into rural areas.

Common conditions that can be treated through HaH care are congestive heart failure, urinary tract infections, shortness of breath, and diarrhea. The HaH model also works well for treating chronic conditions.

A 2020 clinical trial published in the *Annals of Internal Medicine* found that costs for treating acutely ill patients at home were 38% lower compared with a hospitalized group (Levine, et al. 2020). The in-home patients received fewer lab tests, radiology exams, specialist consultations, and lower readmission rates. In addition, a HIMSS white paper on in-home hospitalizations estimated "savings between $5,000 and $7,000 per episode" (Lovett 2022).

This model requires participation of and coordination between payers, providers, HCOs, EMS, employer groups, and platform providers to be successful. Additionally, since HaH is inherently a hybrid care model (virtual & brick-and-mortar care), it should be clinically led and utilize digital transformation methodologies for effective implementation.

Choosing the right patients for at-home care requires involving the care team along with patients in the decision-making process. This is influenced by factors such as patient condition and home factors (access to internet, distance from hospital, family support). However, hospitals can also use sophisticated AI tools such as prescriptive analytics and machine learning to identify factors that can pose obstacles to getting care at home.

Case Examples

- **DispatchHealth** (dispatchhealth.com): According to Dr. Mark Prather, CEO, and co-founder "We've created the most complete platform that solves all aspects of delivering healthcare to the home including clinical logistics, care coordination and delivery of caring medical professionals, all while improving health outcomes and lowering costs. We anticipate the care continuum to continue to move into the home and we expect our platform to enable the movement of that $140 billion marketplace" (Prather 2021). DispatchHealth works with payers, providers, health systems, EMS, employer groups, and others to deliver care in the home to reduce unnecessary ER visits, hospital stays, and readmissions.
- **Medically Home** (medicallyhome.com) of Boston was formed in 2016. In May 2021 Mayo Clinic and Kaiser Permanente announced a collaboration and investment in Medically Home to allow patients to receive acute level of care and recovery services in their homes. Key features of Medically Home's virtual and physical care delivery model include a 24/7 medical command center staffed by clinicians and a care team to deliver care to patients at their bedside. Medically Home estimates that 30% of hospitalized patients can benefit from the model. Nonprofit organizations, such as *Adventist Health*, *ProMedica*, and *UNC Health*, use Medically Home's model of care.

B. *Home Care DHPs: DTx, AI devices, Intelligent Wearables*

Home Care: Digital Therapeutics (DTx)

DTx automates the treatment and management of chronic care while driving down treatment costs: designed for use by HCOs transitioning to at-home and HaH care models.

DTx platforms enable continuous data gathering and algorithmic improvement to customize settings for individual users. These platforms deliver evidence-based chronic and behavioral therapies via software that replace or complement the existing treatment of a disease. In contrast with smart watches and other mobile health and wellness apps – DTx gets

FDA certification which facilitates provider acceptance. *Insider Intelligence* forecasts DTx to be a $56 Billion global opportunity by 2025 (Insider Intelligence 2022).

Case Examples

- **TytoCare** (tytocare.com) – a handheld device that works in asynchronous and synchronous modes. In asynchronous mode, patients can use this device, coupled with AI tools, to diagnose their condition. In synchronous mode, the device can assist telehealth clinicians. With the help of peripherals, the device converts into a stethoscope to listen to the patient's heart and lungs, an otoscope to examine the ear canal and ear drums, a tongue depressor to investigate the mouth and throat, and take vital signs – HR, respiratory rate, and temperature.

- **Propeller Health** (propellerhealth.com) – Asthma or COPD patients attach their inhalers to the Propeller Health–provided digital therapeutics (DTx) sensor, linked to a smartphone. The sensor monitors the amount of medicine consumed by patients which is aggregated and analyzed to customize the dosage and use of the inhaler.

- **Somryst** (somryst.com) – Somryst (insomnia) DTx utilizes CBT to train the brain to sleep instead of relying on medications, meditation, exercise, or hypnotherapy. This treatment is FDA authorized and requires a physician's prescription.

- **RelieVRx** (relievrx.com) – RelieVRx (chronic pain) is a virtual reality (VR) based therapy that uses an amplifier to detect a patient's breathing and uses CBT to address pain through relaxation techniques. It also helps pain by distracting patients with games and educating them on pain management techniques. It is FDA authorized for treating chronic pain.

- **Woebot** (woebothealth.com) – Woebot (depression) is a mental-wellness phone-based app that replaces human therapists and can be used at the patient's convenience. It has been granted FDA breakthrough device status for postpartum depression.

- **reSET and reSET-O** (peartherapeutics.com) – reSET (substance abuse) is designed for use by patients without opioid addiction whereas reSET-O is designed for patients with opioid addiction. These devices utilize a form of neurobehavioral therapy to help patients change behaviors. Both DTxs have been FDA authorized and are available via prescription.

- **EndeavorRx** (endeavorrx.com) – endeavorRx (ADHD) uses video games designed to train young brains to pay closer attention and to stay focused longer. This platform is FDA authorized for ADHD in children.

■ **iSage Rx** (isageapp.com) – iSageRx (diabetes) helps to maintain a steady insulin regimen while achieving low rates of hypoglycemia. FDA approved DTx for Type 2 Diabetics. It is available through prescription.

Home Care: AI Platforms

These platforms help patients avoid hospital settings by managing their care at home and in ambulatory settings.

Case Examples

■ **Amazon** has launched *Alexa Together*, a subscription service, that allows caregivers and family members to remotely monitor aging family members in their homes. They can set customized alerts, such as a warning in case their family member has not used Alexa for a certain amount of time or set up reminders to take medications.

■ **iRhythm Technologies** (irhythmtech.com): iRhythm (Zio) offers diagnostic monitoring solutions designed to improve cardiac health. It uses a wireless Zio patch to diagnose cardiac arrythmias. The patch is applied to a patient's chest and, after the prescribed wear time, returned for analysis, report generation, and physician diagnosis and treatment plan. The FDA has cleared the Zio system to monitor different kinds of irregular heart rhythms.

Home Care: Intelligent Wearables

These platforms help patients meet their wellness goals through continuous monitoring and feedback. They are essential tools in increasing patient engagement.

Case Examples

■ **Apple Watch:** is a smart platform that helps users establish and track exercise goals and monitor users' heart health including heart rates, arrhythmias, blood oxygen, and ECG. It has innovative features such as crash and fall detection that connect users with emergency services, provide user location, and notify emergency contacts. It also provides relaxation and meditation techniques. This watch is an excellent platform for user wellness, monitoring select health conditions and emergency support. Users should determine which of these apps have

FDA clearance prior to using them to monitor and diagnose medical conditions.

- **Google Fitbit:** is a smart platform that helps users track exercise goals and through its health smartwatch includes stress management, heart health, SpO2, skin temperature, and more. Users should determine which of these apps have FDA clearance prior to using them as a means to diagnose medical conditions.
- **Withings Scan Watches** (withings.com): supports clinically validated health monitoring such as ECG measurements, sleep tracking, SpO2 monitoring, and proactive atrial fibrillation notifications. This data is summarized and presented in the Health Mate app on iOS or Android platforms. This platform is designed to collect data from patients and improve its algorithms for its medical grade devices. It has received FDA clearance for blood oxygen sensor and ECG.
- **WELT Smart Belt** (weltcorp.com): works by embedding IoT sensors in the belt buckle which is linked to algorithms that calculate fall risk from abnormal gait patterns. It does this by measuring unstable gait patterns, such as speed and symmetry, and alerts the user through the smartphone app of potential fall risks. The belt gets smarter the longer the user wears it, so users get a more customized plan for their fitness goals over time. Smart belt can monitor the progression of Parkinson's disease, dementia, and diabetes as it acts as a measurement tool.

C. EHRs/Patient Portal and Complementary Solutions

Well-designed and constructed EHRs and their complements are key to a successful digital health strategy. These platforms must be integrated with the telehealth system for effective care management.

Most EHR vendors offer patient portals. This section discusses major EHR vendors and their patient portal offerings. Several vendors have developed patient portals that interface with EHRs to form a digital front door for patients. In addition, niche application/platform vendors integrate with patient portals to enable virtual care through tele video, phone calls, SMS, secure emails, and text messages. Patient engagement requires HIS platforms to support a comprehensive set of patient needs which are enabled through a well-designed digital front door.

Case Examples for EHRs

■ **Cerner** (cerner.com): offers a comprehensive suite of products and services designed around an EHR, computerized provider order entry (CPOE), clinical decision support (CDS), SCM, patient billing, finance, and patient portal.

The Cerner Consumer Framework is an open ecosystem that encourages third-party and partner complements and converts the patient portal into the digital front door. This is evidenced by the following:

o APIs that permit several medical devices to feed into HealtheLife – the patient portal.

o HealtheLife platform adds bidirectional interactions with WELL Health. This enables provider-patient communication through email, SMS text, telephone, and live chat. In addition to patient communication with providers, HCOs can use these features to deliver health information, send flu shot reminders, reschedule appointments, schedule virtual visits, etc.

o HealtheLife supports virtual health solutions, including remote home and mobile monitoring, digital therapeutics, and secure messaging.

o It integrates with GetWellNetwork's patient engagement and Experian for a better financial experience.

■ **Epic** (epic.com): offers a comprehensive suite of products and services designed around an EHR, CPOE, CDS, supply chain, patient billing, finance, and patient portal. Epic offers several APIs and SDKs and encourages third-party vendors to build complementary hardware and software for its EHR.

MyChart, a web portal offered by Epic healthcare organizations, gives patient-controlled access to the same Epic medical records doctors use and provides convenient self-service functions that reduce cost and increase patient satisfaction. MyChart Bedside is used by patients within the hospital to stay in touch with their care team, review their schedules, access personalized patient education, and request help. MyChart supports several functions to increase patient comfort with virtual services such as (a) requesting a copy of a patients record, (b) sharing available health information, (c) Growth charts for children; (d) EyeCare Center, (e) End of life planning, (f) self-scheduling, (g) video visits, and

(h) prescription refills. It is the Number One patient portal for many years on KLAS. Approximately 150 million patients use MyChart.

■ **Meditech** (meditech.com): offers a comprehensive suite of products and services designed around an electronic health record (EHR), CPOE, clinical decision support, supply chain, patient billing, finance, and patient portal. Meditech Expanse EHR offers personalization tools including a library of widgets and shortcuts, customizable order sets, and streamline common tasks to help customize workflows to their specialty and preferences. It offers providers the option to order genetic tests, store results in the patient's chart, and perform pharmacogenomic drug-gene checking.

Meditech offers Greenfield Workspace that offers select FHIR APIs to third-party developers. It also offers patients the following services through the patient portal – (a) secure messaging with providers, (b) schedule appointments, (c) upload insurance and ID cards, (d) complete pre-visit questionnaire, (e) check-in an appointment via smartphone, (f) review results, (g) prescription renewals, (h) virtual visits, etc.

NOTE: Cerner, Epic, and Meditech encourage large clients, such as health systems, to manage the protocol, design, and implementation of IT systems for smaller HCOs. Health systems that choose to undertake IT implementation of multiple hospitals and create a mini-HIT ecosystem economically benefit while aggregating and analyzing data gathered from the platform.

Case Examples of Complements

■ **Apple Health Records:** gives patients control over their data by downloading their health records from participating HCOs through APIs, aggregating their health data from multiple sources such as smartwatch and smartphone apps (such as WaterMinder, Lifesum, Sleep Cycle, Garmin Connect, Google Fit, MyFitnessPal) and sharing their medical information with family caregivers and healthcare providers. Apple Health Records are useful for remote monitoring and other at-home services. For example, UCSD Health is conducting a remote monitoring program that makes data recorded by patients using wearables and other portable devices, like blood pressure monitors and glucometers, available to care providers through the app and then vendor patient portals – such as Epic and Meditech.

■ **Google Health:** Google continues to focus on consumer-facing products like sleep tracking using Google Nest, Fitbit wearables, Care Studio

EHR search tool, and health AI. Google is working on transitioning the Fitbit platform into a patient engagement and diagnostic tool. Google has developed AI/ML models to analyze eye scans to detect early signs of diseases; improve detection of breast cancer; onset of acute kidney injury etc. It is collaborating with Meditech on a project that leverages Google's search and summarization capabilities to create a contextual view of structured and unstructured data from disparate platforms on Meditech's web-based EHR platform.

■ **Microsoft:** has been attempting to leverage Azure (MS cloud platform) to attract health data to the cloud and process this data in a meaningful manner. This initiative has led to the development of the Healthcare Bot powered by AI and the Azure API. This API uses FHIR standard for securely sharing private information between healthcare systems, which aims to make it easier for systems to take in and process health data for users including AI analytics and ML. Healthcare providers use MS Healthcare Cloud for patients and providers: telehealth scheduling/consultations between care providers through MS Teams, patient self-scheduling, telehealth, automated patient triage (COVID-19 specific bots), outbound communication by patients, and cloud-based Nuance (voice recognition, voice biometrics, and dictation) to assist with documentation-related productivity and usability across multi-channel patient engagement – in person, telehealth, messaging.

■ **Salesforce:** care in different healthcare entities translates into patient data being stored in disparate locations, formats, and EHRs. This problem is resolved by Salesforce's CRM platform with their central focus on customers – or patients in the case of healthcare. In addition, HCOs can leverage complementary applications and data aggregation tools that are provided through well-constructed APIs within the Salesforce platform.

Intelligent Clinical Assistants

These intelligent assistants use NLP in conjunction with ML to generate AI models that help improve provider productivity, disease detection, and mitigation.

■ **Microsoft DAX** (Dragon Ambient eXperience) helps improve the patient experience and reduce physician burnout by reducing documentation time. Refer to Chapter 4.

■ **CDS:** AI models used to diagnose and treat diseases such as Sepsis. Refer to Chapters 4, 8, and 9 for additional information.

- **Image AI Models:** used to read and interpret radiological images. Refer to Chapter 4 for additional information.
- **DeepScribe's** (deepscribe.ai) ambient solution uses NLP and speech recognition technology that has been trained on thousands of real scenarios to filter small talk and handle multiple speakers. This platform works through interruptions to ensure clinical notes are accurate. It automatically documents in the office and remote access through DeepScribe's Telemedicine Platform. DeepScribe offers integrations with many of the leading EHR platforms, including AthenaHealth, drchrono, AdvancedMD, Kareo, and Practice Fusion.

D. Supply Chain Management (SCM) Platforms

SCM platforms have moved beyond serving as marketplaces for buyers and sellers. Modern SCM platforms use predictive analytics and increased visibility to help HCOs manage the supply chain.

Case Examples SCM

- **Curvo** (curvolabs.com)**:** provides clinical product intelligence to healthcare organizations. Users can search millions of unique products and view cost and safety information. The search engine mines through trailing 12 months of clinical supply purchase data, including data from FDA UDI, Device Recalls, MAUDE reports, and Orthopedic Network News classifications, and pairs them with market pricing details for value-driven product outcomes.
- **GHX** (ghx.com)**:** provides a set of services to enable a clinically integrated supply chain. For example, (a) transmits electronic billing information to a trading partner when products ship and providing payment information through EDI, (b) collects a variety of data namely accounts payables, supply, and patient records from HCO's cloud-based ERP systems, and (c) uses predictive analytics to convert the data into predictions such as which medical supplies are most effective for different patient conditions and ways to source them cost effectively.
- **Premier** (premierinc.com)**:** has formed an alliance of more than 4,400 US hospitals and health systems and approximately 225,000 other providers and organizations. It has expanded beyond its GPO beginnings, with multiple applications and purchasing tools, population health, and consulting that leverages its platform for members. It supplements group

purchasing with supply chain monitoring and manufacturing to maintain continuity in member hospitals/health systems supply chains.

Premier has partnered with Resilinc (resilinc.com) to help hospitals find medical supplies and reduce disruptions. Resilinc offers an online cloud platform that connects customers and suppliers while tracking manufacturing sites, their suppliers, and inventory levels. The AI-powered EventWatch looks for disruptive events across 189 countries, such as fires or regulatory changes, that can impact supply chains connected to those areas. Premier uses Resilinc's data to inform its contract decisions by monitoring 1,300 suppliers across 15,000 sites. This includes Resilinc's RiskShield product which provides risk scores based on geography, quality, or sustainability practices.

E. Marketplace Platforms

Marketplace platforms are architected to enable transactions between buyers with sellers. They enable demand aggregation, recommendation engines, and connecting buyers and sellers accurately and expeditiously.

Case Examples of Marketplace Platforms

■ **Medely** (medely.com): largest labor marketplace for short- and long-term healthcare jobs. Medely helps healthcare professionals access jobs with the freedom and flexibility to work when and where they want. Healthcare facilities benefit by accessing highly qualified healthcare professionals. Medely also provides healthcare facilities with tools to manage their contingent workforce such as time tracking, billing, and credentials management. Medely clinical specialists, all seasoned RNs, evaluate applicant qualifications for the position of their interest.

■ **RealSelf** (realself.com): online network of plastic surgeons and patients that is a forum for discussions between potential patients and surgeons or experts within their specialty. It serves as a conduit for patients to gather knowledge and for surgeons to gain potential clients. It includes analytical software to allow surgeons to track the number of leads they receive from the site. RealSelf provides unbiased information about cosmetic procedures and the doctors and clinicians who perform them. They have developed a customer satisfaction score based on customer reviews in RealSelf. Patients can rate a treatment as "Worth It" or "Not Worth It."

■ **Modern Fertility** (ro.co): makes fertility tests cheaper and convenient for women by promoting in-clinic or at-home tests. It uses certified labs to process samples. Besides assessing fertility hormones, the company provides customized, physician-reviewed reports and offers education sessions via weekly webinars and one-on-one consultations with fertility nurses. It helps people have a better understanding of their reproductive health.

■ **PatientPop** (patientpop.com): is a SaaS platform designed as a marketing and patient satisfaction tool for physician practices. PatientPop supports physician practices with the following services: develops interactive websites, promotes search engine optimization, reputation management software creates a stellar online reputation to attract patients to the practice, post patient visit surveys, online scheduling, and data sharing by hosting popular practice EMRs on their platform.

■ **Cohealo** (cohealo.com): is a platform that enables sharing in business-to-business situations by de-linking assets from value. Cohealo improves utilization of biomedical equipment (MRIs, CT scans, etc.) through proactive data analytics and sharing expensive capital equipment. According to Cohealo's CEO, Todd Rothenhaus, M.D., "the sharing economy has empowered thousands of consumers to tap into the excess capacity of their cars and homes, delivering value from idle resources. Sharing medical equipment is an eight-figure per year savings opportunity for health systems."

Key Takeaways

1. DHPs must be flexible since they need to adapt to the scope, complexity, and workflow requirements of a range of HCOs for example, ambulatory surgery centers, long-term care facilities, rural hospitals, critical access hospitals, physician clinics, urban hospitals, academic medical centers, and multi-facility health systems.
2. DHP flexibility is influenced by its architecture, governance structure, configuration, types, depth, and range of services offered.
3. This chapter discusses the various types of DHPs used in patient care. While videoconferencing and EHRs are central to the provision of hybrid patient care, it is important for HCOs to understand the variety of complementary platforms that play an important role in their digital health strategy.

4. Telehealth systems can be divided by the number and types of services supported – from primary care to specialty disease management to platforms that support services across the care continuum and finally to platforms that support management of comprehensive chronic diseases.
5. DHPs can support telehealth platforms and EHRs.
6. Advancements in SCM indicate how traditional marketplace platforms have been transformed into innovation platforms to ensure timely management of the supply chain including disposable supplies and instrumentation.
7. *Marketplace platforms offer functional capability to implement desired interactions for buyers and sellers on the platform.* These platforms are architected to enable transactions between buyers with sellers. They enable demand aggregation, recommendation engines, and connecting buyers and sellers accurately and expeditiously. This section also includes sharing critical and expensive equipment such as MRIs and CT scanners.

References

Borbely, Alexandra. 2021. "How Headspace Can Win Over Calm in Mindful Marketing." *Scale Fanatics*. February 3. https://medium.com/scale-fanatics/headspace-calm-marketing-ae52698c3eec.

Carrum Health. 2021. "Hinge Health and Carrum Health Join Forces to Create One-of-a-Kind Comprehensive Musculoskeletal Solution for the Employer Market." April 22. www.carrumhelath.com.

Included Health. 2022. "Included Health Announces All-Included Care™ on Stage at HLTH." *Included Health*. November 15. https://includedhealth.com/announcement/included-health-announces-all-included-care-on-stage-at-hlth/.

Insider Intelligence. 2022. "Digital Therapeutics: DTx Market Trends and Companies in the Growing Digital Health Industry." *Insider Intelligence*. March 15. https://www.insiderintelligence.com/insights/digital-therapeutics-report/.

Jercich, Kat. 2022. "How a Texas Health System Spun up a Virtual ICU-just in Time for COVID-19." *Healthcare IT News*. January 7. https://www.healthcareitnews.com/news/how-texas-health-system-spun-virtual-icu-just-time-covid-19.

———. 2021. "Zoom Announces New Integration with Cerner EHR." *Healthcare IT News*. December 2. https://www.healthcareitnews.com/news/zoom-announces-new-integration-cerner-ehr.

Levine, David M., Kei Ouchi, Bonnie Blanchfield, Agustina Saenz, Kimberly Burke, Mary Paz, Keren Diamond, Charles T. Pu, and Jeffrey L. Schnipper. 2020. "Hospital-Level Care at Home for Acutely Ill Adults: A Randomized Controlled Trial." *Annals of Internal Medicine* 172 (2): 77–85.

Lovett, Laura. 2022. "Hospitals at Home Poised to Save Money, Keep the Patient in Familiar Environment." *Mobihealth News*. March 16. https://www.mobihealth-news.com/news/hospitals-home-poised-save-money-keep-patient-familiar -environment.

Prather, Mark. 2021. "DispatchHealth Raises $200 Million in Series D Financing to Build Largest Systemof In-Home Medical Care." *Dispatch Health*. March 3. https://www.dispatchhealth.com/press-room/dispatchhealth-raises-200-million -in-series-d-financing/.

IT SYSTEMS

II

The goal of Section II is to introduce readers to different aspects of IT systems that are necessary to design and implement digital transformation (DT). This section introduces IT systems through four chapters, each of which addresses key aspects of information systems that must be achieved to support HCO DT efforts: Management of IT Systems; Usability of IT Systems; Big Data, AI Systems, and Interoperability; and Security, Privacy, and Technical Considerations.

In essence, Section II explores the role of senior management, IT governance, IT management, and project management in designing and implementing state-of-the-art systems that result in optimizing user experience. This section also examines ways to improve care provider and patient satisfaction through system design of EHRs and digital systems. Since digital systems, including advancements in interoperability, and population health management (PHM) requirements, result in the generation of big data, this section explores the state of AI tools and requirements to transition EHRs into intelligent systems.

Chapter 10 examines security breaches including the impact of digital health systems on security and privacy of patient data. It explores cybersecurity strategies that consider organizational risk management and recommends methodologies to help HCOs improve their cyber defenses. In addition to impact on patient privacy due to breach in security, this chapter includes operational factors and offers ethical considerations for managing patient privacy. Finally, this chapter explores technical considerations to improve the state of information security and support the transition to digital health through cloud computing, client configurations such as virtual desktops, and network segmentation.

DOI: 10.4324/9781003366584-8

Chapter 7

Managing HCO-IT Systems

Introduction

Senior leadership commitment, including the board of directors, is key to effective IT systems in a healthcare organization. HCO leadership that considers IT as an integral part of its mission uses governance models to support innovative care models for increased provider satisfaction and patient engagement. Innovative governance models include a centralized IT department supported by decentralized technology leadership, empowered functional user committees, project prioritization, design, and support of IT systems.

Chapter 7 emphasizes the hybrid governance model for HCO-IT systems. While IT systems and cybersecurity are best managed through a central IT team, information system requirements of patient care and related functional areas are formulated and designed through decentralized governance and collaboration. The hybrid governance model of a central IT department supported by organization-wide functional and technology decision-makers is effective in supporting digital transformation of HCOs.

Central management of IT systems includes designing and implementing hardware systems including networks, application systems, data analytics, security and privacy of PHI, and user support. Decentralized governance includes governance councils, technology leadership to support patient care systems, technological innovations, and digital transformation, and multidisciplinary teams to support IT projects. Collectively, the decentralized governance infrastructure is empowered to prioritize projects and ensure functional and technological support of IT projects. It is the role of CIOs to collaborate with this governance model to design and implement innovative digital health models to improve outcomes while reducing costs.

DOI: 10.4324/9781003366584-9

This chapter divides the requirements for effective design and utilization of IT systems into five areas. The requirements focus on management support of IT, work transformation methods, governance model, IT management, and project management. Compliance with these requirements results in user satisfaction. In addition, these requirements form the foundations of the digital health strategy for HCOs.

- IT is integral to business strategy.
- Support a work transformation culture.
- IT governance model.
- IT management role – managing technological systems and collaborating with HCO-wide committees and resources.
- Project Management Office (PMO) supports organization-wide projects.

IT Is Integral to Business Strategy

For effective digital transformation efforts, HCOs should consider IT integral to their business strategy. The relationship between IT and HCO management, however, encounters problems due to lack of management commitment and usability of IT systems. This section includes commonly encountered problems and recommendations to improve the relationship between IT systems, user engagement, provider satisfaction, and management support.

1. **Problem:** IT is not involved in formulating the HCO strategic plan.

Recommendation: IT leadership should be part of senior hospital management and strategic decision-making and provide meaningful input in the HCO strategic plan. IT engagement leads to effective alignment of technology with organizational mission.

2. **Problem:** IT work priorities are modified once projects have been approved and initiated.

Recommendation: Management input is critical to the success of the IT function. Therefore, HCO management should collaborate with IT regarding workload prioritization. This ensures that IT projects are prioritized and managed according to HCO management requirements and IT workload.

Managing the IT department requires a multi-pronged approach: (a) leveraging technology through creative engagement with user committees and leadership, (b) emphasizing the use of metrics for support and maintenance functions such as service level agreements (SLAs), and (c) structuring projects through well-defined goals and objectives.

3. **Problem:** Inadequate capital and operating budgets to manage approved projects; maintain hardware, networks, and software systems; and hire appropriately trained and experienced technical personnel.

Recommendation: IT capital and operating funding should be approved by senior management in conjunction with user committees and IT leadership. Funding should consider project scope and outcomes. For example, if desired outcomes from a project are overtime reduction by 50%, then project funding must support engagement of functional users in system analysis and design to achieve the reduction. Care providers should participate in brainstorming sessions to generate system functionalities that meet their requirements.

4. **Problem:** User committees have minimal input in the development of IT roadmap. They do not have decision-making authority to prioritize IT projects and provide input in system design.

Recommendation: User committees should be empowered to develop and implement the IT roadmap that supports the diverse technology needs of the HCO. This requires committees to be responsible for project prioritization, capital funding, system design, and implementation. This structure is most effective when user committees function through an IT executive committee comprising senior HCO leadership.

5. **Problem:** Poorly implemented systems lead to care provider dissatisfaction. This dissatisfaction in turn reduces management trust in IT systems and the possibility of IT-driven innovation.

Recommendation: Encourage pilot projects prior to HCO-wide implementation. Introducing advanced technology through pilots in select areas identifies problems to be rectified prior to house-wide system implementation. While pilots add time and cost to a project, including them is a good strategy for reduced implementation risk of IT projects.

6. **Problem:** Pre-implementation information system provider training is not well configured. Post-implementation support leads to a multiplicity of care processes that result in lower productivity and ongoing system dissatisfaction.

Recommendation: Training programs should accommodate the needs of busy providers including onsite as well as internet based. Training should conform to provider specialties and accommodate provider preferences. System navigation tools and utilities must be included in the training to enable physicians to customize system navigation and workflows to meet their requirements.

User training, including physicians, should require proficiency assessment prior to system access.

7. **Problem:** The hiring, support, and mentoring process does not adequately consider increase in CIO role and responsibilities.

Recommendation: The CIO position is critical to the success of modern HCOs. This position must be well-defined, filled, and supported. In addition to their technological and administrative responsibilities, CIOs must be comfortable in partnering with organization-wide technological leadership roles and functional committees. Most importantly, the proliferation of digital technologies, intelligent devices, big data, AI, cybersecurity, and patient privacy requires close coordination between patient care systems and IT.

Considering IT a "cost department" without leveraging its benefits will inevitably lead to CIO dissatisfaction and lower morale.

8. **Problem:** HCO has outsourced all or portions of IT operations to third parties – vendors and consulting organizations.

Recommendation: Outsourcing IT operations requires oversight by an in-house IT team to ensure desired patient care outcomes. Without this oversight and guidance, it is difficult for HCOs to realize benefits from IT systems.

Support a Work Transformation Culture

Work transformation methods are key enablers of effective IT system design. In addition, the increasing transition to value-based care emphasizes patient engagement, proactive disease management, and improved chronic care management. This change from reactive to proactive care requires an increasing reliance on advanced digital technologies and innovative care models. The key requirement for digital transformation is work transformation methods that support innovative care models to meet the needs of providers and patients.

Requirements: Successful digital transformation requires ongoing commitment from organizational leadership, including Board of Directors and senior management, to implement a culture of Lean Six Sigma (LSS) and PI (LSS/PI) by engaging with care providers and other employees to understand the ongoing impact of work transformation. Successful work transformation efforts help to establish an organizational culture that understands workflow disruptions that result due to new technologies and collaborates with HCO-established support systems to transition to restructured processes. Refer to Chapter 11 for information on how HCOs can establish a change management culture prior to digital transformation efforts.

The following list includes problems encountered by HCO process improvement efforts along with recommendations for improved usability of IT systems.

1. **Problem:** LSS/PI programs focus on improving existing work systems without engaging the IT department, likely suboptimizing PI efforts.

Recommendation: LSS/PI projects should include the IT department to assess modifications to information systems that can disrupt process bottlenecks. *For example, improving the process of appointment scheduling in a physician's office through PI efforts is not as effective as implementing a patient application that enables patients to schedule, cancel, and re-schedule appointments with their preferred provider.*
LSS projects should consider the following steps:

- Utilize tools and techniques to identify functional and process gaps in the current system, including metrics that measure the impact of the existing system.

■ Consider the role of information systems while documenting current process flows. Analyze potential changes to information systems prior to redeveloping proposed process flows.
■ Establish metrics and benchmarks to assess the effectiveness of post-implementation outcomes and next steps.

2. **Problem:** Users lack confidence that PI efforts consider the depth and scope of patient care work models.

Recommendation: The scope of PI projects should be dictated by a team of functional users which may require considering changes to IT systems.

3. **Problem:** IT projects are implemented without adequate functional user involvement in workflow processes and system design.

Recommendation: Vendor-developed IT systems require adapting system design and process flows to user requirements. HCO-IT team should modify the information system using utilities, such as widgets and shortcuts, and human factors engineering (HFE) to optimize user experience. This approach is necessary to ensure that information systems meet system usability requirements. All this is not possible without active functional user engagement which requires "visualization" of the proposed system and associated workflows. Providers should also be trained to use vendor utilities for post-implementation system customization requirements.

4. **Problem:** PI efforts do not effectively use metrics to monitor their outcomes.

Recommendation: Most PI efforts do not succeed due to lack of metric-driven objectives and benchmarks. Project success or failure should be determined through quantitative measures that indicate progress towards outcomes desired from the project, as opposed to user sentiment. It is important for HCOs to transform themselves into a "metrics" driven culture in which PI efforts include desired outcomes and benchmarks to objectively assess project impact. Appropriately designed and utilized metrics and benchmarks can guide IT projects and PI efforts.

5. **Problem:** PI efforts are discontinued post-implementation. This runs the risk of work processes reverting to their pre-implementation state.

Recommendation: LSS/PI efforts require significant time and effort. While projects have a completion deadline, PI projects require post-implementation monitoring to continue process improvements.

6. **Problem:** Users do not implement LSS/PI recommendations since organizational culture is not comfortable with supporting uncertainties resulting from process restructuring.

Recommendation: A change management culture within an organization encourages user participation in system design and implementation as well as well-managed post-implementation transitions. This culture to accept changes in work practices, policies, and procedures is created if users have confidence in post-system implementation improvement efforts. For example, users understand that post-implementation requests will be "heard," system defects will be handled as soon as possible, and approved enhancements will be implemented as promised. Ongoing communication, in-person support, and meeting commitments help clinical users transition through post-implementation changes.

While an HCO workforce can pattern projects after success stories of similar efforts by other HCOs, cultural transformation will only occur when organizations go through their own Lean efforts.

Work transformation methods and associated tools have been discussed in Chapters 11 and 12.

Summary – Management Support of IT Systems

The following list serves as a guide for management support of IT systems based on discussions in the previous sections.

1. CIOs are involved in developing the HCO's strategic plan.
2. CIOs are consulted prior to changes or additions to IT priorities.
3. Capital and operational funding are commensurate with desired outcomes from IT systems.
4. Functional users are engaged in the analysis and design of proposed systems.
5. Decision committees are involved in the development and implementation of the IT Roadmap.
6. Functional prototypes are used to help clinicians develop system design that meets their requirements.

7. Pilots are conducted to reduce project risk.
8. Customized training, including proficiency testing, is required prior to user access.
9. IT systems implementations involve process improvement, quantitative outcomes, and HFE techniques.
10. HCO supports a change management culture.

IT Governance Model

IT governance is a key barometer of its importance in business strategies and user acceptance. In addition to IT department responsibilities for managing security and privacy of patient health information, hardware, software, and network systems, it is important to ensure user satisfaction with redesigned technology-driven processes. This requires the IT department to function as a central department and through a decentralized structure of committees and multi-disciplinary user teams.

The following committees offer a roadmap to help HCOs navigate the technological and process complexities associated with digital transformation. Each committee should be decision-oriented and led by appropriate organizational leaders or functional experts. HCOs can tailor this committee structure to meet their requirements – for example, a *Clinical IT Decision Council* may represent the functional needs and interests of all ancillaries, and a *Provider IT Decision Council* may combine the functional needs and interests of physicians and nursing. Regardless, the HCO governance model should consider the following *committee requirements* for an effective transition towards digital health.

The *IT Executive Committee (ITEC)*, or Steering Committee, is responsible for aligning the direction of IT with the HCOs mission. It comprises senior organizational executives and leaders from functional councils. It approves and oversees IT expenditures and conducts benefit realization studies. The goals of the ITEC must drive the goals and objectives of other operational committees. Key goals of ITEC are:

■ Define the role of technological systems in achieving the organizational mission.
■ Allocate capital and operational funding for the IT department and projects.

■ Develop metrics that represent organizational values and priorities and evaluate progress towards them. These metrics should include project goals (qualitative) and objectives (quantitative). For example, project goals might be to *increase patient satisfaction*, whereas quantitative measures that indicate progress towards project goals could be *patient satisfaction surveys* and *weekly use of patient portal*. Quantitative metrics must be associated with benchmarks that reflect organizational desired outcomes from the project (refer to Chapter 11 for further discussion on CSFs and KPIs).

The Executive Committee can be supported by the following councils that help with project prioritization, desired outcomes, system analysis, and design.

Provider IT Decision Council: chaired by the Chief Medical Informatics Officer (CMIO) or another provider. The council is responsible for provider decisions in clinical projects such as EHRs, CDS, telehealth, and other digital health platforms, training, and support. While IT representatives provide technical support and manage takeaways, the only voting members of this council are providers.

Clinical IT Decision Councils engage clinicians throughout the HCO in prioritizing clinical systems as part of the IT Roadmap. Depending on their needs, HCOs can establish decision councils for nursing, pharmacy, laboratories, imaging, and ambulatory systems. The Provider IT Decision Council may invite chairs of Clinical IT Decision Councils for updates on ancillary and other clinical areas.

The goal of the *Provider IT Decision Council* and *Clinical IT Decision Councils* is to provide strategic and operational guidance for effective design and implementation of clinical systems. The primary goal of these Councils is to establish HCO-wide ownership for technology decisions and outcomes.

IT Regulatory Steering Committee (ITRC) understands regulatory guidance from a variety of sources including CMS, TJC, AHRQ, and state legislations, related to HIT and its use. The ITRC ensures a fiscally sustainable platform for regulatory compliance. This committee is chaired by the Chief Compliance Officer.

Data Governance Council (DGC) establishes a data governance strategy that includes understanding the sources, quality, and analysis of data. This council is also responsible for the review and approval of AI-related issues such as clinical applicability, patient privacy, and assessment for bias. It is led by the Chief Data Officer and includes representatives from all functional councils.

Innovation Council discusses advancements in digital technologies and other systems such as digital health platforms, digital therapeutics, remote patient monitoring systems, and AI algorithms. It consists of members from the Board of Directors and senior leadership team and is led by the Chief Innovation Officer responsible for the Innovation Office. It is important for the Innovation Office and IT department to be aligned when dealing with technologies that impact IT systems.

Computer User Group (CUG) serves as a liaison between IT and the user community on system bugs, functional problems, system enhancements, and updates. The CUG should provide input on service level agreements (SLAs) for key functions (refer to Chapter 11 for examples on SLAs).

User committees, empowered with decision-making capabilities, serve as change management agents for HCOs.

IT Management

Organization of IT departments is influenced by factors such as business strategy, regulatory compliance, and core business operations. In addition to system implementation and project support, the IT team installs and manages client devices, data storage systems, networks, data center, help desk, application support, data analytics, security, and privacy of protected health information. IT stays abreast of technological advancements and communicates with senior management on ways to enhance the organization's core mission. Lastly, IT management supports HCO-wide committees, communicates IT issues, and implements IT policies and procedures.

IT systems increasingly engage care providers through order entry and documentation requirements in EHRs. The reliance on technology is further increased when HCOs transition to digital health and value-based reimbursement models. This requires specialty roles to meet the increasing technological needs. For example, leading HCOs have created information system roles with strategic responsibilities such as networks and communication, security, privacy, data analytics, innovation, and digital transformation (see Figure 7.1).

Depending on their size, complexity, and requirements, HCOs designate the leader of IT as the CIO of the organization. The CIO role is central to the expanded IT role in healthcare (see Figure 7.2). It includes managing IT and project management teams, working with technology and work redesign

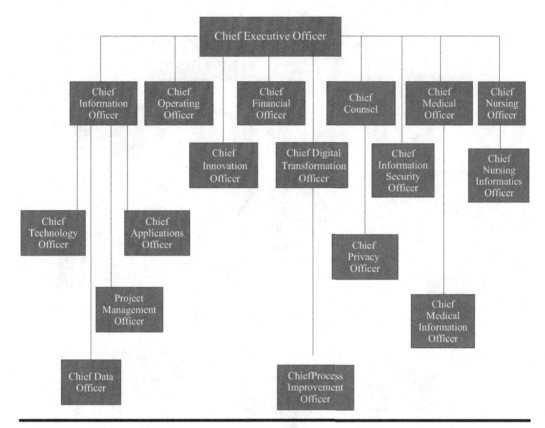

Figure 7.1   Organization chart representing functions recommended for digital transformation.

experts within the organization, managing vendors, working with care providers and key users, and communicating with senior executives regarding the state of IT and its role in meeting strategic and operational goals.

The CIO generally reports to the Chief Executive Officer (CEO) and is a key member of the management team responsible for collaborating with functional experts to leverage information systems for *business advantage* of HCOs.

The following roles are designed to assist HCOs in enabling digital transformation of care systems. The roles support critical functions that can be combined to meet the digital transformation requirements of HCOs. For example, an experienced digital transformation officer can manage *digital technologies, process improvement, and innovation requirements* of the HCO. Within the IT Department, *data* and *application* needs can be combined depending on HCO data analytics strategies. On the other hand, large health systems with broader digital health goals may consider establishing

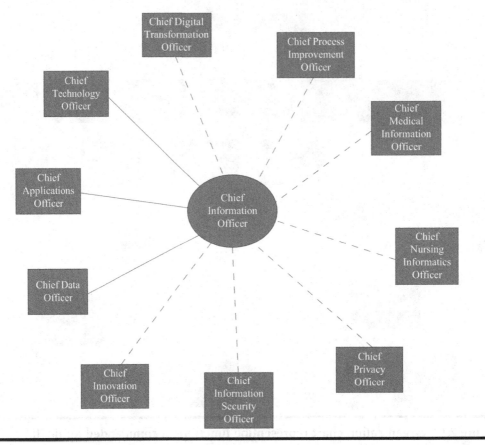

Figure 7.2 CIO relationship with key technology roles/functions within HCO.

individual roles to support IT systems, advanced digital technologies, and digital transformation initiatives. Figure 7.1 illustrates an organization chart representing functions recommended for digital transformation of HCOs.

■ Chief Medical Information Officer (CMIO) – responsible for designing and implementing functionally relevant clinical systems used by physicians. The CMIO chairs the Provider IT Decision Council. This position reports to the Chief Medical Officer and is involved in most councils that address physician needs.

■ Chief Nursing Informatics Officer (CNIO) – responsible for designing and implementing functionally relevant clinical systems used by nurses. The CNIO chairs the Nursing IT Decision Council and reports to the Chief Nursing Officer. This position collaborates with the CMIO to ensure that the resultant EHR represents their combined needs.

■ Chief Digital Transformation Officer (CDTO) – is responsible for the digital transformation of the healthcare organization. This position is generally staffed with MDs and works closely with the Work Transformation Officer. It should report to the CEO. Several health systems have developed a *Digital Transformation Office* (DTO) headed by the Chief Digital Transformation Officer. The DTO must guide the development of hybrid work models and methodologies that advance HCO's strategic mission.

■ Chief Process Improvement Officer – responsible for continuous process improvements using lean process improvement tools, human factors engineering, and hybrid work models. It should report to the Chief Digital Transformation Officer of the HCO.

■ Chief Innovation Officer – responsible for investigating and implementing new technologies, The Innovation Council is led by the Chief Innovation Officer responsible for the Innovation Office which comprises information system and process experts. It is important to align the goals of the Innovation Office with those of the IT Department to ensure that IT can support the assimilation of new technologies within existing systems. This position should report to the CEO.

■ Chief Privacy Officer (CPO) – responsible for the ethical and legal use of information within HCOs. This position should report to the Chief Legal Counsel since it deals with the complexities of privacy within the evolving privacy framework of security breaches and handling of patient data including the de-identification process, transfer to third parties, and sale to vendors.

■ Chief Information Security Officer (CISO) – responsible for implementing proactive hardware and software solutions, policies & procedures, & user training programs. Due to cyber threats and the scale, disruption, and expense of cyberattacks, this position has assumed increasing importance and should report to the CEO.

■ Chief Technology Officer (CTO) – responsible for ensuring user-acceptable throughput, speed, and reliability of HCOs IT systems – namely hardware, software, and telecommunications. CTOs are responsible for ensuring the efficient operation of management information systems (MIS) that supports the CIO's role in fulfilling organizational goals and objectives. This position should report to the CIO.

- Chief Data Officer (CDO) – responsible for managing all data, internal and external to HCOs, including managing, storing, and modeling big data. CDOs are also responsible for understanding HCO goals and objectives and reverse engineering the process to determine requirements and sources of data. This position is responsible for cleansing and normalizing big data including AI, descriptive analytics, and predictive analytics. This position should report to the CIO.
- Chief Applications Officer (CAO) – responsible for managing all application systems whether developed by third parties or in-house personnel. This position is key to digital transformation since it is responsible for functional automation. It should report to the CIO.
- Project Management Office (PMO) – provides project management expertise and assists with implementing work transformation efforts across the HCO. This position should report to the CIO.

Positions that report to other members of the executive team but are responsible for system requirements must work collaboratively with the CIO and members of the IT team to effect the digital transformation of HCOs (see Figure 7.2).

IT Guidelines for Digital Transformation of HCOs

The following guidelines summarize the steps for digitally transforming HCOs through well-designed IT systems.

1. IT analysts and designers must collaborate with vendors, users, and process redesign experts to customize the system for user requirements.
2. System designers should utilize prototypes to engage physicians, nurses, and other functional users in system analysis and design.
3. Project managers should implement pilots in core functional areas (patient care related) to identify system bugs, functional design, and workflow problems prior to full system implementation.
4. IT leadership must collaborate with innovation and digital transformation teams to develop a system configuration that is reliable, cyber-secure, and protects data privacy.
5. IT analysts and programmers must be familiar with interoperability standards, including APIs for system integration between internal

systems, digital devices, and external systems. This includes under-standing middleware technology such as interface engines.

6. IT department should establish the following technical foundations to enable HCO digital transformation efforts.

   a. Move key applications to the cloud to improve data scalability and security.

   b. Segment the network to protect EHI from third-party devices and other vulnerable sources on the network.

   c. Develop HFE expertise to assimilate and present data from intel-ligent devices, home service providers, PGHD, EHRs, and wearable devices in a manner that conforms to care provider requirements.

   d. Use SLAs to manage user support and maintenance.

7. Project management should employ structured methodologies, such as quantitative measures and benchmarks, to support user requirements (refer to the following section on Project Management Office for addi-tional details).

   a. Employ formal communication techniques to update users on project progress and bottlenecks.

   b. Utilize completion timelines for software fixes.

   c. Utilize completion timelines for hardware and network upgrades.

8. IT departments must continue to optimize existing applications through upgrades, system enhancements, work redesign, and user training.

Project Management Office

The Project Management Institute defines a project as a temporary activity a company undertakes to create a unique product, service, or result. PMI describes a framework for evaluating competing demands in the context of scope, time, and cost.

Healthcare IT projects support strategic initiatives, system upgrades, and functional enhancements. All IT projects utilize project management for effective implementation. This includes work transformation methods that align vendor-developed system functionalities with user requirements and are essential to implementing vendor-developed IT systems.

Projects begin with a charter that defines the project's business reasons, scope, goals (critical success factors), metrics and benchmarks of project success (key performance indicators), high-level risks, key milestones (which serve to mitigate high-level risks), key stakeholders, and project subject matter experts and other team members including roles and responsibilities of each. Project charters must be approved by a sponsor or key stakeholders prior to initiation.

The Project Management Office (PMO) is equipped to design and oversee organization-wide projects. This group formalizes IT project management expertise and leads work transformation efforts. A project manager is an expert in project planning and management, defines and develops the project plan, and manages the project implementation life cycle to ensure completion within the allocated time and budget. Project managers develop project plans using the appropriate framework based on the scope and complexity of projects and organizational requirements. In addition to working knowledge of project management methodologies and effective communication, healthcare project managers should possess the following skills:

a. Understand how healthcare is practiced in their HCO – including roadblocks, bottlenecks, and desired outcomes.
b. Engage clinicians in system analysis and design by using PI methodologies, prototypes, and pilots.
c. Encourage HCO leaders and functional experts to generate metrics that can be used to design IT systems and monitor compliance with project objectives.
d. Regularly communicate project status, problems encountered, and anticipated resolution with key stakeholders, including management, care providers, clinical users, and patients.
e. Understand the role of work transformation methods, tools, and techniques, such as LSS and HFE, to align user requirements with system functionality. Refer to Chapter 11 to understand work transformation methods and Chapter 12 to reference commonly used tools and techniques in HCOs.
f. Engage physicians in system analysis and design to ensure that system functionality and workflows meet their requirements.

Systems development life cycle (SDLC) provides a framework for project planning and management. The PMI has mapped the SDLC framework, along with its phases, to project management. This framework was originally established for software development and has been adapted to system implementations which include vendor-developed systems.

SDLC Framework to Implement Technology Projects

The SDLC is a standard framework for planning, managing, and implementing technology systems. The following phases, including requirements, tools, and techniques, offer guidelines for implementing application systems and advanced digital technologies in HCOs.

1. **Planning:** the primary purpose of planning is to decide on project goals and whether the proposed information system can meet HCO objectives. These requirements, along with other planning instruments, are documented through a project charter which contains the following:

   I.   Project goals and objectives.

   II.   Project description and requirements including scope. The description should state what will be included, and what will not be included, in the project. Generally, users are interviewed to help understand roadblocks and functional requirements. Example: will a major system upgrade include optional system enhancements? If so, then which enhancements will be implemented, and what are the desired outcomes from each enhancement?

   III. Project objectives, in addition to completing the project on time and within budget, must include metrics and benchmarks relating to desired outcomes. Metrics must be measurable to assess progress towards project goals.

   IV.   Develop a well-defined criterion for project cost/benefit analysis. Since benefits derived from IT projects can be other than cost savings (user satisfaction), it is important to agree upon "benefit metrics" prior to project approval.

   V.   Formalize the project sponsor and manager, including responsibility matrix for approving project milestones and final deliverables.

   VI.   Establish steering and operational committees to help guide analysis, design, and project outcomes. Assemble a team with the right skills for the project.

   VII. Establish work transformation methodologies, tools, and techniques that will be used for projects. Desired project outcomes should drive system design and process disruptions. Work transformation must be an integral component of every system implementation.

VIII. Establish a project schedule that includes start and end dates and key milestones to assess interim project progress. Project schedule should be driven by its scope and desired outcomes.

IX. Project budget should include support from functional users to design, implement, and support IT systems.

2. **Analysis:** this phase documents detailed business requirements in a structured manner. During this phase the analyst works with functional experts to understand system goals, objectives, and requirements. Since these requirements drive project design, integration, and implementation they are critical to project success. System analysis includes using LSS tools such as process flow charts of current and proposed workflows. These documents must be signed off by key functional users. Since this is a formative phase of IT-related projects, it is important that project teams spend the necessary time and effort to understand and document system functional and data requirements.

3. **Design:** the design phase includes depicting the proposed system using functional prototypes. Proposed workflows are also generated to complement functional prototypes. Since HCOs implement commercial off-the-shelf software, it is possible to develop functional prototypes using vendor-developed customization utilities such as navigation tools, widgets, and shortcuts. Prototypes and workflows should provide functional users with a clear understanding of the proposed system. IT projects must not progress to the development phase prior to system approval by physicians and functional users impacted by the system. This phase also includes developing data models, such as entity relationship (ER) diagrams, to illustrate data relationships.

4. **Development:** the development phase includes configuring the system and dictionaries using vendor-enabled parameters, rules engines, and other development tools. It also includes data integration, conversions, scripting, report writing, and AI projects included in the analysis but not available through the vendor system. IT projects that incorporate applications developed by in-house teams should be managed accordingly.

5. **Testing:** This phase requires user testing of the proposed system to determine accuracy in processing and outcomes. This is accomplished through testing scenarios which are generated through de-identified records of discharged patients. Since these scenarios are based on past patient records with available diagnosis, documentation, tests, and results, they become a reliable source for comparison with the proposed

system. Gaps identified in the proposed system are remedied prior to implementation. The range and number of test scenarios depend on the scope and complexity of the project.

6. **Implementation:** the implementation phase includes work processes prior to moving the new system into "live mode." This includes developing a comprehensive user documentation, user training, and user support. User training can be conducted onsite and available online for completion by users at their convenience. The online option is required for physicians who may not be available during their office hours. It is recommended that users demonstrate system proficiency prior to gaining access to the new system.

7. **Maintenance:** This phase begins once the system has been implemented. It involves working with users in several ways: (a) help desk to gather information about system problems and answer questions around system functionality, (b) walking around to understand user concerns and recommendations, and (c) providing users a convenient way to document enhancement requests. Since the maintenance phase is in effect throughout the life of the new system, it requires a review, analysis, and prioritization process for user enhancement requests – and ongoing communication. These requests should be discussed with the system vendor to explore efficient and effective ways to implement them expeditiously.

The above framework can be operated using different methodologies which provide guidelines for IT projects – including tools and techniques. Healthcare organizations generally implement new technologies or upgrades via two methodologies: (a) waterfall – a sequential model; (b) "agile" – an iterative model.

Waterfall Methodology

This is the commonly used model for adopting new technology in HCOs. Most system implementations, upgrades, and *process improvement* efforts in HCOs utilize the *waterfall* methodology for project planning and implementation. The sequential design of the systems development life cycle (SDLC) framework lends itself to the *waterfall* model. Project plans mostly utilize Program Evaluation and Review Technique (PERT), a network of tasks required to complete the project with an estimated time to accomplish each task, the sequence in which the tasks should be accomplished and critical path. The critical path dictates project completion time since it is a collection of tasks and activities that require the longest time to accomplish. Therefore, the final project completion schedule is extended if proposed modification/additions of tasks during the project extend the duration of critical path (Baltzen 2022).

In the *waterfall* methodology, functional user engagement is important during the planning, analysis, and design phases of the project to ensure optimal workflows and system design around new technological offerings and constraints. This methodology can be used for new system implementations, system functional enhancements, and major PI efforts. Systems can include EHRs, ancillary systems, specialty systems (e.g., cancer, heart health, anesthesiology), revenue cycle management, and general financials.

Advantages of Waterfall

1. Structured project plan, including time estimates for each task and implementation timeline.
2. IT personnel familiarity and comfort with the methodology.
3. Effective for projects with well-defined tasks and IT system upgrades.

Disadvantages of Waterfall

Since most IT projects involve HCO-wide system upgrades and include functional enhancements that impact care providers, they are long in duration. In addition, the scope and complexity of enhancements bring in uncertainties that introduce the following problems when using the *waterfall* methodology.

1. Users (particularly physicians) do not have the time to assist with analysis and design of the proposed system.
2. System agnostic workflows do not reflect provider requirements. This generates a system usability gap which frustrates providers post-system implementation.
3. Organization-wide requirements generally change over the duration of complex projects, impacting time and budget requirements and making it difficult to meet system objectives.

How Can This Methodology Be Improved?

While this methodology uses a "single sweep" through the SDLC phases, the following techniques can be used to improve implementation of technology projects.

1. For pre-developed vendor systems, pilots can be used to configure and test the system around provider specialties. Pilots are implemented in a particular department or patient care specialty to assess system risks, bugs, and vulnerabilities. The lessons learned can be used to improve system design prior to the HCO-wide testing, training, and implementation.
2. Spending time and effort during the analysis phase ensures user comprehension and visualization of their workflows using the proposed technology. This can be especially cumbersome if project scope incorporates an array of subsystems with cross-functional impact. One technique is to use mockups to aid user understanding.
3. Ensure active user participation during the design and testing phases. Incorporate test scenarios that highlight system functionality in commonly occurring situations that are relatable to users. This will elicit active user participation in system design.

Agile Methodology

The Agile methodology for incorporating new technology is an iterative approach that responds to user problems and challenges of technology. It helps with the design and development of systems using multi-disciplinary teams. In HCOs, "customers" who evaluate and modify prototypes can be care providers, support staff, ancillary staff, other users, members, and patients.

The Agile methodology requires that for successful system implementation, the scope of technological change is well understood and manageable. To accomplish this, large system projects can be divided into multiple phases to promote active user engagement and prototyping. This visualization approach promotes iterative improvement of system design and delivers value to users which in turn helps with user acceptance of the transformed system.

This approach promotes the adoption of new technologies and increases end user satisfaction. The primary forms of agile methodologies to develop software include (Baltzen 2022):

■ Rapid prototyping includes extensive user engagement to develop system prototypes that improve system design and user acceptance.
■ Extreme programming (XP) methodology divides a project into four phases – planning, designing, programming, and testing. Each phase is a predecessor to its successor. This methodology is infrequently used in healthcare implementations.
■ Scrum methodology uses small teams to develop software modules. Since Scrum works well in software development projects, it is not widely used in HCO-IT projects.

XP and Scrum methodologies are used to develop application systems. In contrast, rapid prototyping works effectively in healthcare where vendor-developed systems must be embedded in care processes. This methodology engages multi-disciplinary functional teams for system design. This iterative process results in a prototype that can be implemented to meet user requirements.

Healthcare Adoption: Agile methodology is recommended to transform healthcare operations including core process improvements and digital transformation initiatives. This methodology involves many of the steps identified in the Waterfall approach with emphasis on working with multi-disciplinary teams that understand different functional aspects of the system being analyzed. In this approach, prototypes and pilots are utilized to validate system concepts. These tools encourage innovation and ownership by educating users on available technologies, training users on the optimal use of workflow tools, and incorporating spatial constraints, including changes introduced by telehealth. This methodology does not provide well-defined completion timelines, but the resulting system leads to improved user acceptance. If done correctly, the time taken for technology adoption is more aggressive than the Waterfall approach.

Advantages of Agile Methodology

1. System acceptance by care providers, patients, and other users.

Disadvantages of Agile Methodology

The following problems are introduced by the *Agile* methodology:

1. IT personnel should be trained on working with multi-disciplinary teams and using the methodology effectively.
2. Care providers, notably physicians, may not be able to spare the time required to participate in the analysis and design of the proposed system.
3. New technology installs and upgrades that are large in scope may not lend themselves to iterative systems analysis and design.

How Can This Methodology Be Improved?

For complex IT projects, a project management methodology can utilize the sequential project methodology and include Agile methods to design core functionalities. This hybrid methodology should be utilized in situations where it is possible to identify core interactions (for example, patient-related systems) that can be optimized through input from multi-disciplinary teams.

Case Example

The following case example illustrates leadership engagement, use of multi-disciplinary teams, digital technology, workflow design, and Agile development methodology to generate a patient-friendly outcome that assists busy care providers with COVID-related issues.

Virtua Health: Virtua Health is a nonprofit community health system with five hospitals, seven urgent care centers, and 280-plus locations across South New Jersey and Philadelphia.

The Virtua Health leadership directed the implementation of an intelligent digital assistant to meet increasing patient care requirements during the pandemic. In the summer of 2020, Virtua Health's Digital Transformation Office formed an advisory committee comprising medical professionals, legal, IT, marketing employee, and other healthcare representatives to select the right digital technologies to safeguard EHI and augment in-person patient experience to manage the rising volumes of patients due to COVID-19.

The advisory committee embraced the idea of "Get human, and get there quickly," a concept that focused on expanding patient access through AI systems. The committee decided to contract with QliqSOFT to build a web-based, AI-enabled secure messaging solution. The platform engages patients, staff, and clinicians through a chatbot designed with 100% remote care capabilities.

Patient engagement with a chatbot initiates predetermined conversation that guides patients, or their caregivers, to a scripted routine encounter that can be escalated to live text-based or video interaction with a healthcare professional to reach the appropriate outcome. Staff "applied Agile development methodology practices to the chatbot solution to improve the effectiveness of responding proactively to the changing demands of patients and clinicians" (Siwicki 2022).

Key Takeaways

The Managing IT Systems chapter focuses on the following areas for effective IT governance:

1. HCO management that considers information integral to their business demonstrates the following traits:
   a. CIOs are involved in developing the HCOs strategic plan.
   b. CIOs are consulted prior to changes or additions to IT priorities.
   c. Capital and operational funding are commensurate with desired outcomes from IT systems.
   d. Functional decision committees are involved in the development and implementation of the IT Roadmap.
   e. Functional prototypes are used to help clinicians with proposed system design.
   f. Pilots are conducted to reduce project risk.
   g. Customized training, including proficiency testing, is required prior to user access.
2. HCO management supports continuous process improvement culture.
   - LSS/PI projects involve information technology and implement potential changes to the information system.
   - Vendor-developed IT systems are modified to meet user requirements using utilities, redesigned workflows, and human factors engineering.
   - Process improvement efforts emphasize metric-driven objectives associated with desired benchmarks.

- HCO management encourages post-implementation process improvement efforts.
- A change management culture within an organization encourages functional user participation in system design and implementation as well as post-implementation transition.

3. HCO management supports governance models that empower users to prioritize IT projects.
   - The following committee structure can help HCOs through technological and process complexities related to digital transformation.
     o IT Executive or Steering Committee
     o Provider IT Decision Council
     o Clinical IT Decision Councils (represents councils for nursing, pharmacy, laboratories, imaging, and ambulatory systems)
     o Data Governance Council
     o Innovation Council
     o Digital Transformation Office
     o Computer User Group

4. IT management works with its team to manage the installation and support of client devices, data storage, networks, data center, help desk, application support, data analytics, security, and privacy of protected health information. It also supports HCO-wide committees, communicates technology-related issues to senior management, and implements IT policies and procedures. While CIOs report to the CEO, and have three key positions report to them, namely CTO, CDO, and chief application officer, they should collaborate with the CMIO, CDTO, chief process improvement officer, chief innovation officer, chief privacy officer, and CISO.

5. Project management (PM) of IT projects, including experience with PM methodologies and functional requirements of the healthcare entity.
   i. Requirements for effective project management in HCOs.
   ii. SDLC framework to implement technology projects in HCOs.
   iii. Project implementation methods – Waterfall and Agile – offer advantages and disadvantages for IT projects of different scope and complexity.

References

Baltzen, Paige. 2022. *Business Driven Technology*. New York, NY: McGraw Hill Education.

Siwicki, Bill. 2022. "Virtua Health Offers Lessons in Creating a Digital Transformation Office Part 1." *Healthcare IT News*. February 2. https://www.healthcareitnews.com/news/virtua-health-offers-lessons-creating-digital-transformation-office-part-1.

Recommended Readings

Asch, David A., Kevin B. Mahoney, and Roy Rosin. 2019. "3 Ways Health Care Leaders Can Encourage Experimentation." *Harvard Business Review*. October 28. https://hbr.org/2019/10/3-ways-health-care-leaders-can-encourage-experimentation.

Baratta, Angelo. 2006. "The Triple Constraint – A Triple Illusion." *Paper Presented at PMI® Global Congress. 2006 – North America*. Seattle: Project Management Institute.

Indeed Editorial Team. 2022. "The 7 Phases of the System Development Life Cycle (SDLC)." *Indeed*. June 12. https://ca.indeed.com/career-advice/career-development/system-development-life-cycle.

Peter, Weill, and Jeanne W. Ross. 2004. "IT Governance Simultaneously Empowers and Controls." *IT Governance: How Top Performers Manage IT Decision Rights for Superior Result*. Boston Massachusetts: Harvard Business Press.

Raza, Mohammad. 2020. "Agile vs Waterfall SDLCs: What's the Difference?" *BMC Blogs*. August 11. https://www.bmc.com/blogs/agile-vs-waterfall/.

Chapter 8

Usability of Healthcare Information Systems

Introduction

We begin this chapter with a discussion of the evolution of hospital information systems. EHR vendors with a dominant market share were founded decades ago to automate patient registration, billing, and clinical laboratories. These functional modules were subsequently expanded to include pharmacy, imaging, order entry, and flowsheet documentation by nurses and ancillaries. Information systems were designed to support clinical needs while making it easy for service providers to generate billing claims for FFS reimbursement systems.

Over the years, healthcare information systems have expanded to include additional provider functionality such as order entry and clinical documentation. Most of these systems, along with physician documentation tools, have been built on aging technological foundations. While EHR vendors offer utilities to redesign system configuration, the realities of physician workflow requirements, training, one-on-one support, and documentation time continue to be a major source of provider dissatisfaction.

The development of EHRs was fueled by the 2009 Health Information Technology for Economic and Clinical Health (HITECH) Act's meaningful use (MU) incentive program. This program required physician adoption of EHRs and digital technology. MU was led by the Centers for Medicare and Medicaid Services (CMS) and the Office of the National Coordinator for Health IT (ONC). HITECH established the meaningful use of interoperable

DOI: 10.4324/9781003366584-10

EHRs as a critical national goal. The program has the following objectives (CMS 2010):

■ Improve the quality, safety, and efficiency, and reduce health disparities.
■ Engage patients and families in their care.
■ Improve care coordination.
■ Improve population and public health.
■ Maintain privacy and security of patient health information.

The desired outcomes from this program are:

■ Improved clinical outcomes.
■ Improved population health outcomes.
■ Increased transparency and efficiency.
■ Empowered patients.
■ Improve research on health systems.

MU moved most hospitals to deploy EHRs from select vendors. This is represented by statistics outlined in the following article:

> According to KLAS Research, 72 percent of US hospitals deploy EHR systems from one of three leaders in the space: Epic, Cerner, and Meditech. For its US Hospital Market Share 2021 report, the group found that Epic held 31 percent of the hospital EHR market and 42 percent of hospital beds. Cerner came in second, controlling 25 percent of the hospital EHR market and 27 percent of hospital beds. And Meditech came in with 16 percent of the hospital EHR market and 15 percent of hospital beds.
>
> **(Parmar 2022)**

The goals and objectives of the MU program aim to improve the state of patient healthcare while controlling costs. These MU-driven objectives continue to be implemented as part of the Merit-Based Incentive Payment System (MIPS). However, they also encounter a major roadblock: care provider adoption of EHRs. The reasons for this lack of adoption lie not only in state of underlying technology but system design to meet MU, regulatory, and billing requirements. Regardless, incentives associated with adoption of the MU program were largely "successful" in the significant adoption of EHRs and increased patient use of portals.

The expanded use of EHRs improved clarity of provider documentation and made it easy for payers to access clinical information. This has increased payer requirements, implemented through billing rules, for additional documentation to elaborate on the care provided.

About This Chapter

This chapter will explore the usability and adoption of EHRs with respect to care providers and patients. EHR issues that impact care provider satisfaction will be addressed based on the implementation stage during which they occur, responsible parties, and recommendations. It will also address issues related to patient access to their electronic health information (EHI), inability to utilize digital systems to access care, and recommendations. Finally, the chapter will address HCO-IT system development requirements to leverage DHPs and AI solutions. These necessitate data interoperability through a myriad of devices and systems which require human factors engineering (HFE) methods to enable aggregation, and presentation of distributed data to conform to care provider functional requirements.

EHRs, Telehealth, and Healthcare Information Systems

State of Healthcare Information Systems (HIS)

Modern HIS application modules comprise clinical systems, support services, supply chain systems, revenue cycle management, and financials. These systems interoperate with EHRs to support computerized provider order entry, patient information, documentation, medication administration, care plans, and clinical rules to support physicians, nurses, and allied health personnel. HIS also includes specialty applications such as cancer care, cardiology, anesthesiology, and surgical care.

The development of application modules over time, using legacy technological platforms, is well described by Robert Wachter and Jeff Goldsmith, "Mashing up charting, clinical ordering, billing/compliance, and quality improvement within the EHR has been a disaster for the clinical user, in large part because the billing/compliance function has dominated" (Wachter and Goldsmith 2018). In addition to the regulatory and documentation requirements built into EHRs, user interfaces are designed using antiquated design methods such as drop-down menus. Therefore, while EHR vendors have implemented web-compatible "front ends" which include graphical user interfaces, the user experience remains frustrating. For example, users having to click through multiple screens to access desired clinical information.

In addition to UI design, system functionality, and documentation requirements by third parties, vendor-developed EHRs are designed to meet a variety of care provider functional requirements, which render them difficult to navigate. Provider complaints center around the following areas: EHR navigation incompatible with workflow requirements and personal preferences, lack of training, and ongoing support.

The problems with EHR usability extend to provider adoption of digital tools and AI models for clinical decision support (CDS) and population health management (PHM). The section on *Care Provider Usability: Issues and Recommendations* addresses these issues.

Telehealth and EHRs

The pandemic required HCOs to deploy telehealth solutions to diagnose, assess, and treat patients with COVID infections. Leading HCOs capitalized on the transition to telehealth by implementing multi-disciplinary team care models that offered improved patient care while extending support of specialists. These health systems and academic medical centers (AMCs) have improved readiness for value-based care through increased patient access and care involvement. They have transitioned their use of telehealth and hybrid care models to support primary care, behavioral health, remote consultations, and at-home care models for chronic disease management and hospital at-home for acute care.

Several telehealth vendors offer turnkey solutions designed to support HCOs by treating patient overload. However, most telehealth vendors have deployed telehealth solutions that can be integrated with HCO-EHRs to support provider workflows. In addition, telehealth vendors offer solutions for insurance plans and clinical specialties. This requires health systems and other HCOs to implement multiple telehealth platforms to address their digital health requirements resulting in provider workflow challenges. These challenges are exacerbated by a lack of integration with patient information from intelligent devices making it difficult for HCOs to implement workflows across decentralized patient care modalities.

While DHPs and third-party complements focus on increasing patient access and reducing "friction" through synchronous and asynchronous communication options, EHRs remain the primary focal point for care provision and data integration from other systems – either through interoperability or other proprietary platforms (such as interface engines). Therefore, EHR vendors and IT personnel must continue their focus on satisfaction of care providers while improving patient engagement through digital technology.

Usability of EHRs, Intelligent Assistants, and Digital Systems

EHRs, or its subcomponents, are used by physicians, nurses, ancillaries, and allied health professionals to assist in the provision of patient care. While ancillaries and allied health professionals use EHRs to review patient information and document their findings, physicians and nurses use EHRs to manage the entire care process, including chart review, care planning, medication management, communication, orders, and documentation. Therefore, this section addresses EHR usability requirements for physicians and nurse care providers.

The National Institute of Standards and Technology (NIST) definition of *usability*, which has been adopted from the International Standards Organization (ISO), is: "the extent to which a product can be used by specified users to achieve specified goals with effectiveness, efficiency and satisfaction in a specified context of use."

In addition, the Healthcare Information and Management Systems Society (HIMSS) has adapted the NIST definition and defines usable EHRs as follows:

1. Effectiveness, or the ability to perform a given task.
2. Efficiency, or achieving the intended result with minimal time, effort, and expense.
3. User satisfaction.

Since healthcare digital transformation efforts are moving beyond traditional EHRs to big data, automated capture of device-generated data, AI, CDS, and health information exchanges (HIEs), we will elaborate on usability and design principles that apply "usability" to a broad category of systems – including EHRs.

Based on the transition to digital health, we believe that the definition of EHR usability should extend beyond a passive transactional tool to include customized care plans that drive patient care across health systems, CDS, and intelligent analytics that are seamlessly integrated with EHRs to support care provider workflows. This adds the requirement for EHRs to assist in care provision through intelligent virtual assistance for care planning, care management, and clinical decision support. *Therefore, our definition of EHR usability includes effectiveness, efficiency, satisfaction, and intelligent virtual assistance to support value-based care.*

Problems with EHRs

Issues that impact care provider usability of EHRs and satisfaction can be categorized as (a) incompatible system design and workflows with care provider requirements, (b) lack of care provider training, (c) clinically unnecessary documentation requirements, and (d) inability to locate required patient information due to copious addendums. Several HCOs have worked with care providers to meet specialty requirements and preferences by customizing system design and navigation. However, these efforts require a variety of customization tools by EHR vendors, tools that can be used to customize care provider EHR experience, training, and ongoing support.

Notwithstanding these efforts, EHR designs can lead to excessive "clicks," confusing screens and workflows, excessive documentation time, alert fatigue, and an overall frustrating experience for nurses and physicians. In addition to suboptimal EHR workflows, external regulatory requirements by state and federal agencies coupled with payer requirements impose documentation requirements, which impact provider use of EHRs.

These factors, coupled with lack of HFE considerations regarding the design of provider preferred workflows, result in loss of efficiency and increased errors which lead to care provider dissatisfaction with EHRs. The correlation between poor EHR usability and burnout increased for nurses due to the demands and mental stress imposed by the pandemic, in addition to navigating care processes through poorly designed information systems.

The Arch Collaborative EHR Experience Survey examined core EHR satisfaction factors namely system efficiency, functionality, impact on care, and more. The results were aggregated into an overall Net EHR Experience

Score (NEES). According to the report, KLAS used Cerner and Epic EHR data because they offer a large enough representation of specialty data for the study. Hospital medicine providers "are satisfied with their workflow training, EHR functionality ease of learning how to use the system – 70% agreed their EHR had the needed functionality while only 49% of doctors in cardiology and 47% in orthopedics reported feeling that way" (Fox 2022a).

According to Meditech, their Expanse software suite has been ranked by KLAS as the second-best overall behind Epic.

According to KLAS Research's Arch Collaborative Nursing Guidebook 2022, a survey of 16,000 nurses across 35 healthcare organizations indicates a reduction in nurse EHR satisfaction – from 71% of the nurses who found training helpful in 2020 to 59% of those who found training helpful. Nurses in radiology, pediatric and newborn intensive care units, and behavioral health do not agree that the EHR has the needed functionality for their specialties (Fox 2022).

A discussion on commonly occurring problems and recommendations to improve care provider satisfaction follows.

Care Provider Usability of EHRs, CDS, and Digital Systems: Issues and Recommendations

This section presents key issues associated with EHR usability for care providers and recommendations. Most problems associated with lack of system usability are due to poor system design; however, another contributing factor in care provider dissatisfaction is lack of workflow modification to accommodate EHR design. Several system design factors fall under the "pre-implementation" category including system analysis, design, testing, and training. "Post-implementation" factors also play a major role in care provider satisfaction. Based on the above, the usability of EHRs has been divided into five categories. EHR-related issues and recommendations apply to AI models and other digital systems.

1. EHR vendor-controlled usability factors – pre-implementation
2. EHR vendor-controlled usability factors – post-implementation
3. HCO-controlled EHR usability factors – pre-implementation
4. HCO-controlled EHR usability factors – post-implementation
5. EHR usability factors controlled by external parties

Vendor-Controlled Usability Factors – Pre-implementation

1. **Issues:** Poor system design, confusing UI, and lack of customization tools to meet care provider workflow requirements. For example, nested screens for provider navigation can be time-consuming and frustrating.

Recommendations: Conforming EHR functional design to provider workflow requirements is key to provider satisfaction. Vendors must offer user-intuitive interfaces that can be activated via touch screens and voice controls. They must also provide a library of navigation tools and shortcuts, personal order sets, and common tasks such as Quick Orders to assist providers during order entry and care documentation.

Effective digital configurations that conform to physician requirements, and use HFE techniques, are discussed later in this chapter. Since EHR systems are complex functional systems, a comprehensive features list is not possible; however, the following list of functional capabilities can improve provider usability and satisfaction:

- Include shortcuts, including common order sets, frequently used orders by specialty, and physician preferences.
- Modify screen flows, summarize, and prioritize patient data to conform to provider system navigation requirements.
- Automate documentation including flowsheets.
- Locate information efficiently and effectively.

2. **Issues:** Inability to facilitate interoperability between HCO-EHRs, device-generated data, and other systems.

Recommendations: Vendors must offer APIs to permit the exchange of data and third-party complements. While ONC-sponsored TEFCA requires EHR vendors to implement FHIR APIs for data interoperability (refer Chapter 9), this technology should also be used with telehealth platforms and other intelligent devices to aggregate, analyze, and display device-generated patient data. The ability to export aggregated data to external systems, such as Apple Health, for analytics and reimporting into EHRs can assist care providers in patient diagnosis and treatment.

3. **Issues:** Lack of data and function APIs to convert EHRs into intelligent medical assistants.

Recommendations: Several EHR vendors have developed AI models for CDS and analytics to support risk-based contracting and value-based care models. These tools do not always conform to different provider requirements. Therefore, EHR vendors should offer data and function APIs to encourage partners, cloud platform vendors, and independent third parties, to design and develop AI models. Third-party extensions must be appropriately integrated with the functional capabilities of the core platform. Enterprise-wide resource planning (ERP) and customer relationship management (CRM) vendors such as SAP, Microsoft, and Salesforce have used well-designed and maintained APIs to add value for clients while increasing their revenues.

The following use cases represent key examples of AI utilization to enhance EHR functionality and improve provider productivity. Well-developed and implemented AI models help convert "passive" EHRs into intelligent clinical assistants through predictive CDS.

a. Care Planning and CDS: this requires redesigning the EHR to operate as an intelligent clinical assistant, in addition to a documentation tool and repository of patient data. Well-designed EHRs leverage evidence-based care plans based on patient diagnoses, allergies, and conditions. These care plans can enable compliance through notifications and alerts to providers and patients.

b. Population Health Management: PHM care models transition HCOs towards risk-based payment models. Population health can be defined by HCO contractual and public health needs, for example, members with chronic diabetes and their care costs. The goal is to manage patient health while reducing provider risk through proactive patient engagement.

This alignment of interest between providers of care and patients refocuses HCOs towards early stage care models such as disease prevention, early intervention, and rigorous treatment plan follow-up. The goal of PHM is to equalize healthcare opportunities for different patient populations. In value-based care models, providers assume higher risk by accepting premiums in exchange for managing patient lives. All this is aligned through AI models that utilize big data to manage provider financial risks for the covered population.

c. Medical speech recognition: these systems have transitioned to *intelligent ambient solutions* that use deep learning ML algorithms to improve physician workflow and burnout related to EHR documentation. These platforms passively capture and create a detailed clinical note from multi-party conversations during onsite and virtual encounters with patients and integrate in the patient's EHR. This integration is best accomplished through speech recognition systems that are designed as platforms and offer appropriate APIs and SDKs. These embeddable platforms can transfer clinical notes in EHRs, PACS/RIS, other clinical apps, and telehealth. Examples of speech recognition systems are included in Chapter 4.

d. AI Diagnostic Models: facilitate automated radiology reads by HCO-affiliated radiologists, imaging centers, and independent radiology groups to help improve accuracy and efficiency of radiologists in interpreting X-rays, CT scans, Mammography, and other types of diagnostic images. AI algorithms automate repetitive tasks such as processing images for potentially important findings for radiologist checks, making measurements and comparisons, adding quality checks, and enhancing diagnostic accuracy to improve clinical outcomes. Refer to Chapter 3 for additional information on image AI algorithms.

e. Data Extraction: AI models can scan free text systems to extract quality measures, treatments and their effectiveness, and medication errors based on patient conditions and other physician requirements. This analysis of patient data can lead to improved clinical diagnosis and treatment regimens. Data extraction from clinical notes and other free text sources is also useful for medical coding applications. Cloud vendors such as Microsoft Azure, Amazon Web Services, and Google offer AI tools to extract pertinent information from free text EHRs.

f. Predictive Algorithms: These AI models proactively alert physicians of high-risk conditions. For example, "Google is collaborating with delivery networks to build prediction models to alert clinicians of high-risk conditions such as sepsis and heart failure. Each of these can be integrated in EHRs to provide decision support" (Davenport, Hongsermeier and Mc Cord 2018).

g. Generative AI models: these are being increasingly piloted by leading HCOs to serve as intelligent clinical assistants for care providers. Refer to Chapter 9 for additional information.

4. **Issues:** AI models are not utilized by physicians due to poor system design, lack of model integration in physician workflows, and model opaqueness.

Recommendations

■ Depending on the size and diversity of data, an AI model may introduce bias when being used to recommend diagnoses and treatment options for populations other than that used for the AI model. Providers must gain confidence in AI models through "test drives" on their patient population.
■ AI models must be integrated in provider workflows to be used effectively. APIs that work effectively with EHR functional offerings offer a solution.
■ AI algorithmic logic (essentially the recipe), along with the source of big data, is opaque, so providers must trust outcomes which makes acceptance difficult. As a result, AI models must be transparent for provider review, and questions, prior to adoption. Refer to Chapter 9 for FDA guidelines related to categories of CDS software.

5. **Issues:** Integrate data from multiple DHPs and other advanced technologies for aggregation and presentation to care providers. The stress on care providers is exacerbated due to DHPs since they introduce additional workflow, human factors, and data interoperability challenges.

Recommendations: HCOs have contracted with multiple platform operators to extend and enhance their service offerings to handle the pandemic requirements and beyond. Data is generated by telehealth documentation systems, patient-generated health data (PGHD), and social determinants of health (SDOH) to address factors that impact patient health, remote patient monitors (RPMs), digital therapeutics (DTx), and smart wearables.

These systems should serve the following functions: (a) alert remote care providers through well-designed monitoring systems and (b) integrate, normalize, consolidate, and present information for physician review and action. These automated interactions and device-generated data have been further discussed in Chapter 9.

■ NOTE: CRM platforms, such as Salesforce, are designed to support omnichannel strategies such as hybrid care models that incorporate physical, virtual, and automated interactions. These platforms are well-equipped to integrate, analyze, and present contextually relevant data from decentralized sources.

Vendor-Controlled Usability Factors – Post-implementation

1. **Issues:** Delays in handling system errors and functional problems discovered post-implementation.

Recommendations: EHR vendors must prioritize, fix, and implement system problems including breaks and fixes, as soon as possible.

2. **Issues:** Lack of timely follow-through on system enhancement requests. This generally occurs because EHR vendors maintain a queue of enhancement priorities from several HCOs, making it difficult for timely follow-through on HCO enhancement requests.

Recommendations: EHR vendors must offer data and function APIs and a marketplace to encourage extension partners, and third-party developers, to enhance system functionality.

HCO-Controlled EHR Usability Factors – Pre-implementation

1. **Issues:** EHR documentation difficulties have led physicians to append patient assessments and plans of care to prior clinical notes making it difficult for other providers to locate desired information.

Recommendations: Several HCOs have addressed this issue in their EHRs by standardizing the clinical note, including patient assessment and care plan.

2. **Issues:** AI models are not utilized by physicians due to poor system design, lack of model integration in physician workflows, and model opaqueness.

Recommendations: These issues have been discussed under vendor control. However, they require design and implementation input from HCOs.

3. **Issues:** Project funding is inadequate for training, ongoing support, and system enhancements.

Recommendations: A critical aspect of successful healthcare IT projects is adequate funding for pre-implementation training along with post-implementation refresher training sessions, system personalization, ongoing support, and enhancements.

4. **Issues:** PMO's focus on project management is to complete projects on time and within budget.

Recommendation: While it is important for project managers to ensure project completion on time and within budget, effective system implementation requires designing systems around established benchmarks. A key goal should be to achieve desired outcomes post-implementation. This requires active involvement of functional users in system design through process flow charts, system tests, and prototypes. EHR and other system projects should not be considered successful without achieving desired outcomes. Refer to Chapter 7 for additional details on project management.

5. **Issues:** Process flowcharts do not incorporate detailed system navigation by provider type and specialty. Clinicians who *sign off* on proposed process flowcharts may be unaware of system functionality and navigation compatibility with provider requirements.

Recommendations: Since the EHR is an integral tool in redesigned work processes, it is important that system navigation be represented in process flowcharts or through tools that complement process flowcharts. Functional prototypes help engage care providers in system analysis and design.

6. **Issues:** Training sessions are not customized to care provider specialty workflow requirements and preferences.

Recommendations: Provider training must be designed for their workflow requirements. Formal testing must assess additional training needs or customizing system navigation. Post-training sessions must be established with providers to customize EHR workflow to their preferences.

While classroom training is the preferred mode to understand and address provider questions and concerns, providers should be able to utilize online computer-based training. Regardless of modality, training should be designed to accommodate specialty-specific workflows and include proficiency assessment. This will improve care provider satisfaction when using the EHR in production mode.

7. **Issues:** Lack of data interoperability with telehealth platforms, RPMs, and other DHPs negatively impacting care provider review and decision-making.

Recommendations: This issue relates to vendors, third-party developers, and HCO-IT staff since it involves system design and development to meet care provider UI requirements. EHR vendors must offer a platform that accommodates the interoperability of data from different sources. The resultant data should be aggregated, summarized, and presented by HCO-IT and third-party developers to optimize care provider workflow requirements and user experience.

HCO-Controlled EHR Usability Factors – Post-implementation

1. **Issues:** Inadequate post-implementation support is a key contributor to physician and nurse dissatisfaction with EHRs.

Recommendations: HCO-IT trainers and support personnel actively communicate with users about system bugs, functional enhancements, and workflow improvements. Changes must be funneled through a change management committee and made swiftly upon committee approval. The following list offers commonly used methods to provide post-implementation support:

■ Use RN and MD superusers for one-on-one personalized nursing and physician support.
■ Online training for care provider review and practice.
■ Tips and tricks posted within the EHR, for care provider review and use.

EHR Usability Factors Controlled by External Parties

1. **Issues:** Introduction of EHRs has imposed requirements by regulators and insurance organizations for documentation which contributes to the added burden on care providers.
   a. Regulatory requirements focus on capturing structured data to enable interoperability, quality measures, and SDOH to compute population health strategies.
   b. EHRs have made the review and analysis process easier for payers to accept or deny provider claims and incentivize payers to require additional documentation prior to claims approval. These requirements are imposed on FFS programs and vary by payer rules for payment denials.

Recommendations: The following initiatives provide a roadmap for reduction in payer-related documentation requirements:

a. The *Patients over Paperwork* initiative by CMS is designed to streamline provider documentation requirements. A similar effort by private payers to reduce care provider documentation load is expected to follow.

b. Transitioning from FFS to alternate payment models (APMs) such as accountable care organizations (ACOs), capitation, and value-based care reduces payer-related requirements for provider documentation.

Transition to Digital Health

Figure 8.1 is a diagrammatic representation of digitally transformed HCOs that support remote patient care including at-home care. It includes DHPs

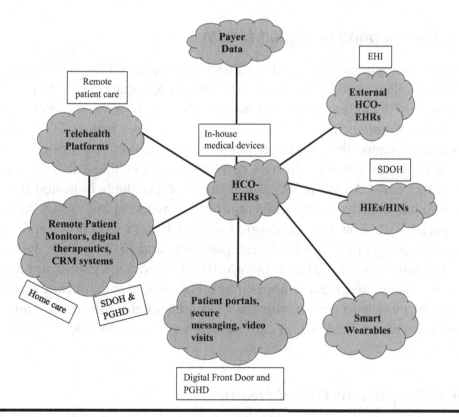

Figure 8.1 Diagrammatic representation of digital healthcare organizations.

that enable virtual care including digital technologies that continuously monitor patients at-home and transfer data over the internet. For example, the HCO EHR gets data input from telehealth platforms, complements, and smart wearables, or it may leverage applications such as Apple Health Records which aggregate patient data from multiple sources. Data feeds from remote systems are analyzed and consolidated for care provider review and treatment. These systems also trigger alerts in brick-and-mortar HCOs.

This ecosystem also supports a digital front door that patients can use to communicate with care providers and add or edit PGHD and SDOH. The HCO EHR also receives digital data via patient-connected biomedical devices within the healthcare facility. A discussion on interoperability requirements to optimize the functional capabilities of facility-based medical devices is included in Chapter 9. HCO EHR interoperates with external HCO-EHRs, RPMs, DTx, smart wearables, and DHPs. This information, coupled with SDOH and PGHD, provides HCOs with a digital foundation to enable transformation to value-based care models.

Physician Adoption of Digital Health

Physicians are generally satisfied with telehealth as an enabler of quality care. This is illustrated in the American Medical Association (AMA) telehealth survey (including video and audio-only visits) between November 1, 2021, and December 31, 2021. They received responses from 2,232 physicians and presented their findings in a Telehealth Survey Report in which "60% of clinicians agree or strongly agree telehealth enabled them to provide high quality care." Additionally, "a majority of respondents indicated that telehealth has improved the satisfaction of their work 54.2%" (AMA 2022).

Physicians are, however, dissatisfied with inefficient workflows and a lack of data integration between telehealth platforms and EHR systems. Problems with data integration in EHRs are exacerbated when aggregating and analyzing data generated from at-home intelligent devices for clinical decision-making. AI models to convert this data into meaningful information are necessary to make these digital care models work towards effective patient care.

Patient Adoption of Digital Health

Traditionally patient care has been conducted in physical settings such as physician offices, ambulatory centers, and hospitals. Prior to the HITECH Act most patients received information regarding diagnosis and test results from the physician or office staff – either telephonically or a follow-up visit. The HITECH Act requires HCOs to demonstrate patient access to their test results and EHI via patient portals. However, in several cases, the distributed nature of care provision required patients to log into multiple portals, namely, hospitals, lab centers, pharmacies, imaging centers, ambulatory care providers, and urgent care centers. Each of these portals has a different user interface and navigation protocols increasing "friction" experienced by patients to access their medical information and take charge of their health.

Leading HCOs have developed unified portals with an intuitive UI and site navigation protocols. In addition to medical information, these portals provide patients access to frequently needed services such re-ordering medications, scheduling appointments for onsite or virtual visits, secure email communication with providers, and bill payment. The pandemic accelerated the use of patient portals by extending services to include telehealth visits and virtual therapy sessions.

These findings are highlighted by McKinsey Consumer Surveys 2020–21 which found that

> 55 percent of patients said that they were more satisfied with telehealth/virtual care visits than with in-person appointments. Thirty-five percent of consumers are currently using other digital services, such as ordering prescriptions online and home delivery. Of these, 42 percent started using these services during the pandemic and plan to keep using them, and an additional 15 percent are interested in starting digital service.
>
> **(Cordina et al. 2022)**

Consumerism in Healthcare: Digital Front Door

According to the 2020 Deloitte Center for Health Solutions' biennial survey (Betts, Giuliani and Korenda 2020) (the Deloitte 2020 Survey of US Health Care Consumers) consumers are becoming increasingly active and engaged in their health care:

- ▪ Willingness to disagree with their doctor.
- ▪ Tracking their health conditions and using that data to make decisions.
- ▪ Accessing and using their medical record data and wanting ownership of it.

- About a third to half of consumers are comfortable using at-home diagnostics.
- Engaging in healthy behavior/prevention.

HCOs have traditionally measured patient satisfaction on the care provided in onsite settings. Few recognize the impact of digital interactions on patient satisfaction and extension of the patient relationship with the HCO. The *digital front door* has become a key strategy in the move towards consumerism of healthcare by reducing patient "friction" to access healthcare services. Timely and easy access to providers, health information, and other services contributes to patient engagement, improved outcomes, and satisfaction. This is a precursor for HCO participation in risk-based programs and value care models.

A *digital front door* strategy should include access to the patient portal, and other systems such as CRM through the web and mobile app, that provides patients convenient access to the following services:

a) Enable consultation with providers through synchronous (telemedicine and phone call) and asynchronous (email and text) communication tools.
b) Access EHI.
c) Capture PGHD including medical devices.
d) Capture social determinants of health (SDOH).
e) Medication refills and home deliveries.
f) Scheduling appointments for services/reminders.
g) Consolidated bill payment.
h) Export patient data to external systems, such as *Apple Health Record*, for aggregation and analytics to improve patient diagnosis and treatment.

A quote from Helen Waters, Executive Vice President & COO of Meditech, emphasizes the importance of interoperability with external systems, "through our system patients can incorporate personal health data from home monitoring scales, monitors, and share their data with Apple Health, and their care management team monitoring their conditions, which is a key piece to the digital front door."

In-house Software Development

HCOs require customization of EHR, application development, integrating disparate systems, and data analytics to accommodate care provider

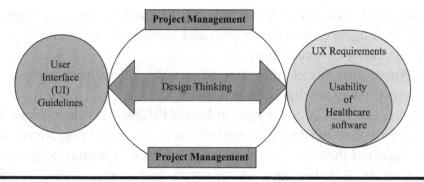

Figure 8.2   Aligning EHR usability, UI, UX, design thinking, and project management.

information requirements and workflows. These efforts should preferably be accomplished by in-house IT teams since they will be responsible for ongoing support and maintenance. IT teams must understand that advanced development efforts require working knowledge of UI design guidelines, rapid development framework and design thinking, to optimize user experience (UX). These tools, techniques, and methodologies are discussed in the following section. Figure 8.2 illustrates the relationship between EHR usability, UI, UX, design thinking, and project management. These relationships are further discussed in the HFE section.

HCO-IT Development Efforts: Integrate, Data Repositories, and Applications

HCO-IT teams can engage in several development efforts such as data integration, data analytics, functional enhancements, and workflow customization strategies using HFE techniques.

1. Consolidate multiple versions of applications, or similar applications from multiple vendors, into a singular application. Depending on the number and state of legacy applications, this effort will require data conversions and consolidation.
2. Move applications to the cloud. Ensure cloud configuration supports the healthcare industry, including cloud-supported AI tools, HIPAA privacy, and security requirements.
3. Generate data repositories for analytical efforts. These repositories consolidate information from internal and external sources and are optimally cloud hosted. Information is standardized, normalized, and cleansed prior to use.

4. Implement EHRs that include CDS, AI, productivity enhancement, and other "intelligence" to support provider workflows and patient care, and increase provider satisfaction.

5. Implement care models that support remote patient monitoring as part of a comprehensive digital health solution.

6. Integrate external systems with in-house EHR(s), to collect, consolidate, and personalize information from different sources. Integration can be accomplished through APIs that can be reused to accommodate new applications. Together these systems can democratize data availability, access, and input. For example, API-level integration between Salesforce and Epic permits Piedmont care teams, that support virtual, onsite, and at-home care, to access and input patient medical information and SDOH. Patients can get a consolidated view of their medical condition, including clinical guidance, via the patient portal (Salesforce 2020).

7. Develop specialty applications, unavailable through commercial software, to meet HCO needs.

8. Generate a platform that integrates legacy applications with a uniform UI. In addition to developing a software platform, this effort requires functional integration and data consolidation across legacy systems.

Human Factors Engineering (HFE): UI/UX and Design Thinking

The field of HFE encompasses the concept of human-computer interface to minimize user errors when interacting with information systems. HFE incorporates several disciplines, including psychology, physiology, biomechanics, user interface design, user experience, and industrial and systems engineering, which deal with different facets of the human element in system design. HFE is considered synonymous with terms such as ergonomic (popular in Europe), human factors, usability engineering and human-computer interface (HCI – UI and UX design principles) (Rice University n.d.).

HFE facilitates system design around the way people interact with their work environment. In healthcare, this means designing computer systems and medical devices to work effectively during the provision of care. The goal is to design work systems and care processes that make it easy for users to do the right thing and reduce errors (USF Health 2021).

In healthcare, advanced information systems and EHRs have introduced added emphasis on improved UX with information technology that is designed to anticipate the next steps for busy clinicians. HIT system design considerations have taken on added meaning for care providers whose mode of operation has transitioned to point-of-care order-entry, documentation, and virtual care platforms. Unfortunately, most EHR systems focus on windows like UI as opposed to optimizing the UX on the computer system – a key requirement for busy professionals.

Success in HFE efforts related to optimizing UI and UX is measured through improved user efficiency, effectiveness, and satisfaction, which translates to usability. In healthcare, "user intuitive" system designs can be challenging due to technology limitations, regulatory controls, payer requirements, and HCO-imposed constraints. These challenges require EHR vendors and IT departments to apply UI and UX principles to support provider workflows for improved system usability and safety.

Describing UI, UX, and Design Thinking

Every application has a UI which is the point of interface between human and computer. It consists of input devices, output devices, and application interface. Input devices consist of keyboard, trackpad, microphone, touch screen, fingerprint scanner, e-pen, and camera. Output devices consist of monitors, speakers, and printers. Application interface consists of pages, screens, buttons, drop-down menus, fields, forms, search fields, notifications, and other visual elements that enable a human to interact with the device.

Cognitive scientist Don Norman defines UX as follows: "'User experience' encompasses all aspects of the end-user's interaction with the company, its services, and products" (User Testing n.d.).

Scott Jenson, former Product Strategist at Google, describes the difference as follows, "The UX focuses on the user and their journey through the product. The UI tends to be the specifics of screens, focusing on labels, visual style, guidelines, and structure" (User Testing n.d.). In the context of healthcare applications, a UX designer needs to understand care provider requirements to ensure that the system is customized to support care provider requirements and preferences. These UX recommendations are translated into screen designs for an effective UI.

Example of UI/UX

- Google search engine – uses a minimalistic user interface to generate excellent user experiences. A user interface that requires meta data or a search process that takes measurable time to generate desirable outcomes would result in a poor user experience.
- EHRs – a computer order entry system may have an excellent UI and UX so long as providers can locate and order tests efficiently and effectively. On the other hand, the screen design (UI) may be excellent for online order entry, but UX will be poor if providers have difficulty ordering specialty tests.

Earlier in this chapter we described the desired outcomes from a care provider usable EHR. We now turn our attention to designing principles for usable EHRs and other software. HCOs digital health system includes EHRs, DHPs, telehealth systems, digital front door, aggregation, and presentation of data from different intelligent devices, CDS integrated in EHRs, and other application systems. Therefore, HIS vendors and IT designers must familiarize themselves with UI/UX design principles that can lead to usable digital health systems.

Design thinking is a methodology that encourages user-centric design within the agile development framework. It works as a component of system analysis and design within SDLC project management.

Aligning Software Usability, UI, UX, Design Thinking, and Project Management

Figure 8.2 represents the relationship between Software Usability, UI, UX, design thinking, and project management. *Design thinking* works with the agile development framework and helps formalize the planning, analysis, and design stages of the SDLC in project management. The process of *design thinking* uses UI guidelines to generate a usable software which meets the outcomes desired in UX guidelines.

The following description of design guidelines for UI, UX, and design thinking has been adapted for healthcare information systems.

User Interface (UI)

UI design focuses on improving people's interactions with computers. It predicts user requirements and creates intuitive inputs that take users to their desired functionality in the digital system. A well-designed UI ensures a consistent, cohesive, and visually attractive interface to make interaction with digital devices intuitive using icons, buttons, visual components, color, responsive design, and information architecture. UI tools are constantly evolving. However, the most prevalent in healthcare can be summarized as follows:

▪ **Input controls:** should be graphical user interfaces (GUIs) including touch screens and point and click inputs. Users interact with applications through visual representations using trackpads that operate cursors on a computer screen. The cursor clicks on buttons, text fields, checkboxes, radio buttons, drop-down lists, list boxes, etc.

▪ **Voice interfaces** – these interfaces are gaining a significant foothold in modern digital platforms. Users interact with these systems through voice commands. Smart assistants, such as Siri on smartphones or Alexa on Amazon devices, use voice control. In healthcare, Microsoft Nuance voice recognition systems, in addition to recognizing care provider voice commands, help capture and document ambient discussion between provider and patients, making it significantly easier for care providers to complete patient notes.

HCOs rely on HIS vendors for UI design and implementation. Additionally, digital health systems generate patient information from disparate sources using multi-disciplinary team of care providers. This information is consolidated, filtered, and presented to nurses and physicians in a clinically meaningful and friendly manner using UI design principles and AI tools.

Physicians have different design requirements for patient information based on their specialty and preferences. This understanding should be part of the UI/UX design team so that information can be customized to meet physician requirements.

The UI is a critical part of any software product. When it is done well, users don't even notice it. When it's done poorly, users can't get past it to efficiently use a product. To create successful UIs, most designers follow interface design principles which represent high-level concepts used to guide software design. The following guidelines have been adapted from Jakob Nielsen's *10 Usability Heuristics for UI Design* for healthcare information system design efforts (Nielsen 1994a).

UI Design Guidelines

The following user interface design guidelines have been developed keeping in mind users in healthcare including providers and patients.

1. **Simplicity:** Keep the interface simple and uncluttered to improve system usage for providers and patients. Information should be adequate for decision-making. Unnecessary information or visuals should be excluded. "Screen crowding" is a major complaint by busy providers and disincentivizes them from using the system.
2. **Readability:** system designers should consider features to aid in scanning and readability of healthcare users – spatial relationships between items and page structure based on importance, strategic use of color and texture, different sizes, fonts, and arrangements of the text. For example, color is used to convey medical emergencies.
3. **Consistency:** use patterns in language (terminology), layout, and design (menus, color, fonts, capitalizations, etc.) consistently throughout the application to facilitate user familiarity and efficiency. Once users become familiar with navigation protocols in one part of the application, they should be able to navigate to other parts of the application with ease.
4. **Error handling:** UI designs should prevent users from making serious errors for example, gray out fields inappropriate for patient, disease, or treatment, do not allow alphabetic characters in numeric entry fields. If users make an error, the interface should offer simple, constructive, and specific instructions for recovery.
5. **Feedback:** UI design should keep users informed about what is going on, through timely feedback. Well-designed systems should provide feedback on processing status.
6. **Memory Assists:** Minimize user memory load by making elements, actions, and options visible. Avoid making users remember information from one screen that needs to be used on a subsequent screen. It is better to design online forms that fit on a single screen as opposed to extending to multiple screens.
7. **Efficiency of Use:** offer tools that can be used by frequent users to improve efficiency. For example, shortcuts such as common orders, personal orders, and personal order sets can improve physician efficiency in order entry. Navigation customizations limit the number of screens required to complete physician tasks including a number of clicks. The

design should effectively balance the need for uncluttered screen design and fewer screens for providers to complete their tasks.

8. **Help and Documentation:** If necessary, provide contextual documentation to help users complete their tasks. For example, if users are unfamiliar with a function, hovering over it should prompt a brief description of the function and its operations.

User Experience (UX)

Don Norman's original definition of UX is at the core of every thought experience design – it's all-encompassing and always centered around the human being it's interacting with. Health systems designed for patient care cater to different user types and specialties that can be broadly divided into two classes: care providers and patients. For example, the EHR serves different care providers and their requirements while the patient portal offers patient information derived from the EHR along with functionalities that drive patient engagement. Therefore, in the world of patient care, UX must be designed and architected separately for care providers and patients.

UX guidelines represent outcomes from well-designed information systems. At the core of these guidelines is how well information systems meet the needs of users. UX design requirements include system usability, whereas the other independent requirements contribute to increased usability of information systems.

Factors that Influence UX

At the core of UX is ensuring that users find value in what you are providing to them. Peter Morville represents this through his User Experience Honeycomb (usability.gov). UX design guidelines have been adapted for healthcare applications.

UX Design Guidelines

1. **Useful:** whether the application serves user needs. Consider the following examples:
   - Healthcare example 1: A suite of clinical modules that are integrated within an EHR meet the needs of care providers, while data gathered through the EHR, and ancillary systems, populate a well-designed portal that meets the needs of patients, the applications

are considered useful. In this example, the assumption is that care provider and patient needs are well understood and represented in the EHR and portal.

- Healthcare example 2: Patients with chronic diseases receiving at-home care will get excellent care if providers are promptly notified of trigger events and receive remotely collected patient information in a timely and clinically meaningful manner.
- Healthcare example 3: A frequent source of provider dissatisfaction is the inability of EHR vendors to modify their systems to meet provider requirements. Modern EHRs are addressing this problem by transitioning to an "open" architecture in which they make APIs available to third-party vendors and partners to develop software and hardware complements that enhance system functionality.

2. **Usable:** users are able to achieve their end goals effectively and efficiently. Consider the following examples:
   - Healthcare example 1: EHRs that require care providers several clicks to access clinical information are not considered usable.
   - Healthcare example 2: Patients who cannot reorder prescription medications via a smartphone app will not consider the modality usable.

3. **Findable:** refers to whether the navigational structure within an application is intuitive and information is easy to locate. Consider the following examples:
   - Healthcare example 1: Well-constructed vendor EHRs offer sophisticated tools and programming options to customize EHR navigation around care provider preferences. This makes it easy for care providers to locate needed information.
   - Healthcare example 2: Patients would consider a portal design "findable" if they can locate information and desired functionality without the need for formal instructions.

4. **Credible:** users trust the application system in terms of ethics, durability, and accuracy. Consider the following examples:
   - Healthcare example 1: EHRs that break down often are not considered credible by users. Users will refuse to use them.
   - Healthcare example 2: providers lose confidence in CDS upon discovering that it supports algorithms that are biased against a particular patient population.
   - Healthcare example 3: inconsistent patient data across the EHR will discourage care providers from using the system.

5. **Desirable:** applications achieve desirability through high quality and branding. Consider the following healthcare example:
   - In healthcare, over the past 10 years most US hospitals have consolidated their use of EHRs to three vendors. This is related to the desirability of these EHRs by demonstrating higher quality than competitors.

Design Thinking

Design thinking was introduced by Nobel Laureate Herbert A. Simon in his 1969 book, *The Sciences of the Artificial*, who subsequently contributed many ideas to its principles. Design thinking involves designing a system around user needs and experience. It considers user-centric design earlier in the system development life cycle and works well with the agile development framework. "The design thinking ideology asserts that a hands-on, user-centric approach to problem-solving can lead to innovation, and innovation can lead to differentiation and competitive advantage" (Gibbons, 2016). It has been used to great effect by Google, Apple, Airbnb, IBM, PillPack (an Amazon company), UberEATS, Bank of America, and Stanford Hospital's Emergency Department.

The following phases highlight the design-thinking process (Gibbons 2016) that has been adapted to healthcare systems. While these phases are designed to be addressed sequentially, iteration is strongly encouraged to allow participants with different backgrounds, expertise, and interests to contribute. Also, since later phases may alter the nature and scope of the problem, it is good practice for participants to circle back to early phases such as empathize and define to make sure that they reflect any modifications.

Guidelines for Design Thinking

1. **Empathize:** Conduct interviews to develop an understanding of users. Healthcare organizations generally facilitate such processes through committees comprising key functional users. With the transition to consumerism there is increased emphasis on patient engagement. This makes it necessary for the committee to include patient perspectives requiring different services.
2. **Define:** Combine and categorize findings and observe where user problems exist. For HCOs, research must be categorized by user type

since each user has different requirements and preferences that introduce different design challenges.

3. **Ideate:** Generate a range of creative ideas. This includes brainstorming
   with team members, as well as other users, to incorporate the requisite
   functional expertise.

4. **Prototype:** Build real, tactile representations for a range of ideas.
   Visualization is the most impactful of ideas. In 1990 the IT department
   at Georgetown University Hospital was tasked by the CEO to develop
   an EMR using a fourth-generation language and graphical user interface.
   The primary goal of this effort was automating medication management and reducing medication errors. The proposed system was named
   patient care information system (PCIS) since commercial off-the-shelf
   software (COTS) was not available to fulfill GUMC's needs. The author,
   along with an implementation committee including the IT team, developed a functional prototype using a grant from Sun Microsystems
   (Oracle).

5. **Test:** Return to your users for feedback. Continuing with the PCIS case
   study. The prototype was presented to the GUMC user community over
   several months for feedback and prioritization.

6. **Implement:** Put the vision into effect. Finally, the IT team implemented
   the requested and approved modifications and the system, PCIS was
   piloted in a medical specialty.

Lessons Learned: PCIS Development Process

This user-supported design and implementation process taught us several
valuable lessons, namely:

■ System design should be personalized for user type.
■ Ongoing user feedback should be encouraged, organized, and
  responded to proactively.
■ Always deliver what is promised and communicate with users – notably
  care providers. Any delays should be communicated along with a new
  completion date – to the extent possible.

While EHR and advanced HIT systems are now commercially available, HIT
departments can use design thinking in conjunction with UI design guidelines to design and configure vendor systems. These frameworks can also be

used to organize data, generated from the integration of remote automating systems to HCO-EHRs, for a streamlined provider workflow.

Design Thinking: Airbnb

While Airbnb is data-driven, their teams often start with a creative hypothesis, implement a change, review how it impacts the business, and repeat the process.

Airbnb co-founder Joe Gebbia shares his early design school experience.

> If we were working on a medical device, we would go out into the world. We would go talk with all of the stakeholders, all of the users of that product, doctors, nurses, patients and then we would have that epiphany moment where we would lay down in bed in the hospital. We'd have the device applied to us, and we would sit there and feel exactly what it felt like to be the patient, and it was in that moment where you start to go aha, that's really uncomfortable. There's probably a better way to do this.

This experience pushed Gebbia to make "being a patient" a core value of their design team (First Round Review n.d.).

Key Takeaways

1. The state of IT systems has altered dramatically with the advent of the HITECH Act and the Meaningful Use (MU) incentive program. MU was implemented in three stages resulting in significant adoption of EHRs.
2. According to KLAS Research, "72 percent of US hospitals deploy EHR systems from one of three leaders in the space: Epic, Cerner, and Meditech."
3. EHRs are a key source of frustration for physicians and nurses. Specialty physicians and nurses are more dissatisfied than primary care providers, due to lack of EHR functionality and workflow adaptability to their requirements.
4. Surveys indicate that physicians and patients are generally satisfied with telehealth systems.

5. Patients are not satisfied with the functionality of patient portals due to the need to access multiple portals from different entities, lack of integration, and lack of desired functionality.

6. Care Provider EHR Usability: Issues & Recommendations have been divided into five categories: (a) EHR vendor-controlled (pre-implementation issues and recommendations), (b) EHR vendor-controlled (post-implementation issues and recommendations), (c) HCO-controlled (pre-implementation issues and recommendations), (d) HCO-controlled (post-implementation issues and recommendations), (e) Factors controlled by outside parties.

7. Consumerism in Healthcare: A digital front door strategy provides access to patient portal with the following capabilities: easy-to-access EHI, medication refills, scheduling appointments for services, reminders, consolidated bill payment, and provider consultations through asynchronous (email and text) and synchronous communication tools (telemedicine and phone call).

8. HCO-IT staff software development projects center around aggregating different data sources, displaying summarized data sets, and analytics.

9. It is important for vendors and HCO-IT design teams to understand HFE principles in relation to UI and optimizing UX (and system usability), by utilizing design thinking in software development and system implementation projects.

References

AMA. 2022. *2021 Telehealth Survey Report.* https://www.ama-assn.org/system/files/telehealth-survey-report.pdf.

Betts, David, Shane Giuliani, and Leslie Korenda. 2020. "Are Consumers Already Living in the Future of Health?" *Deloitte Insights.* August 14. https://www2.deloitte.com/us/en/insights/industry/health-care/consumer-health-trends.html.

CMS. 2010. *Factsheet.* July 13. https://www.cms.gov/newsroom/fact-sheets/cms-and-onc-final-regulations-define-meaningful-use-and-set-standards-electronic-health-record.

Cordina, Jenny, Jennifer Fowkes, Rupal Malani, and Laura Medford-Davis. 2022. "Patients Love Telehealth – Physicians Are Not So Sure." *Mckinsey.* February 20. https://www.mckinsey.com/industries/healthcare-systems-and-services/our-insights/patients-love-telehealth-physicians-are-not-so-sure.

Davenport, Thomas H., Tonya M. Hongsermeier, and Kimberly Alba Mc Cord. 2018. *Using AI to Improve Electronic Health Records.* December 13. https://hbr.org/2018/12/using-ai-to-improve-electronic-health-records.

First Round Review. n.d. "How Design Thinking Transformed Airbnb from a Failing Startup to a Billion Dollar Business." *First Round Review.* Accessed October 2022. https://review.firstround.com/How-design-thinking-transformed-Airbnb -from-failing-startup-to-billion-dollar-business.

Fox, Andrea. 2022. "Nurse EHR Satisfaction Slides during Pandemic." *Healthcare IT News.* August 29. https://www.healthcareitnews.com/news/nurse-ehr-satisfac-tion-slides-during-pandemic.

———. 2022a. "Physician EHR Satisfaction Varies by Specialty, Says Klas Report." *HealthCare IT News.* September 21. https://www.healthcareitnews.com/news/ physician-ehr-satisfaction-varies-specialty-says-klas-report.

Gibbons, Sarah. 2016. *Design Thinking 101.* July 31. https://www.nngroup.com/ articles/design-thinking/.

Nielsen, J. 1994. "Enhancing the Explanator Power of Usability Heuristics." *Proc. ACM CHI'94 Conf.* Boston, MA, 152–158.

Parmar, Arundhati. 2022. "How Health Systems Can Successfully Manage and Grow Their Provider Networks with an EHR." *Medcity News.* June 27. https://medci-tynews.com/2022/06/how-health-systems-can-successfully-manage-and-grow -their-provider-networks-with-an-ehr/.

Rice University. n.d. *What is Human Factors/HCI.* Accessed September 2022. https://psychology.rice.edu/what-human-factorshci.

Salesforce. 2020. "Trailblazer Q&A: Piedmont Healthcare's Andy Chang." *Salesforce News.* March 9. https://www.salesforce.com/news/stories/trailblazer-qa-pied-mont-healthcares-andy-chang/.

User Testing. n.d. *UI vs. UX.* Accessed September 2022. https://www.usertesting .com/resources/topics/ui-vs-ux.

USF Health. 2021. *Human Factors in Healthcare.* March 1. https://www.usf-healthonline.com/resources/health-informatics/human-factors-in-healthcare/.

Wachter, Robert, and Jeff Goldsmith. 2018. "To Combat Physician Burnout and Improve Care, Fix the Electronic Health Record". *Harvard Business Review.* March 18. https://hbr.org/2018/03/to-combat-physician-burnout-and-improve -care-fix-the-electronic-health-record.

Chapter 9

Big Data, AI, and Interoperability

Introduction

Healthcare is an information industry. Prior to adoption of the HITECH Act of 2009, most healthcare entities utilized paper medical records. Even when the original source data existed in digital form, such as lab results and radiology reports, it was printed and filed in the official paper medical chart. Therefore, this hidden trove of data could not be effectively converted into meaningful information to improve the quality of patient care.

The following confluence of events contributed to the explosion of digital information in healthcare: (a) adoption of certified EHRs as the official patient record, (b) device-generated data from medical monitors, namely vital signs, insulin and pain pumps, defibrillators, and pacemakers on HCO networks, (c) interoperability of digital patient data between healthcare entities via health information exchanges (HIEs), and (d) adoption of telehealth and DHPs to support virtual and hybrid care models comprising healthcare across the care continuum. These models include at-home care and hospital at-home care models that generate patient data from remote patient monitors (RPMs), digital therapeutics (DTx), smart wearables, and other sources.

Healthcare data generated from the confluence of events is primarily objective and lends itself to machine learning (ML) models. This data exists in structured (e.g., sections of EHRs, device-generated data, and smart wearables) and unstructured (e.g., clinical notes, and imaging) forms which can be parsed, summarized, and analyzed through natural language processing

(NLP) algorithms. These self-learning models can assist care providers in a variety of ways, for example, predicting complications for high-risk patients post procedure, enabling preventative measures for improved quality, and reducing cost of care.

This chapter provides an understanding of big data, AI, and interoperability in the context of healthcare. It concludes by assessing the relationship between these technologies and digital transformation of HCOs.

Big Data

How Is Big Data Generated?

Big data can be described as a collection of structured and unstructured datasets too large to handle via traditional software programs and therefore requires specialized analytics. In fact, 80% of data currently generated is unstructured which is roughly mirrored in healthcare. Big data in healthcare is generated from internal sources such as EHRs, imaging systems, medical devices, IoT-enabled devices, interoperability, payer data, and remote/home-based care through telehealth, RPMs, DTx, smart wearables, and remote documentation by care providers. Refer to Figure 9.1 for a diagrammatic representation of digitally transformed health systems and other HCOs with potential data sources that are internal, external, and remote.

As Figure 9.1 illustrates, documentation regarding patient-generated health data (PGHD) and social determinants of health (SDOH) can be obtained from patients, family members, and care givers. These terms are defined in the official website of the Health and Human Services (HHS). PGHD are health-related data created, recorded, or gathered by or from patients (or family members or other caregivers) to help address a health concern. SDOH are the conditions in the environments where people are born, live, learn, work, worship, and age that affect a wide range of health, functioning, and quality-of-life outcomes and risks.

Big data analytics can analyze and predict patient diagnosis, treatment, medication safety, and patient characteristics. They can also improve provider productivity by converting speech to text, recognizing patterns in radiological images, and extracting relevant clinical data from unstructured data sets such as discharge summary and progress note. HCOs transitioning to Medicare Advantage and other risk-based arrangements understand the importance of managing the health of member population which requires

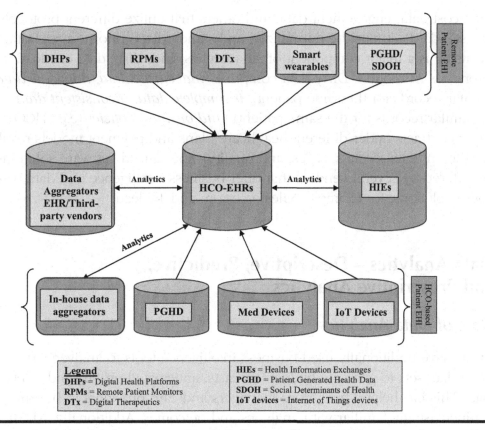

Figure 9.1 Potential data sources for digitally transformed HCOs: internal, external, and device generated.

leveraging population health data and SDOH to manage risks, reduce costs of chronic disease management, disease prevention, and improve patient outcomes.

Data Aggregation

Data aggregation is collecting patient data from different sources to create a unified data asset. It forms the foundation for PHM and transition to value-based care. For example, aggregating data from a homogeneous population can help generate prediction models for similar patients.

Data Cleansing

Since big data is an aggregate of disparate data sources such as HCOs of different size and scope, EHRs, imaging data, socio-economic data, claims data, cost data, engagement data, and others that utilize different protocols and standards, it must be normalized and standardized prior to use. Data cleansing is a major component of AI analytics since dirty data can lead to erroneous AI models. Dirty data comprises *inaccurate data, duplicate data* (similar records for the same patient), *incomplete data, inconsistent data* (dissimilar records for the same patient), *and business policies* (e.g., HCO payer contracts under different healthcare plans and payment models result in different data formats, types, and quality). Specialized software solutions are offered by several vendors that offer business intelligence and data warehouse solutions, for example, Salesforce.com and Tableau.

Data Analytics – Descriptive, Predictive, and Prescriptive Analytics

State of Data Analytics

HCOs have traditionally used business intelligence tools to analyze structured data sets to generate budget forecasts, anticipated profits, and safety data. This has helped healthcare managers and care providers in becoming increasingly familiar with analytics and outcomes. Additionally, AI/ML systems have gradually gained acceptance due to availability of big data, cloud computing, and sophisticated computational AI tools to generate ML algorithms.

ML algorithms can be designed to be predictive with a higher degree of accuracy. And their prediction accuracy improves with additional patient data, helping patients adhere to treatment protocols and care providers with improved accuracy of diagnosis and outcomes. These systems can also provide alerts when patients are not in healthcare settings. For example, an Apple watch can continuously monitor heart rate and provide alerts if the patient rate goes above the desired level.

Figure 9.1 illustrates potential sources of big data in HCOs that utilize digital technologies to generate advanced analytics. The diagram indicates EHI derived from HCO-based patient care, at-home care, and interoperability platforms such as HIEs. A significant source of big data is remotely generated through smart wearables, health apps, and at-home care devices such as RPMs, digital platforms, digital therapeutics, and PGHD including SDOH. Data provided by ongoing intelligent monitoring and treatment devices supports patient engagement and provider diagnosis and can be used by in-house IT, HIEs, EHR vendors, and third-party aggregators to generate PHM analytics and AI-based clinical decision support.

Descriptive, predictive, and prescriptive analytics are commonly used to analyze data of all sizes and types, including cloud-stored big data. AI predictive analytics is frequently used in healthcare – which, like descriptive analytics, utilizes retrospective data to "understand" the data but goes further by developing regression models that predict future events based on patient EHI. AI models utilizing predictive analytics are routinely embedded (or integrated) in EHRs to convert them into intelligent systems.

Descriptive analytics employ tools and techniques on past data to understand patterns and trends. These analytics provide insights into events that occurred. The following examples illustrate HCO use of descriptive analytics.

- Understand healthcare operations. For instance, ER trends such as *patient wait time* and *patients who leave without being seen* are routinely monitored to ensure compliance with HCO policies and standards. HCOs use process redesign, operational changes (establishing a fast-track center for lower acuity patients), and spatial optimization to close the gap between current outcome measures and desired targets.
- Monitor the safety and quality of care via scoreboards. These scoreboards drive improvement plans by monitoring key indicators such as *serious safety events, pressure ulcers (various stages), falls*, and *medication errors*.
- Analyze data from member population for risk-based arrangements (such as Medicare Shared Savings Plan) to understand health risks and costs associated with the member population.
- Athenahealth analyzed their patient records to identify 62,000 hypertensive women of childbearing age who were prescribed ACE inhibitors which put them at risk. The women's doctors were advised to either prescribe a different hypertension medicine or urge the women to use contraception (Bush and Fox 2016).

Predictive and prescriptive analytics – *predictive analytics* leverage ML algorithms and training data sets to predict future outcomes based on patterns and trends discovered in the data. *Prescriptive analytics*, on the other hand, can provide the most favorable course of action – in addition to predicting events. For example, it can use past diagnosis and treatment information to recommend a course of patient treatment. Providers prefer to use AI models for clinical decision support rather than a recommended course of action. Therefore, most AI algorithm developers utilize predictive analytics to provide decision support. This also mitigates risk of potential litigation.

While predictive analytics can be used in a variety of situations, including patient care, supply chain management, operations management, and billing, the following serve as examples of use cases.

- Treatment – precision medicine to provide customized treatment for patients.
- Prevention – proactive monitoring and wellness programs for early disease detection and treatment.
- Safety – reduce medical errors.
- Cost – reduce overall healthcare expenditure by enabling a favorable switch to value-based care models.

Examples

1. **Predictive analytics to improve operational management:** A *Forbes* article (Marr 2016) details how hospitals with the Assistance Publique-Hôpitaux de Paris used big data to generate algorithms that predicted future admissions trends. Forbes states:

   The result is a web browser-based interface designed to be used by doctors, nurses, and hospital administration staff – untrained in data science – to forecast visit and admission rates for the next 15 days. Extra staff can be drafted in when high numbers of visitors are expected, leading to reduced waiting times for patients and better quality of care.

   These types of predictions utilize simulation models.

2. **Predictive analytics to improve disease management:** Chronic Obstructive Pulmonary Disease (COPD) is complex and expensive to manage. According to the Centers for Disease Control and Prevention (CDC), the costs attributable to COPD increased from $32.1 billion in 2010 to $49 billion in 2020. In addition, total absenteeism costs were $3.9 billion in 2010 with an estimated 16.4 million days of work lost because of COPD (CDC 2018).

Case Example: Propeller Health (Propeller Health n.d.) has developed a solution to monitor and manage medication adherence of inhalers for effective Asthma and COPD management. It uses sensors that attach to inhalers, track medication usage, and transfer that data to an app on the patient's phone. The app helps patients through reminders, identifying triggers, symptoms, trends, and other analytics. Providers are alerted if patient adherence is not well controlled. Providers can access all data gathered through Propeller Health in the patient's EHR or on the Propeller Health platform through Propeller APIs. Propeller utilizes ML algorithms to identify patients whose inhaler use has increased and alerts both the patient and their care providers.

The Cleveland Clinic enrolled 39 patients, with COPD and at least one hospitalization or ER visit the year prior to their enrollment, into a program that required the use of Propeller Health's platform and sensors. The results demonstrated a reduction in COPD-related hospital utilization from 3.4 trips pre-enrollment to 2.2 trips post use of the Propeller platform (Dietsche 2019).

AI and Healthcare Systems

AI algorithms attempt to create human-like thinking and reasoning skills in computer systems. These algorithms incorporate machine learning, neural networks, deep learning, and natural language processing. The following description of each technology is followed by applications relevant to healthcare systems.

Machine Learning (ML) – ML is a set of algorithms that learn from data and use those learnings to discover patterns of interest as well as generate outputs desired by the algorithms. ML models follow the functions learned from data feeds but may need revisions depending on actual vs. desired output. Additional data sets allow ML to learn and mature to the desired state.

Neural Networks – neural networks are a subset of ML. Algorithms in neural network models are capable of self-determining the accuracy of their predictions/outcomes.

Deep Learning – deep learning uses layers of choices – each refining the previous – to perform specific tasks with increasing accuracy. Deep learning comprises complex neural networks with the ability to handle abstract images and ill-defined problems. Like neural networks, deep learning is a subset of ML.

Natural Language Processing (NLP) – NLP combines the science of linguistics and AI. NLP systems are used to define and extract data from unstructured data sets such as clinical notes. Examples of NLP algorithms in healthcare: speech recognition, spell checks, coding assistant, and text extraction. These examples, and others, have been detailed in the following section.

Machine Learning Systems

ML systems, neural networks, and deep learning systems are used to develop predictive models for different applications in healthcare. The following examples illustrate models offered by vendors and institutions.

Examples

1. Virtual Health Assistants (VHAs) used by healthcare organizations are AI-based systems designed to interact with customers since they can respond to human speech. These systems are developed using NLP, ML, and AI-enabled bots (not to be confused with chatbots) and can assist patients in several ways including:
   - Scheduling, changing, or canceling appointments.
   - Ordering recurring medications.
   - Contacting regarding available test results and reminders.
   - Answering questions such as procedure preparation requirements.
   - Answering common patient billing questions.

   HCOs should solicit VHA vendors with experience and expertise in healthcare in order to understand, select, and embed these systems in their operations.
2. Chatbots use ML algorithms and NLP to provide real-time assistance to patients. They have proven to be extensions of HCO digital health strategy and can be used to promote patient-centric care in several ways. Chatbots can play a key role in HCO platforms through real-time patient engagement, triage, and transfer to healthcare professionals.

   Conversational chatbots come with different maturity levels. Chatbots with lower maturity levels support pre-built responses to well-defined questions, while chatbots with higher maturity levels can mimic human interactions by contextually interpreting questions and providing customized responses. Finally, prescriptive chatbots go beyond questions and answers and offer therapeutic solutions. For example, Woebot designed by researchers at Stanford University supports mental health assistance using cognitive behavioral therapy (CBT).

3. Babylon Health offers a digital healthcare app using AI, video, and text for consultations with doctors and specialists, which has been adopted by health services and the NHS in the UK. The company has also created a digital care assistant to advise people on how to diagnose and manage suspected COVID-19 infections (Babylon Health n.d.).

4. AI diagnostic algorithms are being used by HCO-affiliated radiologists, imaging centers, and independent radiology groups to help improve accuracy and efficiency of radiologists in interpreting X-rays, CT scans, mammography, and other types of diagnostic images. AI algorithms automate repetitive tasks, process images for potentially important findings for radiologist checks, add quality checks, and enhance diagnostic accuracy to improve clinical outcomes. Measurements such as volume, dimension, shape, growth rate, and more can be extracted from images and analyzed to reveal anomalies, patterns, relationships, and insights.

   A 2020 study from American College of Radiology (ACR) indicates a 30% increase in the clinical adoption of AI-based algorithms by radiologists – up from none in 2015. It is anticipated that over the next 10–15 years average radiologists will practice with 20–40 algorithms, depending on their subspecialties (Siwicki 2021).

5. Mass General Brigham has developed over 50 image algorithms for use in their clinical practice "some of which have been FDA-cleared and made available via Nuance's AI Marketplace" (Siwicki 2021).

6. Researchers in MD Anderson have developed medical ML algorithms "to predict acute toxicities in patients receiving radiation therapy for head and neck cancers" (Raeke 2019).

Natural Language Processing Systems

ML models leverage NLP to generate algorithms. This technology has applicability in several areas within healthcare.

Examples

1. Summarize digital text into summaries and synopses for researchers or ML algorithms.

2. Identify uncoded diseases in unstructured medical documentation such as clinical notes. This improves patient treatment protocols and outcomes.
3. NLP algorithms in conjunction with ML can assist medical coding systems by:
   - Extracting clinical information from unstructured text.
   - Synthesizing detailed charts into key points to make the coding process efficient and effective.
4. Speech recognition platforms capture and create a detailed clinical note from multi-party conversations during in-person patient encounters. These systems improve patient throughput, reduce clinical documentation time, and improve provider satisfaction. Examples of speech recognition systems that offer ambient clinical intelligence can be found in Chapter 4 (Microsoft DAX) and Chapter 6 (Deepscribe).
5. Anti-spam software scan emails for spam or phishing using NLP's text classification capabilities.

Generative AI Systems

Generative AI falls under the ML category and has been gaining acceptance in healthcare applications. It uses significant number of parameters in conjunction with large data sets to generate new content. While there are several types of generative AI systems, the most commonly used in healthcare are large language models (LLMs) that serve as foundations for models that serve specialty needs. For example, LLM-based generative AI systems such as OpenAI's ChatGPT-4 (based on the GPT LLM) and Google's Bard (based on the PaLM LLM) are used to generate text based answers to queries.

Generative AI models are based on neural network architecture and unsupervised learning. Caution should be exercised while using these models since they lend themselves to inventing references, copyright violations, and generating misleading content.

Examples: HCOs are partnering with EHR, speech recognition, and cloud vendors to pilot generative AI use cases such as searching for disparate patient data including clinical references across the care continuum, responding to written patient queries to care providers, and generating visit summary based on data captured during a patient visit.

Bias in AI Models

Bias in healthcare AI systems can lead to undesirable consequences. AI model bias can occur due to *incorrect algorithmic model and data used to train the model.*

For example, if data used to train a scheduling algorithm is disproportionately skewed towards older patients who fail to make their appointments, then in another healthcare setting, this model will switch appointments for elderly patients who are running late to patients on the waiting list. A balanced training data set might have identified a link between missed appointments and lack of access to transportation, regardless of patient age.

Training data bias can be remedied by properly identifying data, expanding data to include a representative sample of the patient population, or modifying the algorithm.

AI/ML models can be based on *supervised* (defined data sets) and *unsupervised* (ill-defined data sets). However, bias can be introduced regardless of the extent of training data definition.

- **Supervised ML:** begins with big data that is reasonably well classified and labeled. The algorithmic models learn from the defined data set and deliver outputs. The actual outputs undergo a reasonability test by comparing with expected outputs. Algorithms continue to be modified until an acceptable match is achieved between actual and desired outputs. Prediction accuracy for supervised ML models is impacted by *overfitting* or *underfitting*. *Overfitting* occurs when training data is narrowly focused, whereas *underfitting* occurs due to lack of complexity in training data. HCOs must assess AI models to confirm the absence of this bias prior to adoption.
- **Unsupervised ML:** begins with large data sets that are neither labeled nor classified. Unsupervised ML models can identify patterns related to a specific disease such as diabetes along with associated symptoms and outcomes using de-identified patient data. These models can be used to classify data and add labels which can be fed into a supervised ML model for predicting outcomes. Unsupervised ML models are used to identify spam emails from unsolicited bulk emails.

Managing Big Data and AI Models

Providers and HCOs should consider the following areas while licensing AI models from vendors and third-party developers.

1. **Training Data Quality:** Big data used for training AI models must meet the following criteria to ensure well-developed models:
   - Well understood, cleaned, and normalized for aggregation, stratification, and analytics by different algorithmic models.
   - Reflects desired outcomes of the ML model.
   - Avoids inherent biases that skew outcomes.
2. **Privacy and Security:** Since data can be exchanged with multiple sources, including EHRs from different care providers, medical devices, and smart wearables, it is important to de-identify and secure data that is used to train AI models. Data privacy and security methods are discussed in Chapter 10.
3. **System Design:** Due to the complexities of AI models, vendors design algorithms that focus on a particular disease or problem, for example, imaging AI algorithms that are trained to search for single finding from a modality. Since radiologists look for several findings, concurrently, in a modality that workflow requires deployment of multiple algorithms, resulting in a convoluted configuration. This illustrates the need to ensure that AI models are designed around provider clinical protocols and workflow preferences.
4. **Workflow Integration:** AI models offer the opportunity to improve the provision of healthcare by converting EHRs into intelligent systems that assist providers in diagnosing and treating patients. Understandably, however, providers are reluctant to use AI models that disrupt the flow of patient care. Therefore, it is important for providers to determine if AI models are integrated in EHRs to generate a seamless provider workflow.
5. **Sources of AI Models:** HCOs can purchase AI toolsets and models from EHR vendors, third-party developers, and cloud vendors. The following sources offer some examples.
   a. EHR vendors such as Epic and Cerner have added capabilities for AI-based CDS.
   b. AI giants such as Google, Amazon, Microsoft, and Apple have released code sets that can be compiled into deep learning models.

    c.   AI Marketplaces link radiologists with AI algorithm developers through platforms that support APIs for data and functions exchange. For example, appropriately architected PACS, speech recognition, and EHR/RIS platforms can be used by vendors of AI models to assist radiologists.

6. **Model Transparency:** Providers must explore the validity of AI models prior to adoption. The following serve as a starting point (refer to Examples of Non-devices -Criteria 4 under FDA Guidance on Clinical Decision Support Software):
   - Logic used in AI models.
   - Integration examples of AI models with HCO EHR.
   - Will AI models "train" from HCO patient data?
   - Will HCO patient data be used to train other AI models by vendor?
   - Benefit analysis of AI models in their work environment.
   - Are model outcomes predictive or prescriptive?
   - Model performance using HCO patient data.
   - Does the model qualify as a medical or non-medical device according to FDA guidelines?

The following FDA guidelines qualify CDS software as a medical device or non-device. It is important for HCOs to understand these guidelines, including FDA requirements from vendors.

FDA Guidance on Clinical Decision Support (CDS) Software

CDS Software Qualifying as a Medical Device: FDA has issued Guidelines on the criteria for Clinical Decision Support Software to qualify as a medical device.

> Software function that analyzes patient-specific medical information to detect a life-threatening condition, such as stroke or sepsis, and generate an alarm or an alert to notify a healthcare professional (HCP). This software is a device function. It does not meet Criterion 3 because it is intended to provide a specific diagnostic output or directive, including an alarm which supports time-critical decision-making.

(Section 12, Page 22 (FDA 2022))

Requirements: vendors of CDS software that qualifies as a medical device should get FDA clearance prior to sale.

CDS Software Qualifying as a Non-device: The 21st Century Cures Act defined CDS Software that could operate outside of the US Food and Drug Administration (FDA) regulatory requirements. As a result, FDA has issued a guidance to describe criteria which must be met for a CDS software to be considered a non-device under the device definition in section 520(o)(1)(E) of the FD&C Act (FDA 2022a). The four criteria that must be met for a CDS software to be considered a non-device CDS are:

1. Your software function does NOT acquire, process, or analyze medical images, signals, or patterns.
2. Your software function displays, analyzes, or prints medical information normally communicated between HCPs.
3. Your software function provides recommendations (information/options) to an HCP rather than providing a specific output or directive.
4. Your software function provides the basis of the recommendations so that the HCP does not rely primarily on any recommendations to decide.

Examples of Non-devices – Criteria 1 and 2

■ Information whose relevance to a clinical decision is well understood.
■ A single discrete test result that is clinically meaningful.
■ Report from imaging study.

Examples of Non-devices – Criteria 3

■ Lists of preventive, diagnostic, or treatment options.
■ Clinical guidance matched to patient-specific medical information.
■ Relevant reference information about a disease or condition.

Examples of Non-devices – Criteria 4

■ Plain language descriptions of the software purpose, medical input, and underlying algorithm.
■ Relevant patient-specific information and other knowns/unknowns for consideration.

Requirements: Criteria 4 of FDA's guidance advises that the software product or its labeling should provide the basis for its findings in plain language to allow HCPs to evaluate the basis of recommendations. Specifically, the FDA recommends the following measures for CDS software developers to meet this criterion:

■ Include purpose of the CDS software or its intended use, including the intended HCP user and patient population.
■ Identify the required input medical information, with instructions on how the inputs should be obtained, their relevance, and data quality requirements.
■ Provide a plain language description of the underlying algorithm development and validation that forms the basis for the CDS implementation.

Population Health and Precision Medicine

Population Health Management (PHM) and Value-Based Care

According to the Centers for Disease Control and Prevention (CDC) "90% of US's $4.1 trillion in annual health expenditures are for people with chronic and mental health conditions" (CDC 2022). The diseases included in this group are heart disease and stroke, cancer, diabetes, obesity, arthritis, Alzheimer's disease, epilepsy, and tooth decay.

FFS payment models have progressively increased healthcare expenditures with minimal improvement in population health and patient outcomes. On the other hand, value-driven care organizations like Kaiser Permanente continue to attract seniors, payers, employers, and care providers. Since 2012, CMS has been modeling and implementing their Medicare Shared Savings Program (MSSP) in physician and hospital-led Accountable Care Organizations (ACOs) to reduce cost of care while positively impacting patient health. ACOs have been created across the US to participate in risk-sharing programs sponsored by CMS and private payers.

Prior to entering arrangements with payers through alternative payment models (APMs), HCOs use AI analytics to understand diseases, associated costs, and risks associated with the member population. A key requirement of value-based programs is proactive care management that emphasizes an ongoing relationship between providers and patients. This relationship helps providers manage patient risk factors through wellness programs, earlier disease detection and intervention, and incorporating SDOH in PHM.

Analytics

Value-based care and PHM systems combine data from diverse sources such as EHRs, other clinical data, patient billing information, patient monitoring devices, and SDOH.

To support data stratification at different levels of granularity for risk assessment and disease management PHM requires access to patient data from several provider organizations that store EHI in proprietary EHRs and follow different documentation protocols. Data stored as text or scanned files, using proprietary protocols, makes it difficult to aggregate and process. ACOs undertaking PHM initiatives can either manually extract relevant clinical data from text/scanned files or use NLP models, in combination with ML, to extract relevant information to assess patient risk.

For example, PHM AI analytics models correlate SDOH, including economics and living circumstances to understand member population's diabetes diagnosis, educate providers, integrate that information in EHRs, and encourage regular visits by at-risk members for proactive management of complications. This can be further extended through at-home visits by care providers.

Precision Medicine

In his 2015 State of the Union address, President Obama announced the launching of Precision Medicine Initiative – a bold new research effort to revolutionize how we improve health and treat disease.

"Doctors have always recognized that every patient is unique, and doctors have always tried to tailor their treatments as best they can to individuals. You can match a blood transfusion to a blood type – that was an important discovery. What if matching a cancer cure to our genetic code was just as easy, just as standard? What if figuring out the right dose of medicine was as simple as taking our temperature?"

- President Obama, January 30, 2015

According to the US Food & Drug Administration, most medical treatments are designed for the "average patient" as a one-size-fits-all approach, which may not be successful for some patients. Precision medicine, interchangeably known as "personalized medicine" is an approach for targeting medical treatments that consider differences in people's genetic patterns, lifestyle, environmental, and cultural factors. The goal of precision medicine is not to design a unique therapeutic intervention for each patient, such as a personalized drug regimen, but to target the right treatments to patients who will best benefit from it.

For example, University Hospitals in Cleveland is working on pharma-cogenomics, which Maulik Purohit, MD, associate chief medical information officer, describes as "the ability to understand the interaction of medication with an individual at the individual level" (Wider 2022).

"Precision medicine could mean higher medication prices for specific subgroups of patients, but it is a way to avoid the costs of unnecessary and inappropriate treatments for individuals not responsive to specific therapeutic approaches" (Gameiro, et al. 2018).

Analytics

The future of precision medicine will enable healthcare providers to tailor treatment and prevention strategies to people's unique characteristics, including their genome sequence, microbiome composition, health history, lifestyle, and diet. To get there, we need to incorporate many different types of data, from metabolomics (the chemicals in the body at a certain point in time), the microbiome (the collection of microorganisms in or on the body), and data about the patient collected by healthcare providers and the patients themselves. Success will require that health data is portable, that it can be easily shared between providers, researchers, and most importantly, patients and research participants.

Examples

Consider the following advancements in precision medicine:

- What if a combination of bio- and nanotechnology, and AI could sense potential adverse drug reactions before they happen, intervening to prevent previously unforeseeable events?
- With smart pills and wearables tracking a patient's physiology in real time, a service can alert the patient to the optimum moment for taking drugs and warn against treatments when there is a chance of adverse reactions.

Impact of AI on Digital Transformation

AI systems play a significant role in the digital transformation of healthcare. Developing a digital front door that offers patients access to a wide array of services and information requires HCOs to digitally transform their operations while using AI systems for communication alerts, wellness apps, and other portals. In addition, remote care models require automated interactions using AI systems to monitor patient health, trigger prompt alerts, and ensure patient medications are administered timely and accurately.

The road to digital transformation of HCOs goes through well-designed and well-implemented AI systems.

Interoperability

Case for Interoperability in Healthcare

In the 1970s, healthcare applications were developed by different vendors to support different HCO functions, namely laboratories, radiology, pharmacy patient registration, patient billing, and financials. Data transmission between disparate application systems was supported by HL7 standards for patient admission, discharge, and transfer (ADT) to eliminate duplicative entry of patient information, facilitate communication across disparate systems such as requests for lab tests and results linked to the patient, and patient billing.

The 2009 HITECH Act accelerated the development, certification, and adoption of EHRs. According to the *HIPAA Journal*, "Prior to the HITECH Act 2009, the rate of EHR adoption throughout the healthcare industry was just 3.2%. By 2017, 86% of office-based physicians and 96% of non-federal acute care hospitals had adopted EHRs" (HIPAA Journal 2022).

HITECH and 21st Century Cures Act led to the expansion of HIEs to enable data interoperability across HCO information systems. Healthcare Information and Management Systems Society (HIMSS) defines interoperability as the ability of different information systems, devices, and applications (systems) to access, exchange, integrate and cooperatively use data in a coordinated manner, within and across organizational, regional, and national boundaries, to provide timely and seamless portability of information and optimize the health of individuals and populations globally. (HIMSS 2022).

Interoperability Benefits

Improving patient care by exchanging data with other HCOs to generate a longitudinal health record is a key interoperability goal. This has been accomplished by HIEs in several ways including physician query and response from HIEs and using record locator services (RLS). A comprehensive discussion on HIEs and their services is discussed later in this section. Interoperability can support value-based care and PHM to manage high-risk or at-risk patient populations. Several HIEs have been formed to support ACOs to manage care costs, improve patient access to their healthcare, and increase patient satisfaction.

HIEs are helpful in streamlining healthcare workflows. The following illustrate ways in which healthcare can be facilitated through interoperability of patient data.

1. Care transition to different care settings, for example, acute care to long-term care.
2. Care coordination between caregivers, care providers, and patients can be facilitated through real-time sharing of patient data.
3. Physicians can access lab results upon completion and confirmation by the lab.
4. Medication reconciliation can be accomplished across patient encounters in different care settings.
5. Patient portals that aggregate data from different care settings for a comprehensive view for patients.

Interoperability Challenges

EHRs and data interoperability have been accepted as necessary conditions to advance the state of US healthcare and enable the following capabilities – patient disclosure and access, equal opportunity for quality patient care independent of socio-economic status, monitoring by public health agencies, and improved outcomes. However, several challenges persist in advancing interoperability. The following list incorporates major challenges towards nationwide interoperability.

1. **Lack of standardized national patient identifier:** this issue has been discussed over the past two decades with no solution. Nationwide HIEs, such as TEFCA, must implement a national patient identifier or a workaround.

2. **Growing number of data sources:** With the advent of device and machine-generated data it has been increasingly difficult to transfer and utilize large and diverse EHI for patient care.

3. **Staff workflow complexities:** unstructured data imported from external systems negatively impacts staff productivity, since it must be converted into structured data sets in EHRs to accommodate physician workflows.

4. **Patient information blocking problems:** blocking problems can be encountered by factors such as the state of the patient's EHR and provider refusal.

5. **HCO Configuration:** HCOs comprise systems that range in scope, services, and operational complexity – from large integrated health systems and AMCs that provide comprehensive healthcare services to physician offices, urgent care clinics, ambulatory surgical centers, and nursing homes. Different HCOs generate customized and proprietary data which can only be used by receiving organizations as unstructured text.

6. **Security/Privacy:** Access to patient EHI by HIEs, and other networks, to advance the state of interoperability requires HCOs to provide access to EHI with a corresponding increase in security and privacy risks of patient data.

7. **Legacy Systems:** The use of legacy systems, and lack of technical capability, in several HCOs reflects financial constraints which prohibit compliance with ONC's interoperability requirements. While upgrading application and data systems to the cloud require monthly premiums, they impose lower demands on capital expenditures and improve EHI security in comparison to on-premises data centers. HCOs that wish to transition away from legacy infrastructure may consider Software as a Service (SaaS) or other cloud arrangements.

8. **Document Requirements – Payers:** Access to transparent provider documentation that can be analyzed for payment denials increase payer demands for additional documentation. This increases provider reluctance for participation in HIEs.

9. **Document Requirements – Public Agencies:** Government regulatory requirements such as the *21st Century Cures Act* introduce additional documentation and process demands on HCOs and providers.

Interoperability and Digital Health: Changing Role of Key Stakeholders

Arguably the lynchpin to the virtualization of healthcare has been the gradual transition towards nationwide interoperability.

Figures 9.2 and 9.3 reflect the changing role of key stakeholders in the healthcare ecosystem because of the growth of interoperability and adoption of digital health. Key stakeholders include HCOs (traditional providers of care), payers, employers, regulators, and patients. These changes have demonstrated a roadmap for employers and payers to reduce cost of care, increase patient engagement, population health management, and improved outcomes.

As Figure 9.2 indicates, prior to the growth of interoperability and adoption of digital health, most patient care was supported by HCOs. This landscape significantly changed due to the emergence of nontraditional providers of care such as independent DHPs, employers, payers, and retailers (refer to Figure 9.3). The decentralized care resulting from virtual models emphasized by nontraditional providers requires HCOs to digitally transform their systems to enable participation in value-based reimbursement models with

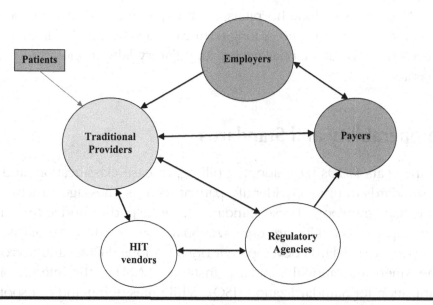

Figure 9.2 Provision of healthcare – prior to adoption of digital health and HIEs.

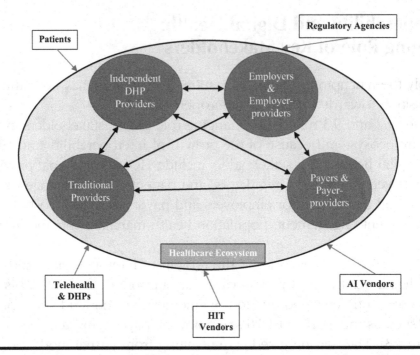

Figure 9.3   Provision of healthcare – post adoption of digital health and HIEs.

nontraditional and traditional providers. This model increases reliance of traditional and non-traditional care providers on nationwide interoperability.

■ NOTE: HCOs include hospitals, health systems, academic medical
centers, physician offices, long-term care facilities, ambulatory surgery
centers, ambulatory pharmacies, ambulatory laboratories, and imaging
centers.

Interoperability and Standards

Over the years HCOs have adopted billing, disease classification, and identifier standards to uniquely identify patient records, message structure,
and message transport. These standards have helped to bridge the terminology gap across healthcare organizational systems. Most standards are
developed by standards development organizations (SDOs) and accredited
by the American National Standards Institute (ANSI) or the International
Organization for Standardization (ISO). While messaging and transport standards are key to interoperability at all levels, terminology standards help in
message normalization, and interpretation, to enable semantic exchange of
data sets across systems.

The following categories of standards encompass the myriad of health data standards for HCOs: vocabulary/terminology, content, transport, privacy and security, and identifiers.

Coding Systems

Coding systems are critical in structuring, classifying, and normalizing data sets to enable interoperability across healthcare enterprises. The following healthcare coding systems are key to healthcare payment, treatment, and operations – Healthcare Common Procedure Coding System (HCPCS) – extension of CPT, Codes for Dental Treatment (CDT), National Drug Code (NDC) – identify medications in the US, RxNorm – codes for clinical drugs, Current Procedural Terminology (CPT), Logical Observation Identifiers Names and Codes (LOINC), Systematized Nomenclature of Medicine – Clinical Terms (SNOMED-CT), and International Classification of Diseases (ICD).

Since the scope of this effort focuses on the concept of standardization and interoperability, we will discuss a subset that is frequently used across HCOs – CPT, ICD, LOINC, and SNOMED-CT. Each of these is designed for a specific purpose and used to map different terminologies to standard code sets. Readers interested in understanding the entire set of healthcare coding systems can find them on the Internet.

a) CPT 11: used for billing outpatient and office procedures. This code set is supported by the American Medical Association (AMA).

b) ICD-11: used for medical classification of diseases. The US version of this code set is maintained by CMS and National Center for Health Statistics (NCHS).

c) LOINC: common code sets for laboratory and clinical tests (vital signs or clinical documents). LOINC provides the code for tests or measurements *question* in HL7 messages. It is maintained by the Regenstrief Institute, a US nonprofit medical research organization.

d) SNOMED-CT: clinical health terminology code set that represents the *answer* for clinical tests and observations in HL7 messages. It is a collection of medical terms providing codes, terms, synonyms, and definitions used in clinical documentation and reporting.

Since SNOMED codes can be mapped to ICD-10, they enable mapping disease classification with clinical tests and observations. This facilitates semantic-level interoperability (refer to Levels of Data Exchange in this chapter). The International Health Terminology Standards Development Organization owns SNOMED-CT.

Content Standards

Content standards define the structure and organization of e-messaging systems. HCOs can use these standards to move data sets across organizational systems without the need to re-enter data. For example, patient information entered into an organization's registration system can be transferred to other systems using these standards. Commonly used standards include HL7 v2, HL7 v3 – for messaging; Clinical Document Architecture (CDA) and Consolidated CDA (C-CDA) – for clinical documents; and USCDI – for standard set of data elements. These standards are discussed later in this chapter.

Transport Standards

Transport standards define the format, document architecture, data elements, data linkage, and transfer methods for interoperability. Commonly used standards that pertain to digital health transformation include Digital Imaging and Communications in Medicine (DICOM) used to store and retrieve medical images in PACS, Direct Standard (XDR/XDM) – secure and direct health message exchange, FHIR – API-supported data exchange, Integrating the Healthcare Enterprise (IHE) – health data exchange, and National Council for Prescription Drug Program (NCPDP SCRIPT) – electronic prescription exchange.

Health Level Seven (HL7®)

Health Level Seven International is a not-for-profit, international organization for developing standards supporting data transmission between healthcare entities. It refers to the framework and international standards that support transfer of clinical and administrative data. HL7 got its name from the 7th layer of the OSI (Open Systems Interconnection) Model which consists of the physical, data, network, transport, session, presentation, and application layers. The HL7 framework offers formatting techniques for the application layer while assuming compatibility with OSI's lower six layers.

HL7 continues to play a major role in the current state of interoperability across QHINs which will be discussed later in this chapter. The following section briefly discusses the history of HL7, its evolution, and current state.

Evolution of HL7: The earlier version of HL7 was developed with the goal of interfacing data sets between best-of-breed ancillary, patient registration, patient billing, and finance. Some key messages were ADT, which include triggers to indicate patient status – admission, transfer, or discharge, moving demographic data based on queries or events, order entry to electronically order ancillary tests and associated results, and patient billing. ADT message types are one of the most popular and high-volume within the HL7 framework.

In 2000, HL7 released standards for structured clinical documents through their CDA®, an XML-based markup standard, designed to specify the encoding, structure, and semantics of clinical documents for exchange. CDA is based on a framework for transmitting clinical statements between incompatible systems. CDA maintains continuity of care by supporting the exchange of Continuity of Care Documents (CCD®) such as discharge summaries and progress notes. In general, EHR documents including text, images, and other forms of multimedia can be managed through this standard. CDA has been upgraded to include the Consolidated Clinical Document Architecture (C-CDA).

In 2014 the JASON report, created by a government advisory panel including private and public sector representatives, generated a report that resulted in the Argonaut Project to accelerate the use of FHIR® in healthcare information exchange under the HL7 umbrella. FHIR standards were enhanced by Substitutable Medical Applications and Reusable Technologies (SMART®) which defines how third-party apps launch within an EHR. SMART on FHIR enables additional security and makes it easier to build applications that integrate with EHRs, patient portals, and data warehouse. It also supports portability of third-party applications that use FHIR API for health data exchange.

HL7's FHIR combines the best features from HL7 v2, HL7 v3, and CDA while leveraging the latest web service technologies. Therefore, FHIR can be used in mobile apps which makes it easy for patients to access their EHR – a major step towards consumerism. FHIR can also facilitate the exchange of financial information and other data not directly linked to patient care. It includes specifications for an API, based on web standards to create a comprehensive interoperability solution for healthcare.

FHIR is being modified to support brokered exchanges by routing FHIR API transactions between QHINs to promote nationwide interoperability. The 21st Century Cures Act made SMART a certification requirement for interoperability.

Summary of HL7® Standards

- HL7: facilitates ADT messages to downstream systems such as ancillaries and billing.
- C-CDA: allows EHRs and other health IT systems to process documents while enabling access on web browsers and mobile devices.
- FHIR®: designed for the web and can be used in mobile phone apps.
- SMART on FHIR: allows HCOs to plug third-party medical apps into their EHR.

Privacy and Security Standards

National patient privacy and security requirements are discussed in HIPAA Privacy (2003) and Security (2005) rules. The European Union uses the General Data Protection Regulation (GDPR) to regulate privacy and security for all processing and storage of data relating to people – including health information. HIPAA Security and Privacy rules, and risk management strategies, are discussed in Chapter 10.

Identifier Standards

Identifier standards are critical to uniquely identify patient records across a spectrum of healthcare organizations. A few commonly used are Enterprise Master Patient Index (EMPI), to uniquely identify patients across a healthcare organization, and Medical Record Index (MRN) identify patient care history in a healthcare organization.

USCDI – Standardizing Data Sets (ONC n.d.)

USCDI: The Cures Act adopted the USCDI standards to help data sharing among providers and patients. According to the ONC, the USCDI helps to standardize data elements, providing a roadmap to health IT vendors/developers to build products and solutions that can help improve health outcomes at both the individual and population levels.

A USCDI *Data Class* is an aggregation of *Data Elements* organized by a common theme. A *Data Element* is the level of data exchange. The relationship between *Data Class* and *Data Element* can be demonstrated using the laboratory *Data Class* which consists of the *Data Elements* tests, values/results, specimen type, and result status.

USCDI has established a core set of data essential to support patient care which replaces the Common Clinical Data Set in use cases such as:

- Transitions of Care documents.
- Clinical information reconciliation and incorporation.
- How patients view, download, and transmit their health data.
- Electronic reporting to public health agencies.
- C-CDA documents.
- Data access via APIs.

USCDI data elements include data not previously captured by EMPI such as race, ethnicity, email, and SDOH.

Until October 6, 2022, EHI for the purposes of IB was limited to data elements represented in USCDI v1. Post October 2022, the requirements to comply with IB requirements expand EHI to include all ePHI data elements in the Designated Record Set (DRS) which includes the group of medical and billing records maintained by (or for) a covered entity (45 CFR §164.501).

USCDI continues to be reviewed, revised, and implemented to advance the state of interoperability. Recently, ONC has proposed Draft USCDI v4 which if finalized will result in 19 data classes that include 112 data elements.

Levels of Data Exchange

HIMSS defines four levels of interoperability exchange with increasing levels of clinical usability – Foundational, Structural, Semantic, and Organizational (HIMSS n.d.). Each level advances the state of data exchange in healthcare IT systems.

Foundational: this level supports basic connectivity requirements for exchanging organizational data sets with external systems. It does not involve data reformatting or interpretation by IT systems; therefore, a professional is required to interpret transferred data to understand its impact on patient care.

Example: HCO system requests a clinical note from an external organizational system which sends it in PDF format; however, it requires a clinician to extract relevant clinical data and enter structured data fields within the HCO's EHR for interpretation and analysis.

Structural: This level defines the format of data exchange which helps with data packaging and exchange across HL7 compatible systems. The assumption in this level is that the systems involved in the exchange must be able to receive and understand trigger events. Data standards like HL7 and FHIR support structural interoperability but do not require message standardization to enable semantic normalization.

Example: ADT messages are commonly used to transmit patient demographics at a healthcare entity. ADT message types provide information for many trigger events, for example, patient admission (ADT^A01), patient transfer (ADT^A02), and patient discharge (ADT^A03). HL7 messages are transmitted via TCP/IP lower layer protocol (LLP) for real-time interfaces and File Transfer Protocol (FTP) for batch processing.

Semantic: This level defines the format of data exchange and enables the use of transmitted information by receiving systems. This meaningful exchange is enabled through standardized and coded data sets. This interoperability level is important in healthcare since different HIT systems incorporate different terminology. Semantic interoperability can be enabled via publicly available standard code sets (previously described) and AI/NLP model processing. It can assist with improved data analytics (e.g., PHM), patient care, and billing.

The following examples offer two semantic interoperability scenarios:

■ "Whooping cough" is the common term for "pertussis" and systems exchanging this data must be able to recognize this similarity.
■ AI/NLP models extract clinical data from a note and convert into standard codes for meaningful data exchange.

Organizational: This level involves exchanging data between organizations. This level of data interoperability requires a framework that standardizes policy, governance, and technology requirements. Participating organizations consent to policy requirements to ensure secure and integrated flow of patient data across organizations.

Example: Trusted Exchange Framework and Common Agreement (TEFCA) defines the framework under which Qualified Health Information networks (QHINs) or large HINs can enable nationwide data exchange.

TEFCA involves standardization at the policy, governance, and technological levels across QHINs to enable secure movement of data across different systems and accommodate workflows across disparate systems.

∎ *NOTE: Depending on the sophistication of data exchange, each level impacts operational systems. HCOs should identify workflow requirements, and redesign operational systems, to effectively implement data exchange. Organizational-level data interoperability is optimized when participating organizations exchange data at the semantic level.*

Interoperability – Framework and Networks

The road to nationwide interoperability has been paved with roadblocks. However, a combination of standards coupled with public/private partnerships has matured the state of meaningful health information exchange (HIE) and health information networks (HINs) across a variety of stakeholders comprising the healthcare ecosystem, namely, HCOs, state, federal agencies, payers, vendors, physicians, other care providers, pharmacies, research organizations, clinical laboratories, and patients.

ONC laid out three high-level goals in their interoperability roadmap:

1. 2015–2017 – Send, receive, find, and use priority data domains to improve healthcare and quality outcomes.
2. 2018–2020 – Expand data sources and users in the interoperable health IT ecosystem to improve health and lower costs.
3. 2021–2024 – Achieve nationwide interoperability enabling a learning health system with the patient at its center.

The following discussion begins with regional and state-level HIEs/HINs, transitions to nationwide HIEs, and concludes with a description of TEFCA – a framework to integrate major HIEs across the US.

Local, State, and Regional Interoperability Standards and Networks

HIEs provide technology to enable secure exchange of data. HIEs can operate at local, statewide, regional, and community levels depending on ownership and revenue models. They are run by state governments, private organizations, or a collaboration of state and private organizations. They generally operate as nonprofit organizations with several funding sources such as state, federal, and member dues/charges. HIEs exchange EHI by either operating as a gateway between member organizations or centrally storing and forwarding EHI. HIEs that store EHI can provide value-add services.

HIEs use different technologies to send queries to participating healthcare entities with many using geofencing to search for patient data within a defined geographic area of the patient's home location or last healthcare entity. Queries that locate patient information return it to the HIE, that in turn sends it to the requesting location. Additional technical protocols for data location and exchange, such as RLS and FHIR-APIs, are included in descriptions of nationwide HIEs.

In addition to data interoperability, HIEs provide value-added services based on member requirements and use cases. The following use cases represent examples of services offered by HIEs across the US.

a. Provide data utility by supporting member organizations in establishing APMs, CMS Quality Payment Programs (QPP), and payer-negotiated performance measures. Statewide HIEs also support data exchange between private HIEs established for ACOs and software vendors.
b. Support e-prescribing.
c. Provide security and privacy services.
d. Support data aggregation and advanced analytics.
e. Support population health analytics.
f. Support collection and exchange of SDOH through public health and clinical data exchange.
g. Provide patient portals for access to clinical data and other value-add services.
h. Support alert systems to inform providers when their patients have been seen elsewhere within the network.
i. Select HIEs use Integrating the Healthcare Enterprise-based brokering infrastructure to exchange FHIR payloads between members.

Local, state, regional, and community HIEs advance the state of interoperability while providing technical services for small, rural, and critical access hospitals. On the other hand, mid to large health systems find less value in HIE participation since many have pre-established data exchange protocols with partner HCOs that support specialty care for the patient population.

Example: Chesapeake Regional Information System for Our Patients (CRISP) is a nonprofit designated HIE for the state of Maryland and regional HIE provider for Maryland, DC, West Virginia, Connecticut, and Alaska. CRISP is a Health Information Organization (HIO) that provides several services to its members through their portal, access to member-stored clinical data, Prescription Drug Monitoring Program (PDMP), and alerts to providers if their patients register at another CRISP participating HCO – for example, ER visit, inpatient admission, or discharge (CRISP n.d.).

Nationwide Interoperability Framework and Networks (HealthIT.gov) (ONC 2015)

The ONC established the National Health Information Network (NHIN) in 2004 to develop and implement a framework for interoperability at the local, regional, state, and national levels. The idea for the framework was to develop a common set of nationwide legal, technical, data use, service level agreements, and policy rules with the goal of promoting trusted data exchange.

In 2012, ONC transitioned NHIN to *The Sequoia Project*, a nonprofit chartered to advance implementation of secure, interoperable nationwide HIE. Under *The Sequoia Project* NHIN was renamed eHealth Exchange. *The Sequoia Project* supports two independent interoperability initiatives that share information under a common trust framework and set of rules – the eHealth Exchange (formerly NHIN) and Carequality framework. These initiatives became independent of the Sequoia Project in 2018.

The following networks enable nationwide data exchange and are a combination of public/private efforts – eHealth Exchange, CommonWell Health Alliance, Carequality, DirectTrust, and Civitas Network for Health.

eHealth Exchange

eHealth Exchange is a nationwide HIE based on the concept of *one connection-to-many* that enables secure sharing of clinical information between federal and non-federal HCOs over the Internet. The eHealth Exchange spans all 50 states and is the largest HIE infrastructure in the US. Participants include large provider networks, hospitals, pharmacies, regional HIEs, and federal agencies (Department of Defense, Veteran's Health Administration, and Social Security Administration), representing 75% of all

US hospitals, thousands of medical groups, more than 8,000 pharmacies, and 120 million patients. It establishes a twofold path to interoperability – via Data Use and Reciprocal Support Agreement (DURSA) that is entered into by members who wish to exchange EHI, and shared governance including technical requirements such as C-CDA and FHIR-APIs (eHealth Exchange n.d.).

CommonWell Health Alliance

The CommonWell vendor-neutral trade alliance is a health data–sharing network. It uses RLS that allows caregivers and others to locate and access records associated with a patient regardless of where the care was delivered. Services include patient ID management, advanced record location, and query/retrieve broker services, allowing a single query to retrieve records for a patient from member systems. CommonWell members span the continuum of care including hospitals, ambulatory practices, post-acute and long-term care, pharmacies, and patient health records (CommonWell Health Alliance n.d.).

Carequality

Carequality is a vendor-neutral framework that builds consensus and enables exchange across vendor networks, HIEs, RLS providers, clinical information networks, consumer groups, and personal health record networks. Carequality is a public-private collaborative that enables health data sharing between and among disparate vendor, payer, and other networks. Patient information is generally shared in the form of C-CDA documents. In 2016, CommonWell and Carequality announced an agreement to increase health IT connectivity by combining their networks (Carequality n.d.).

DirectTrust

DirectTrust maintains the policies, standards, and practices that support direct messaging in the network. This framework includes a technique for health data sharing between members – public key encryption (PKE) and digital certificates managed under the public key infrastructure (PKI). Accredited health information service providers (HISPs) provide direct address to enable message exchange on the DirectTrust Network. Message exchange is done using PKE, an asymmetric cryptography system that encrypts sent messages and decrypts received messages using different keys. DirectTrust Network supports health plans, health departments, registries, and any party that wants to securely exchange health data – including patients that wish to communicate with providers (DirectTrust n.d.).

Civitas Networks for Health

In 2021, Strategic Health Information Exchange Collaborative (SHIEC) and the Network for Regional Healthcare Improvement (NRHI) combined to form Civitas Networks for Health, a national collaborative comprised member organizations working to use HIE, health data, and different stakeholders to improve health. As the largest network of its kind in the country with over 180 members, Civitas represents local health innovators moving data to improve outcomes that together cover more than 95% of the US population (Civitas n.d.).

TEFCA (ONC 2022)

The Trusted Exchange Framework and Common Agreement (TEFCA) is a contractual and operational framework for sharing data between member organizations with the goal to establish an interoperability standard of EHI across the county. It is sponsored by CMS/ONC with rigorous technical and governance requirements for its QHINs. It requires member organizations to support data exchange via push and query-based pull capabilities.

TEFCA has two distinct yet compatible goals: the Trusted Exchange Network (TEF) and Common Agreement (CA). The Trusted Exchange Framework (TEF) includes the technical platform (based on established standards) whose architecture involves interconnecting QHINs using FHIR-APIs for EHI access across member HCOs.

The Sequoia Project serves as the Recognized Coordinating Entity (RCE). It is responsible for developing, updating, implementing, and maintaining the Common Agreement which serves as a legal contract between the RCE and HIN that will become a QHIN once designated by RCE. It establishes the governing approach that requires flow down to all participants within the QHIN – notably cooperation and nondiscrimination among competitors, HIPAA privacy and security rules, and confidentiality.

Use Cases for TEFCA: Exchange of payment, treatment, and operations, EHI use and disclosure by public health agencies, benefits determination by governmental agencies, and third parties that support individual EHI access services.

While there is no mandate for HCO participation in TEFCA, it is highly likely that as use cases expand, non-participating HCOs will consider joining a TEFCA network.

QHINs: Existing regional and state HIEs/HINs can elect to apply for a QHIN designation or become participants and sub-participants in a QHIN that is compatible with their philosophy and technical architecture. Key requirements for QHINs are:

- **Security Certification:** QHIN applicants are required to demonstrate appropriate cybersecurity and privacy controls through third-party certification such as HITRUST.
- **FHIR® Exchanges:** TEFCA requires QHINs to demonstrate exchanges beginning with unbrokered FHIR API-based exchange across QHINs and moving to QHINs brokering FHIR payloads by routing FHIR-APIs transactions between QHIN Participants and Sub-participants.
- **FHIR Bulk:** Access data on groups, cohorts, and populations to support population health, quality reporting, and analytics such as clinical decision support, big data analysis, and SMART on FHIR applications.

Biomed Device Integration (Entity-Based)

Entity-based biomed devices have become increasingly sophisticated in terms of their technical architecture and functional offerings. However, since these devices coordinate a variety of patient care functions, it is important to integrate them in ways that optimize care provider workflows.

Most medical device systems use IoT and other sensors for real-time location services (RTLS), Radio-Frequency Identification (RFID) technologies, and barcodes and are compatible with HL7-level message exchange. These devices can be integrated either through point-to-point interfaces or middleware.

The device functions commonly used in HCOs include *nurse call system, temperature monitoring, hand hygiene, patient tracking, digital patient room signage, interactive patient entertainment/patient education system, caregiver to patient assignment, and wireless beds. integration.*

To be effective, these devices' functions must be appropriately integrated with communication devices/methods and HIS. Since a variety of communication devices and methods accommodate care provider preferences, we begin by discussing options regarding communication devices/systems.

A. Communication Devices/Systems

These devices can be used for caregiver–caregiver, patient–caregiver, and physician–caregiver communication for safety and overall experience of patients and staff. Different communication devices/systems can be used depending on caregiver preferences, however, that complicates achieving desired workflows. Adding to the challenge are the security and privacy concerns inherent in these communication methods.

Stakeholder discussions can identify the best workflow and communication devices/systems. The best solution will integrate with existing directories (phone directory, on-call lists, presence info, etc.) to allow seamless and secure communication among care providers regardless of device type, within and outside the healthcare facility.

Commonly used communication devices/systems: Vocera badge – hands-free communication device, Cisco wireless telephone – portable wireless telephone that operates as an extension on the enterprise telephone system, desk phone, mobile phone, pager, messaging via HIS, direct secure messaging, and secure text.

B. Integrating Medical Devices, Communication Devices/Systems, and Information Systems

Achieving the desired workflow by integrating medical devices, communication devices/systems, and HIS requires that the right information be available to the right caregiver on the right device at the right time. These workflow configurations are best facilitated via middleware since it can accommodate future changes in medical devices, communication devices/systems, and information systems. Since middleware integration efforts can vary significantly based on workflow requirements, they should be carefully examined prior to implementation.

Potential uses

■ Nurse call integration with communication devices (direct patient–caregiver communication).
■ Medical device alarms (IV Pump, Bed, etc.) sent to caregiver.
■ EHR information communicated directly to caregiver (stat orders, Lab results, etc.).
■ Device or patient location information can be communicated to caregiver or group of caregivers via their preferred device, for example:

- Patient returned from surgery.
- Patient or equipment left department when not supposed to.
- Patient discharged and has left the room – environmental services automatically contacted.

■ Medical Telemetry alerts/alarms sent directly to caregivers.

C. Asset Tracking

Asset tracking works via RFID technologies consisting of tamper-resistant tags attached to an asset and tracked via receivers. These systems can be configured to support a role-based view of assets and locations.

Potential uses

■ IV pumps – track pumps when needed for patient care and for easy location by bio-medical personnel during preventive maintenance. The smart tags affixed to pumps alert appropriate staff when pump enters soiled storage room and needs to be cleaned.
■ Department-specific equipment – asset tracking can locate equipment on a map. Especially useful for equipment that moves with a patient throughout the hospital and may not be in the right location if the patient is discharged from another department.
■ High dollar or rental medical equipment – easily track the location of equipment. Set alerts if equipment is not in its designated location. This facilitates finding rental equipment when it needs to be returned.
■ Identify under-utilized equipment – tagged devices that have not moved from inventory in a defined time period or have not been in a patient room in a defined time frame would be considered underutilized.
■ Use chokepoints at exits to send alarm or notification when equipment exits a facility.

Key Takeaways

1. Healthcare has been an information-intensive industry, but the recent shift towards digital health has generated increasing amounts of data from EHRs, telehealth, device-generated data, home healthcare, PGHD, public agencies, and HIEs.
2. The availability of big data, shift towards value-based care, and cost reduction methods have accelerated development of software and hardware-based AI models and platforms.

3. Healthcare uses predictive analytics for most of their clinical decision support software.

4. AI algorithms incorporate ML, Neural Networks, Deep Learning, and NLP. Recently, generative AI models using ChatGPT are being piloted by HCOs.

5. Bias of AI models and their opaqueness make it difficult for healthcare practitioners to accept AI models.

6. It is important to integrate CDS software and other AI models into the provider-patient care workflow.

7. Strategies to manage AI models include transparency of their functions and learning data. The recommendation to ensure model transparency is enabled by recent FDA guidance on *non-device* CDS software that requires compliance with four criteria including requirement for developers to label their product with the basis of its findings to allow health providers to independently evaluate the basis of recommendations.

8. CDS software that detects life-threatening diseases such as sepsis is classified as a *device* by the FDA.

9. Interoperability has transitioned from local, regional, state, and nationwide HIEs/HINs to ONC-sponsored nationwide interoperability through TEFCA. This strategy integrates other large HINs (called QHINs) for nationwide interoperability.

10. The TEFCA framework includes a common agreement that must be agreed upon by QHIN participants and supports the FHIR API standard for inter-QHIN communication.

References

Babylon Health. n.d. "About Us." *Babylon Health*. Accessed October 2022. https://www.babylonhealth.com/en-us/about.

Bush, Jonathan, and John Fox. 2016. *Bringing the Power of Platforms to Health Care*. November 10. https://hbr.org/2016/11/bringing-the-power-of-platforms-to-health-care.

Carequality. n.d. *Carequality*. Accessed November 2022. https://carequality.org.

CDC. 2018. "COPD Costs." *CDC*. February 21. https://www.cdc.gov/copd/infographics/copd-costs.html.

———. 2022. *Health and Economic Costs of Chronic Diseases*. September 8. https://www.cdc.gov/chronicdisease/about/costs/index.htm.

Civitas. n.d. *Civitas Networks for Health*. Accessed December 2022. https://www.civitasforhealth.org.

CommonWell Health Alliance. n.d. *CommonWell Health Alliance*. Accessed September 2022. https://www.commonwellalliance.org.

CRISP. n.d. "CRISP Connected Providers." *CRISP*. Accessed September 2022. https://www.crisphealth.org/about-crisp/connected-providers/.

Dietsche, Erin. 2019. "Cleveland Clinic Study Finds Propeeler Health Platform Helps Reduce Hospitalizations among COPD Patients." *Medcity*. June 12. https://medcitynews.com/2019/06/cleveland-clinic-study/?rf=1.

DirectTrust. n.d. *Direct Trust*. Accessed November 2022. https://directtrust.org.

eHealth Exchange. n.d. *eHealth Exchange*. Accessed September 2022. https://ehealthexchange.org.

FDA. 2022. "Clinical Decision Support Software." *FDA*. September 28. https://www.fda.gov/media/109618/download.

———. 2022a. "Your Clinical Decision Support Software: Is it a Medical Device?" *FDA*. September 27. https://www.fda.gov/medical-devices/software-medical-device-samd/your-clinical-decision-support-software-it-medical-device.

Gameiro, Gustavo Rosa, Vikto Sinkunas, Gabriel Romero Liguori, and Jose Otavio Auler-Junior. 2018. "Precision Medicine: Changing the Way We Think about Healthcare/Clinics." *NIH, National Library of Medicine*. November 23. https://www.ncbi.nlm.nih.gov/pmc/articles/PMC6251254.

HIMSS. n.d. *Interoperability in Healthcare*. Accessed September 2022. https://www.himss.org/resources/interoperability-healthcare.

HIPAA Journal. 2022. *HITECH Compliance Checklist*. https://www.hipaajournal.com/hitech-compliance/.

Marr, Bernard. 2016. "Big Data In Healthcare: Paris Hospitals Predict Admission Rates Using Machine Learning." *Forbes*. December 13. https://www.forbes.com/sites/bernardmarr/2016/12/13/big-data-in-healthcare-paris-hospitals-predict-admission-rates-using-machine-learning/?sh=41610b0779a2.

ONC. 2015. November 17. https://www.healthit.gov/faq/what-sequoia-project.

———. 2022. *Trusted Exchange Framework and Common Agreement (TEFCA)*. September 27. https://www.healthit.gov/topic/interoperability/policy/trusted-exchange-framework-and-common-agreement-tefca.

———. n.d. *USCDI*. Accessed January 2023. https://www.healthit.gov/isa/united-states-core-data-interoperability-uscdi/.

Propeller Health. n.d. *Propeller Health*. Accessed December 2022. https://www.propellerhealth.com.

Raeke, Meagan. 2019. "Predicting Head and Neck Cancer Treatment Toxicities with Machine Learning." *MD Anderson Cancer Center*. September 16. https://www.mdanderson.org/publications/cancer-frontline/predicting-head-and-neck-cancer-treatment-toxicities-with-machine-learning.h00-159306201.html.

Siwicki, Bill. 2021. "Mass General Brigham and the Future of AI in Radiology." *Healthcare IT News*. May 10. https://www.healthcareitnews.com/news/mass-general-brigham-and-future-ai-radiology.

Wider, Janette. 2022. "Transformative Trends 2022/One Hospital System Makes Precision Medicine a Reality." *HC Innovations Group* 33.

Chapter 10

Security, Privacy, and Technical Considerations

Introduction

Privacy and security of protected health information (PHI) are critical to the success of digital health strategies and survival of HCOs. The US Department of Health and Human Services (HHS) website states "The HIPAA Privacy Rule provides federal protections for personal health information held by covered entities and gives patients an array of rights with respect to that information." PHI is a subset of personally identifiable information (PII) which according to NIST "encompasses any information that can be directly or indirectly linked to an individual's identity." PII applies to medical, educational, financial, and employment information.

The HIPAA Privacy Rule defines 18 identifiers that convert health information into PHI. It allows for disclosure of PHI for Treatment, Payment, and Operations (TPO) and can be used for research purposes by removing all identifiers and de-identifying health data.

As healthcare has begun its transformation towards digital care models, cybersecurity, and identity theft have increasingly become a source of frustration and concern. Cybersecurity breaches extend beyond direct infrastructure attacks on healthcare providers to business associates including providers of cloud services, applications, and medical device vendors. Cyberterrorists recognize that attacking vulnerabilities in the decentralized yet connected digital health ecosystem will breach ePHI.

This chapter examines healthcare cybersecurity breaches, their impact on HCOs, and compliance strategies including risk management frameworks that can be customized to address the security needs of HCOs based on their business needs and risk appetite. Strategies are also presented for compliance with HIPAA privacy requirements. Lastly, the chapter covers technological advancements that present technically viable options for cybersecurity. These advancements include network configuration, cloud computing, and hardware clients to support the functional and security needs of digital health.

HIPAA and ePHI

The Health Insurance Portability and Accountability Act (HIPAA) of 1996 was signed into law in order to "improve the portability and accountability of health insurance coverage." During the early 2000s HHS mandated compliance with HIPAA privacy and security rules for organizations handling protected health information (PHI) including covered entities and business associates. While HIPAA privacy applies to PHI stored in any medium – ePHI, paper, or tape – HIPAA security focuses on ePHI, the electronic portion of the designated record set (DRS).

HIPAA rules require administrative, physical, and technical safeguards, to protect the security and privacy of patient information. These rules require protecting computer systems including hardware, applications, and data against inappropriate access, backups, disaster recovery plans, and encrypting ePHI.

In case of a security breach, HIPAA-covered entities must comply with HHS's breach notification rule. The FTC recently mandated the application of *Health Breach Notification Rule* to entities that handle healthcare data but are not covered by HIPAA. Breach notification requirements have been discussed further under HIPAA Privacy.

Confluence of Events: Growth of ePHI

The significant growth of ePHI was fueled by a confluence of events over the past decade: the HITECH Act, growth of the internet for e-commerce, use of ePHI by covered entities, the adoption of telehealth and other digital technologies to manage the rapidly accelerating COVID-19 pandemic and alternate payment models (APMs).

COVID-19 accelerated the adoption of telehealth systems and complementary DHPs. The ability to offer virtual care through different video, audio, and other telehealth options was largely successful in helping the US healthcare system transition through the peak of the pandemic. However, that brought with it a transition towards proactive management of patient care through portals that were converted into a *digital front door* – platforms that offer an array of services and options to increase patient engagement. In addition, at-home care models to treat chronic and acute diseases using intelligent devices increased the generation, transfer, and storage of digital patient data.

The increase in adoption of APMs accelerated the growth of ePHI. HHS Health Care Payment Learning and Action Network (HCP LAN) indicates that healthcare payments continue their transition towards value-based models – from 23% in 2015 to 40.9% in 2020 (HCPLAN 2021). HCP LAN uses an APM framework that includes shared savings, shared risk, bundled payment, population-based payments, integrated finance, and delivery system payments, to value-based care (HCPLAN 2017).

The explosion of digital patient data has come with a downside. The realization by bad actors that ePHI is worth more on the dark web than a credit card has led to an exponential increase in cyberattacks. These attacks exploit system vulnerabilities that are gateways to large quantities of ePHI. Once a system is breached, a network system malware encrypts files, rendering them unusable. Cyber-terrorists demand ransomware in exchange for decryption keys.

It has become apparent that with healthcare's increasing push towards distributed access and controls, cyberattacks and breaches must be managed and controlled by covered entities, business associates, and non-covered entities that handle healthcare data.

Protecting ePHI security is a key requirement for compliance with HIPAA privacy. However, factors such as sale and handling of ePHI to third parties for non-treatment, payment, and operations can also compromise patient privacy. These factors will be discussed later in this chapter.

We begin with statistics related to cyber breaches and ransomware including the ever-expanding target areas for cyber criminals.

Ransomware Statistics and Observations

The increase in the number, severity, and outcomes of cyberattacks has been alarming. The following survey from Sophos highlights the perspectives of IT professionals on the state of ransomware in healthcare.

Sophos launched the *State of Ransomware in Healthcare 2022* where 5,600 IT professionals, including 381 in healthcare, from 31 countries participated in the research. Select findings from the report are (Mahendru 2022):

- Ransomware attacks on healthcare almost doubled – 66% of healthcare organizations surveyed were hit by ransomware in 2021, up from 34% in 2020.
- Healthcare organizations that paid the ransom got back only 65% of their data in 2021. Furthermore, only 2% of those who paid the ransom in 2021 got ALL their data back.
- Forty-four percent of healthcare organizations that suffered an attack in the last year took up to a week to recover from the most significant attack, whereas 25% of them took up to one month.
- Only 78% of healthcare organizations have cyber insurance coverage and 97% of these organizations have upgraded their cyber defenses to improve their cyber insurance position.

While this survey includes healthcare IT professionals from several countries including the US, it highlights the following observations regarding cyberattacks (a) ransom payments are not effective in retrieving lost patient data. Healthcare security organizations such as CISA, MS-ISAC, and federal law enforcement do not recommend paying ransom in case of cyberattacks, and (b) HCOs must obtain cyber insurance coverage as part of their cybersecurity risk management solution.

HHS's Health Sector Cybersecurity Coordination Center issued a *threat brief* about EHRs. According to the *brief* the average total cost of a data breach for the healthcare industry was $9.23 million in 2021 (HHS 2022). The brief makes the following observations:

- Top threats against EHRs are phishing attacks, malware, and ransomware attacks, encryption blind spots, cloud threats, and employees. Forty million patient records were compromised in 2021.
- "EMR/EHRs are valuable to cyber attackers because of Protected Health Information (PHI) it contains and the profit they can make on the dark web or black market." PHI can include names, dates of birth, Social Security numbers, account numbers, email addresses, internet protocol (IP) addresses, and more.

Tables 10.1, 10.2, and 10.3 have been generated using data reported by healthcare organizations to the U.S. Department of Health and Human Services, Office of Civil Rights. The HHS-OCR Breach Portal Data includes "Archived" and "Under Investigation" Breaches of Unsecured PHI Affecting 500 or more individuals as of September 2, 2022 (HHS OCR n.d.).

The breach data has been divided into three six-monthly intervals starting January 1, 2021. OCR classifies breach data by "Type of Breach" and "Location of Breach" (refer to Tables 10.1, 10.2, and 10.3). An examination of the data highlighted **breach types** – *Hacking/IT Incidents* and **breach locations** – *Email* and *Network Server* as the most frequent type and location of breaches.

The OCR classification of *Type* and *Location* of breach is represented in Tables 10.1, 10.2, 10.3 as:

1. All[1] Type of Breach: *Hacking/IT Incident*; Improper Disposal; Loss; Theft; Unauthorized Access/Disclosure; Unknown; Other.
2. All[2] Location of Breach: Desktop Computer; Electronic Medical Record; *Email*; Laptop; *Network Server*; Other Portable Electronic Device; Paper/ Films; Other.

An examination of Tables 10.1, 10.2, and 10.3 reveals the following:

■ The majority of security breaches occur as a result of hacking/IT incidents in the network server.

Table 10.1   Security Breach Data (HHS-OCR Portal): Jan–June 2021

Archived + Under Investigation		Jan–June 2021			
Type of Breach	Location of Breach	Incidents		Affected Individuals	
		Number	Percentage	Number	Percentage
Hacking/IT Incidents	Email	76	20.7%	3,422,435	12.2%
Hacking/IT Incidents	Network Server	195	53.0%	23,630,091	84.3%
Subtotal			73.7%		96.5%
All [1]	All [2]	368		28,019,964	

Table 10.2   Security Breach Data (HHS-OCR Portal): July–Dec 2021

Archived + Under Investigation		July–Dec 2021			
Type of Breach	Location of Breach	Incidents		Affected Individuals	
		Number	Percentage	Number	Percentage
Hacking/IT Incidents	Email	71	20.5%	2,093,174	9.2%
Hacking/IT Incidents	Network Server	182	52.4%	19,387,809	85.1%
Subtotal		253	72.9%		94.3%
All [1]	All [2]	347		22,791,762	

Table 10.3   Security Breach Data (HHS-OCR Portal): Jan–June 2022

Archived + Under Investigation		Jan–June 2022			
Type of Breach	Location of Breach	Incidents		Affected Individuals	
		Number	Percentage	Number	Percentage
Hacking/IT Incidents	Email	83	23.9%	1,634,892	7.9%
Hacking/IT Incidents	Network Server	168	48.3%	16,116,779	78.3%
Subtotal		251	72.1%	17,751,671	86.2%
All [1]	All [2]	348		20,582,446	

- The number of security breach incidents reduced from 368 in January–June 2021 to 348 in January–June 2022. Concurrently, the number of individuals impacted during the same periods went from 28 million to 20.6 million – a drop of 26%. While this is encouraging news, this downward movement may be an aberration. HCOs should continue their remediation efforts to mitigate security risks.
- A Pareto analysis of the data reveals that the top 20% of security breaches impact the vast majority of individuals. Further data analysis for each of the above tables reveals the following:

- January 2021 and June 2021: 20% of the largest hacking incidents (74) impacted 92.8% (26 million) individuals.
- July 2021 and December 2021: 20% of the largest hacking incidents (70) impacted 92% (21 million) individuals.
- January 2022 and June 2022: 20% of the largest hacking incidents (70) impacted 87.6% (18 million) individuals.
- The above analysis speaks to the impact of a few cyber breaches dominating the healthcare landscape. Business associates (BAs) who provide services to a vast array of HCOs were involved in several high-impact cyber breaches. Therefore, HCOs should assess BA security configurations and protocols as part of their due diligence. Additionally, ongoing assessments and security certifications must be established in BA agreements.
- In addition to BAs, cyberattackers target a variety of participants within the healthcare ecosystem, smaller hospital systems and clinics, health plans, large health systems, and cloud vendors. These observations make it imperative that all covered entities must assess and manage cybersecurity risk.

Cybersecurity Vulnerabilities: Third-Party Vendors

The past three years have seen significant increases in HCO security breaches that have led to ransomware, system downtime, and identity theft. Cybercriminals target entities (covered and non-covered under HIPAA) to gain access to ePHI and sell on the dark web. Most cyber criminals use a multi-threaded approach to ransomware: threat to sell ePHI, threat to publicize attacks, and denial of service by encrypting infected files and making them unusable. This complicates the recovery of EHRs and provision of patient care.

A majority of cyberbreaches occur as a result of third-party cybersecurity vulnerabilities. The following discussion considers examples of third-party security vulnerabilities and their prevalence.

Medical Devices: In a September 12, 2022, release, FBI Cyber Division Private Industry Notification states how unpatched and outdated medical devices provide cyber-attack opportunities (FBI 2022a). Medical device vulnerabilities arise due to poor hardware design (security not designed into the device), device software management (device software not updated since it requires special upgrades and patching procedures), and ineffective operational management (default device configurations unchanged by HCOs).

Connected medical devices are increasingly used in HCOs and patient homes to monitor, collect, and transfer ePHI which exacerbates the impact of security vulnerabilities associated with medical devices. Several medical devices used in home care and hospital-based care utilize the Internet of Things (IoTs).

The FBI notification references a January 2022 report conducted by a cybersecurity firm, which found "53% of connected medical devices and other Internet of Things (IoT) devices in hospitals had known vulnerabilities. Approximately one third of healthcare IoT devices have an identified critical risk potentially impacting technical operation and functions of medical devices."

The notification also references a mid-2022 report released by a healthcare cybersecurity analyst that states "medical devices that are susceptible to cyberattacks include insulin pumps, intracardiac defibrillators, mobile cardiac telemetry, pacemakers, and intrathecal pain pumps" (FBI 2022a).

Healthcare payment processors: In its September 14, 2022, release the FBI notification provides examples of cyber criminals targeting healthcare payment processors to redirect healthcare payments and costing victims millions in losses. In these attacks, cyber criminals target healthcare payment processors by using publicly available PII and social engineering techniques such as phishing emails to redirect victim payments (FBI 2022).

Third-party developers and FHIR APIs: A report published October 13, 2021, by Approov titled "Knight Ink Research Report: Playing with FHIR: Hacking and Securing FHIR APIs" found vulnerabilities in FHIR APIs used by third-party developers and aggregators (Approov 2021). Most of these developers do not design data transfer and handling protocols in their system, such as segmenting ePHI from non-healthcare data.

The findings highlight the need for EHR vendors and HCOs to validate system configuration and security provisions of third-party app developers, data aggregators, and third-party vendors that require access to EHR data via FHIR APIs.

Meta Pixel: is a third-party analytics tool that can be installed on websites to provide analytics on ads for Facebook and Instagram. An investigation indicated that 33 of the top 100 hospitals in the US use this tool on their websites to evaluate patient preferences. Several hospitals installed Meta Pixel on password-protected portals that sent information about patient health conditions, etc. to Facebook. The breach has been submitted to

HHS-OCR who will assess patient damages for violation of medical privacy (Wider 2022).

Regulatory Controls – For Medical Device Manufacturers

Vulnerabilities in connected medical devices can be exploited by cyber terrorists to attack networks. This has been demonstrated by the increase in cyberattacks that target medical devices and the networks to which they are connected.

To secure medical devices to prevent medical disasters and privacy violations, the House and Senate have considered companion bills *Protecting and Transforming Cyber Health Care Act or the PATCH Act of 2022*. While the PATCH Act did not pass in 2022, the FDA, in collaboration with MITRE, updated the "Medical Device Cybersecurity Regional Incident Preparedness and Response Playbook." This guideline emphasizes the need for a diverse team to participate in cybersecurity preparedness and response exercises. For additional information refer to the FDA website (FDA 2022).

HIPAA Security and Cybersecurity Frameworks

Compliance with HIPAA privacy and security rules is mandatory for HCOs. It is achieved by translating HIPAA security requirements into controls. However, the increasing sophistication of HCO cyberattacks requires a framework-oriented approach that offers a comprehensive set of objectives and controls to secure HCOs. Since cyberattacks impact the core business of HCOs, it is recommended that risk management be considered in the design and implementation of cybersecurity risk mitigation strategies. A comprehensive and flexible approach that can be tailored to include organizational risk management is presented in security and privacy frameworks.

Cybersecurity frameworks help organize and implement an effective cybersecurity program while meeting HIPAA requirements. They incorporate a set of policies and procedures to help HCOs organize cybersecurity risk management activities. Frameworks help organizations understand their cybersecurity risks and generate customized measures for risk mitigation. They have been developed by for-profit organizations, industry cybersecurity groups, not-for-profit organizations, and governmental agencies. Several security frameworks have gained recognition for meeting the cybersecurity needs of HCOs.

Advantages of Cybersecurity Frameworks

The following are the principal advantages of using Cybersecurity Frameworks:

- Frameworks are flexible and can adapt to different types and sizes of HCOs.
- Frameworks provide a compilation of requirements for HIPAA requirements (cybersecurity and privacy).
- Frameworks provide access to industry standards, best practices, guidelines, and controls.
- Framework objectives are outcome-based which are achieved through, controls using tools, techniques, and processes decided by individual HCOs.
- Provide HCOs an opportunity to assess HIPAA compliance – informally and formally.
- Risk-based cybersecurity frameworks help identify and prioritize cyber risks and bridge the gap between cybersecurity risk and organizational risk management practices for remediation.
- Frameworks provide a common language and systematic methodology to manage cybersecurity risk across an HCO and other participants in its ecosystem such as vendors, suppliers, and customers.

Commonly Used Cybersecurity Frameworks

The National Institute of Standards & Technology (NIST) Cybersecurity Framework helps HCOs organize their cybersecurity strategy while satisfying government requirements around HIPAA privacy and security. The Health Information Trust (HITRUST) Alliance, a not-for-profit organization, has also developed a cybersecurity framework that combines controls and standards from several pre-existing frameworks. The following discussion includes commonly used Cybersecurity Frameworks in healthcare.

NIST Cybersecurity Framework

Since publishing "An Introductory Resource Guide for Implementing the Health Insurance Portability and Accountability Act (HIPAA) Security Rule," NIST has provided standards to comply with HIPAA security requirements. To better assist HCOs meet HIPAA security requirements against cyber threats, NIST has incorporated their updated standards (NIST SP 800-53 r5) (NIST CSRC 2020) into a Cybersecurity Framework and mapped these to HIPAA security rules.

The NIST Framework has been developed by the federal government, in collaboration with private businesses, and is widely used by US businesses. It is required for governmental organizations, and its adoption is voluntary for private health entities. While the NIST Framework is a risk-based approach, HCOs continue to use a compliance-based approach to cybersecurity and privacy. The NIST Framework comprises a core, implementation tiers, and profile (NIST 2018).

Core

The core comprises five functional areas, divided into categories and subcategories. Subcategories are the objectives (desired outcomes) that must be achieved for effective risk mitigation. Each objective is linked to a set of resources, including security controls and standards. NIST Framework relies on controls provided in NIST SP 800-53 r5, supplemented by applicable references in other cybersecurity frameworks such as ISO/ISE 27001, COBIT 5, and ISA 62443. These references help cybersecurity designers operationalize objectives included in NIST Framework.

OCR has released a crosswalk between the HIPAA Cybersecurity Rule and NIST Framework. This crosswalk includes standards from other cybersecurity frameworks some of which are mentioned in the "Other Cybersecurity Frameworks" section. HCOs planning to implement a security and privacy framework should refer to links in this section and consult security experts. Implementing a framework-based cybersecurity program relies on detailed controls and standards which can be time-consuming and expensive (HHS OCR 2016).

NIST has released the initial public draft (IPD) of "Implementing the Health Insurance Portability and Accountability Act (HIPAA) Security Rule: A Cybersecurity Resource Guide." This Publication 88-66 Rev 2 includes guidelines to protect advanced technologies such as cloud computing, smart personal devices, digital platforms, and telehealth from cyberattacks (Marron 2022).

Core: Functional Areas

NIST Framework functional areas comprise the risk management life cycle – *identify, protect, detect, respond, and recover* – managed continuously for an effective cybersecurity program. These functions form a good starting point for cybersecurity strategies regardless of whether HCOs plan on following the entire framework. The five functions are:

■ *Identify:* involves identifying organizational assets subject to cybersecurity risks namely equipment, applications, data, people, and subsystems. During this stage, assets that support critical operations can be identified and treated with higher priority.
■ *Protect:* involves implementing appropriate safeguards namely password management, firewalls, anti-malware systems, end-point encryption, training, data security for data in motion through end-to-end encryption, and formal policies and procedures. The *identify* and *protect* functions focus on preventing cyberattacks.
■ *Detect:* includes security monitoring and detection in the event of a cyberattack. If detected during early stages, many cyberattacks can be managed to limit damage to critical systems. Detection is best accomplished through around-the-clock monitoring using security incident and event management (SIEM) solutions which use advanced analytics on security logs, events, and data files to detect anomalies and threats.
■ *Respond:* well-designed cybersecurity systems *respond* proactively and retroactively to cyberattacks. The proactive function responds to potential cyber threats. For example, security systems that respond to multiple failed logins by locking down system access are designed to prevent potential cyberattacks. The *respond* function includes response planning, communication, and mitigation.
■ *Recover:* this function involves restoring impacted systems which includes managing the safety and integrity of backups within the context of recovery planning and communication.

Implementation Tiers

NIST framework implementation tiers describe the degree of compliance of cybersecurity risk management programs with HCO business objectives and framework characteristics. There are four tiers as described below:

■ *Tier 1: Partial Level* – represents HCOs whose cybersecurity risk management practices are not formalized nor integrated with their risk management program. In this tier, HCOs do not understand risks posed by the external ecosystem of cyber supply chain partners, vendors, payers, and patients.

- *Tier 2: Risk Informed Level* – represents HCOs with formal cybersecurity risk management practices that are not consistently and evenly applied organization-wide. In this tier, HCOs understand risks posed by the external ecosystem of cyber supply chain partners, vendors, payers, and patients but do not formally manage them.
- *Tier 3: Repeatable Level* – represents HCOs with formal risk management practices integrated with cybersecurity-related risks. Cybersecurity programs are prioritized evenly across the organization. In this tier, HCOs formally manage risks posed by their external ecosystem partners.
- *Tier 4: Adaptive Level* – represents HCOs that continuously adapt their cybersecurity activities using lessons learned from their business environment and advances in cybersecurity technologies and best practices. In this tier, HCOs formally, and continuously, collaborate with their ecosystem partners. Since the level of cyber threats, protective technologies (AI, ML, and pattern recognition), and business requirements constantly change, Tier 4 is effective in reducing cybersecurity breach risks for critically important programs.

Profile: Customizing the Framework

NIST Framework's Cybersecurity Profile recommends using HCO's business objectives, cybersecurity threats, and HCO risk tolerance to generate a customized set of requirements and controls. HCOs should customize the framework after due consideration of the variables. For example, the probability of cybersecurity threats cannot be predicted, and HCO risk tolerance levels are dictated by threats to patient care, loss of reputation, and fines which cannot be underestimated.

Risk Management Considerations for Implementing the NIST Framework

HCOs can implement cybersecurity programs by customizing the Framework and using tools and techniques to achieve desired outcomes in the subcategories. The following example illustrates how risk management can be incorporated in HCO-cybersecurity programs.

Example: An HCO with a well-renowned cardiac program has determined that ongoing access to their EHR and related systems is critical to their success, and in case of a cyberattack, system disruptions to the cardiac program cannot last more than eight hours. In this scenario, organizational systems associated with the cardiac program must be *identified, protected*, and in case of system breach, *detected, responded to, and recovered from* within eight hours. This requires an investment in protective systems, 24×7 monitoring, proactive detection, and response. In addition, the HCO needs to ensure a cloud-based backup environment that can be restored in case of a cyberattack.

Due to the critical nature of the cardiac program, the HCO must operate their cybersecurity program at the *Tier 4 level*. In this tier, the HCO collaborates with ecosystem partners to ensure compliance with cybersecurity best practices, and continuously adapts its cybersecurity activities using lessons learned from its business environment and advances in cybersecurity technologies such as pattern recognition, ML, and malware detection.

While this strategy does not guarantee the eight-hour turn-around-time in case of a cyberattack, the practices required to demonstrate cybersecurity Tier 4 level compliance will help to achieve the HCO's goal.

HITRUST Common Security Framework (HITRUST CSF)

The HITRUST is based on the ISO/IEC 27001 framework (refer to "Other Cybersecurity Frameworks") and includes controls and standards from different information security frameworks, including NIST 800-53, HIPAA, PCI, CMMC, and others (HITRUST lists approximately 45 major security and privacy standards, regulations, and frameworks).

The HITRUST Framework amalgamates requirements from different sources to help HCOs comply with HIPAA rules, PCI DSS, and other standards. This Framework, like the NIST Cybersecurity Framework, is hierarchical in structure and comprises *control domains*, that consist of control objectives that are accomplished through controls. HITRUST CSF specifies multiple control requirements for each control to meet the business and technical requirements of an HCO.

HITRUST provides different types of assessments and certifications based on the level of assurance and effort required. It has been selected as a certification body for HIEs/HINs that wish to qualify as QHINs under TEFCA's security requirements. Therefore, HITRUST will continue to support the secure interoperability of patient information for nationwide treatment, payments, and operations. For additional information refer to the HITRUST website (HITRUST n.d.).

Payment Card Industry Data Security Standards (PCI DSS)

In addition to NIST security and privacy requirements, HCOs that accept, process, store, or process credit card information must comply with PCI DSS requirements. These requirements are governed by the Payment Card Industry Security Standards Council (PCI SSC).

The PCI DSS standard is designed to ensure security of credit card information for all organizations. This standard has four levels based on the annual volume of credit or debit card transactions processed which determine organizational compliance requirements. HCOs that process, store, or transmit credit card information must comply with these requirements. Key PCI DSS requirements are included below. Most HCOs can meet these requirements by complying with HIPAA security and privacy rules.

HCOs can obtain PCI DSS certification by complying with six objectives which can be met through 12 requirements. The objectives, and associated requirements, are briefly described below. These security practices are commonly employed in HCOs. Since the PCI DSS requirements evolve with the online threat landscape, readers are advised to refer to the PCI SSC website for additional details (PCI SSC n.d.).

1. Secure network – use updated firewalls, strong passwords.
2. Protect cardholder data – encrypt cardholder data at rest, and in transit.
3. Manage system vulnerabilities – build/maintain secure application systems, protect them through anti-virus solutions.
4. Access controls – protect physical and digital access to cardholder data. Assign unique IDs to users accessing the system.
5. Monitor and test network – maintain access logs for cardholder data; regularly test security systems & processes.
6. Information security policy – implement a security policy for all users of the information system.

Other Cybersecurity Frameworks

The NIST Cybersecurity Framework cross links with the following Frameworks to comply with HIPAA and manage cybersecurity risks. The ISO/ISE 27001, COBIT 5, ISA 62443, and NIST SP 800-53 r5 standards help cybersecurity designers with operationalizing objectives contained in the NIST Framework. In addition, the SOC 2 Framework is used by cloud-based vendors for cybersecurity certification. For additional details on these frameworks refer to web links attached in the brief description.

ISO/IEC 27001 Framework

The International Organization for Standardization (ISO) and the International Electrotechnical Commission (IEC) provide a framework that is broad yet comprehensive in detail. Built on an international basis (EU) with stricter data protection standards, this framework is designed to ensure Privacy and Security while reducing vulnerability to cyberattacks (ISO n.d.).

COBIT 5 Security Framework

Developed in 1996, the Control Objectives for Information Related Technology (COBIT) is a broad-level framework for governance and management of enterprise IT. It is popular for its relative simplicity and can be a supplement to a detailed effort to comply with the current advanced cybersecurity threats (ISACA n.d.).

ISA 62443 Framework

The International Society of Automation (ISA) published a comprehensive family of standards to protect automation and control systems. The ISA 62443 Framework is designed to secure equipment and operations for industries that comprise the US critical infrastructure against cyberattacks. It is endorsed by the United Nations (ISA n.d.).

SOC 2 Framework

The System and Organization Controls (SOC) Framework was developed by the American Institute of Certified Public Accountants (AICPA). It can be customized to the scope and threat risks posed to individual cloud/data storage vendor organizations. The resultant reports focus on appropriateness of system design (Type I) and operational effectiveness (Type II). It is recommended that HCOs obtain SOC2 compliance reports from cloud-based vendors (NDNB n.d.).

Resources and Guidelines to Manage Cybersecurity Risks

While cybersecurity frameworks help to organize HCO security and privacy defenses and HIPAA compliance, the following resources and guidelines can assist in establishing an effective cybersecurity risk management program in HCOs.

Governmental Resources for Cybersecurity

Utilize services offered by the Cybersecurity & Infrastructure Security Agency (CISA) and AHA's Cybersecurity and Risk Advisory Services. Regardless of HCO-cybersecurity expertise, it is desirable to stay in touch with resources that are informed of impending cyberthreats and advances in risk management strategies.

AHA members can get help from their risk advisory services, while CISA provides free cybersecurity services, open-source tools, and free tools offered by public and private organizations. HCOs can sign up for CISA's free cyber hygiene services (CISA n.d.), including vulnerability scanning, to protect from cyberthreats. In case of cyberthreats or cyberattacks HCOs must contact the local FBI office and CISA.

Cybersecurity Guidelines

Cyberattacks have transitioned from large multi-entity healthcare systems to standalone rural, community, and critical access hospitals that do not have the resources to initiate a cybersecurity program. Attacks on smaller health-care entities are not widely publicized and generally result in the entity succumbing to ransomware.

The goal of HCOs must be to proactively monitor and prevent cyberattacks (or limit their destructive potential) by implementing well-designed protection, detection, and response systems. The following cybersecurity guidelines are categorized as *General Considerations, Identification, Protection, Detection, Response, and Recovery.* The reader may recall that this order is similar to the five functions recommended in the NIST cybersecurity framework.

General Considerations

1. **Congruency with workflows:** design security policies, procedures, implementation tools, and techniques that minimize "friction" in user workflows – including care providers and patients.
2. **Organization structure:** the organization structure should encourage collaboration between the CIO and CISO by striking a balance between system functional requirements and security.

3. **Cybersecurity personnel qualification:** utilize certified security personnel – in-house staff, or external consultants – to design, establish, and review cybersecurity programs.

4. **Third-party preparedness:** ensure third-party cybersecurity risk management preparedness. This assessment must be ongoing since digital health involves care coordination across multi-disciplinary teams, different entities, and digital systems.

5. **Managed service providers:** HCOs that do not possess in-house resources should contract with managed security service providers or managed detection and response (MDR) providers of security services including firewall management, intrusion detection, virtual private network (VPN) management, vulnerability scanning, and anti-malware services.

6. **Continuous management:** cultivate a culture of continuous monitoring, user training, timely security updates, and system upgrades as part of a well-structured cybersecurity program.

7. **Cyber insurance:** purchase a cyber insurance policy that adequately protects the HCO against liability, expenses, and revenue loss. HCOs that wish cyber protection against higher loss may consider cyber insurance from multiple insurance providers. In these situations, it is advisable to use insurance brokers to coordinate with multiple insurance providers who may need to work in tandem. For example, the insurance company that assumes primary coverage will charge more per million dollars of coverage than subsequent coverages.

   Cyber insurance providers (or brokers) require HCOs to respond to detailed requirements checklists. This offers HCOs an opportunity to assess their cybersecurity risk management program, generate a gap analysis, and remediate deficiencies. It helps improve HCO preparedness against cyberattacks as part of obtaining cyber insurance coverage.

8. **Cybersecurity certification:** get cybersecurity certification by utilizing a cybersecurity framework, such as NIST or HITRUST, to implement a comprehensive cybersecurity risk management program. Getting certification can be expensive depending on the gap between the framework's requirements and the current state of HCO-cybersecurity program. However, it will reduce exposure to cyberattacks and potentially lower insurance costs.

Recommendation: The US government should sponsor a nationwide cybersecurity certification program for all hospitals including rural hospitals, CAHs, clinics, and specialty centers. The certification program should be developed for different risk levels, size, and scope of organizations handling ePHI. This will improve overall HCO preparedness against cyberattacks. This certification program can also be linked to obtaining cyber insurance.

Identification

Inventory and identify assets namely equipment, applications, data, and people that support, or are associated with, ePHI. These assets must be treated with higher priority with regard to cybersecurity. The importance of each asset to the organizational risk management strategy can dictate cyber-security risk management practices.

Protection

1. **Password Controls:** require strong passwords including automatic lockouts after three attempts. Require periodic change of passwords. HCOs must develop system access solutions that support physicians who would otherwise jot down passwords in non-secure locations. As in all security controls, HCO-IT security teams must balance strong passwords with mandatory change frequency and risks of password exposure.
2. **Proxy Access:** give home caregivers proxy access to the patient portal. However, depending on patient requirements, access limitations can frustrate caregivers and lead to patients sharing their passwords with caregivers. This can lead to security and privacy breaches. This problem can be remedied by EHR vendors defining additional roles that can provide increased access to caregivers.
3. **Multifactor Authentication (MFA):** Enable MFA on systems that are vulnerable to cyberattacks or compromise ePHI such as emails and EHRs.
4. **Software updates:** regularly update apps, web browsers, and operating systems.
5. **Encryption:** encrypt devices such as laptops, tablets, smartphones, removable drives, backup tapes, and cloud storage solutions that contain ePHI.
6. **Virtual Private Networks (VPNs):** Use VPN to send and receive emails to encrypt data in motion.

7. **Anti-malware Systems:** Ensure that the HCO is protected by antivirus/antimalware software and that virus signatures are kept up to date.
8. **CISA – Security Vulnerabilities:** Implement security patches that address known vulnerabilities in vendor application systems as soon as available. Refer to CISA for known exploited vulnerabilities (CISA n.d.).
9. **CISA – Guidance for Cloud Services:** If applicable, implement controls outlined in CISA's guidance related to cloud services (CISA 2021).
10. **Training:** Implement an annual security training program that includes phishing emails and social engineering techniques used by hackers to trick users into undesirable actions. This training program should include a formal assessment of employee understanding of cybersecurity threats and best practices, including their role.
11. **Network segmentation:** Segment HCO network to limit damage to mission-critical applications and ePHI. For example, moving third parties and vulnerable IoT biomedical devices on separate sub-networks can protect HCO-wide ePHI from cyberattacks that originate from infected third-party systems or biomedical devices connected to the EHR. Network segmentation is discussed in the *Technical Considerations* section in this chapter.
12. **Network Access:** Disable all nonessential ports and protocols across the HCO.

Detection

1. **Intrusion Detection System (IDS):** Ensure that cybersecurity/IT personnel are trained to identify and assess unusual network behavior. Detection is best accomplished through around-the-clock monitoring using Security Incident and Event Management (SIEM) services which use advanced analytics on security logs, events, and data files to detect anomalies and threats.

    HCOs that do not possess in-house expertise and systems can contract with a managed security service provider of SIEM services. Additional details are included in the *Technical Considerations* section of this chapter.

Response

1. **IDS – Automated Response:** program IDS to generate alarms upon encountering a suspicious event and shut off sensitive part(s) of the HCO network.

2. **IDS – Manual Response:** For manual response, train IT teams to locate areas infected on the network and take them offline. Additional information for detection and analysis can be found in CISA's Ransomware Guide, September 2020, which consists of two sections. Part 1: Ransomware Prevention Best Practices; Part 2: Ransomware Response Checklist.

Recovery

1. **Backups:** backup systems can be configured on premises or in the cloud. HCOs that have moved their ePHI stored applications to the cloud will likely consider cloud backups. However, HCOs that rely on-premises systems should consider the following for effective recovery from cyberattacks.
   - The ability to recover from a cyberattack requires backup of complete patient data, application executables, and images of preconfigured OS and associated software applications. One copy should be stored offline. In addition, a parallel hardware configuration system should be maintained in a separate location that can be linked back to the HCO.
   - An increasingly cost-effective and viable solution involves backup solutions offered by cloud vendors.
   - Backups should be tested as part of the business continuity plan. Appropriately configured, tested, and maintained backups ensure a high probability of recovery in case of a cyberattack. Information on cloud options is included in the *Technical Considerations* section of this chapter.
2. **Business Continuity Plans:** HCOs should implement a comprehensive business continuity plan that incorporates different severities of cyberattacks including system encryption and unavailability due to ransomware. Downtime procedures should include backup communication systems and rapid restoration of critical data. Test exercises must be conducted regularly to ensure every member of the crisis response team, including the main points of contact, understand their roles and responsibilities.

HIPAA Privacy

Introduction

The HIPAA Privacy Rule, published in 2002, was designed to protect the confidentiality of patients and their health information while enabling its availability for healthcare. The Rule requires the implementation of safeguards to protect the privacy of individually identifiable PHI and establishes limits and conditions on the uses and disclosures that may be made of PHI without an individual's authorization. The Rule also gives individuals rights over their PHI.

The Privacy Rule defines the "what" of PHI in terms of who can use it, under what circumstances, including the patient, whereas the HIPAA Security Rule defines "how" to securely enable the requirements in the Privacy Rule. However, the notable difference is that the Privacy Rule applies to all PHI, regardless of how it is created, used, stored, or disclosed (electronic, paper, or oral) whereas the Security Rule applies to ePHI.

The Privacy Rule applies to covered entities which include healthcare providers, health plans and insurers, healthcare clearinghouses, and third-party service providers to covered entities (business associates). The criterion for a business to be classified as a covered entity is that its functions or services involve the use and disclosure of individually identifiable health information. Covered entities are briefly described below.

Healthcare providers include hospitals, clinics, physicians, and other providers that transmit ePHI to *health plans* which include health insurance companies, HMOs, and public health payers. *Healthcare clearinghouses* include medical claim & electronic record processing organizations, community health information systems, and "value add" networks that reformat data to enable information exchange. *Business associates* (BAs) include a vast array of service providers to HIPAA-covered entities, including HIT vendors, third-party administrators, billing companies, cloud service providers, consultants, pharmacy benefit managers, collection agencies, claims processors, and medical device manufacturers.

Covered entities must enter into a HIPAA-compliant BA agreement which includes responsibilities of the business associate with respect to HIPAA and PHI.

Breach Notification: On September 2021, FTC issued a *Policy Statement* that clarified the HIPAA Omnibus Rule by requiring breach notifications from any vendors who handle health information. The HIPAA Omnibus Rule applies to subcontractors who handle PHI on behalf of covered entities (CEs) and other BAs to be HIPAA compliant. The FTC *Policy Statement* extends BA requirements to entities not covered under HIPAA and includes personal health record (PHR) vendors, PHR-related entities that collect information from multiple sources, for example, manual inputs from consumers and APIs, and service providers for PHR vendors and PHR-related entities. The

Policy Statement notes that companies offering these services "should take appropriate care to secure and protect consumer data."

Example of Privacy Violation (FTC 2022)**:** In August 2022, the Federal Trade Commission (FTC) sued data broker Kochava Inc., for selling data that tracks people at reproductive health clinics, places of worship, and other sensitive locations. FTC alleges that Kochava uses geolocation data from hundreds of millions of mobile devices to identify people and trace their movements. Kochava's business model is based on customizing data for clients to use in advertising and analyzing foot traffic.

21st Century Cures Act (Cures Act)

Widely used electronic health systems and digital patient data have enabled interoperability through national network integration and data exchange. As a result, the 2016 Cures Act authorized the Secretary of Health and Human Services to identify "reasonable and necessary activities that do not constitute information blocking," providing patients control over their EHI, and business-to-business exchanges such as hospital and provider practice, two hospitals, provider and labs, vendors and HINs, and other entities. HHS' goal through the Cures Act is to improve interoperability, empower patients, and reduce provider burden.

Information Blocking (IB): ONC describes Information Blocking (IB) as any practice that the healthcare provider, HIT developer, Health Information Network (HIN), or HIE know is unreasonable and is likely to interfere with access, exchange, or use of EHI. It distinguishes it from other kinds of conduct that interfere with health information exchange. The definition requires three criteria to be met to demonstrate IB: *Interference* – an act or conduct that interferes with the ability of authorized persons or entities to use EHR; *Knowledge* – when the decision to block information is made knowingly; *No Reasonable Justification* – when considering a public policy.

Information Blocking Report: ONC has published a report (ONC 2022) that displays data on claims or suggestions of possible information blocking. The data was analyzed through their Report Information Blocking Portal. Between April 5, 2021, and September 10, 2022, the total number of possible information blocking claims was 429 with a majority of the complaints received from patients, and third parties on behalf of patients. Surprisingly, a majority of claims were against healthcare providers.

Impact of Digital Technologies

Healthcare digitization has improved access to primary care, urgent care, chronic care management, and acute care, e.g., post-operative care. However, digital health configurations have decentralized the storage, transfer, and use of ePHI across multiple systems: for example, telehealth platforms that facilitate video conferencing between patients and care providers, and at-home care models using smart digital technologies collect, store, and process ePHI. The decentralization of patient information is exacerbated in care models where technological components from different platforms and intelligent devices interoperate to provide a longitudinal EHR.

It is necessary for HCOs that are configuring digital health architectures to ensure that each participating vendor incorporates data security and privacy in every component of their system development life cycle. This requires understanding system components, data storage, and contracts with third parties to ensure that privacy and security of ePHI are not compromised.

Privacy Regulations

Data Sharing: Privacy Aspect

In July 2022, the American Medical Association (AMA) released the results of a nationwide survey, which found that most US consumers oppose selling their health data. According to the press release, the survey (AMA 2022) indicated that while patients are comfortable with physicians and hospitals accessing their health data, they are not comfortable with social media sites, employers, and technology companies having access to the same data.

The findings from the survey underscore the configuration of digital architectures that utilize advanced technologies, owned, and operated by different vendors, and store ePHI. These vendors do not fall under the CE designation and absent legislative controls may elect to package and sell patient data for monetary gains without patient knowledge.

Regulations

Currently, some of the confusion regarding enforcing the ban on information blocking comes from which agency is responsible for enforcing the ban. For example, while HHS's Office of Inspector General (OIG) has primary authority to investigate information blocking claims, it must coordinate with ONC (collector of the complaints), Center for Medicare and Medicaid Services (CMS), Office of Civil Rights (OCR), and Federal Trade Commission (FTC) to avoid confusion.

American Data Privacy and Protection Act (ADPPA)

The ADPPA bill (CRS 2022) would establish requirements for companies, including nonprofits and common carriers, that handle personal data including information that can identify individuals. The bill includes the following requirements (a) most companies must limit the collection, processing, and transfer of personal data which is reasonably necessary for their business (analogous to HIPAA's *minimum necessary* rule); (b) establishes consumer data protections; (c) prior to engaging in targeted advertising, the bill requires companies to provide individuals with a means to opt out of such advertising; (d) companies are prohibited from transferring personal data without consent from the individual. Some large data holders and data service providers would face different or additional requirements.

ADPPA contains a private right of action and generally preempts state laws. The private right of action would allow injured individuals to sue covered entities in federal court for damages, along with requiring that small or medium businesses be provided an opportunity to address the violation. This bill has several outstanding issues that need to be resolved prior to passage.

Privacy Frameworks

NIST

NIST has developed a Privacy Framework that can be used by HCOs to manage privacy risks related to cybersecurity and data operations. The NIST Cybersecurity Framework helps to organize and manage cybersecurity risks and resultant privacy risks. *In addition to cybersecurity, patient privacy can be compromised by system, product, or service operations with data whether in digital, paper, or voice format.* An organization may make data operation decisions within applicable laws and regulations but increase the risk of patient privacy.

Privacy risk assessments can help HCOs understand the values to protect, methods to employ, and ways to balance implementation to lower risks related to data operations. For example, HCOs that are working with third-party DHPs, data aggregators, and other service providers need to ensure that the availability and use of patient data are balanced with privacy. Since HCO digital data operation decisions require balancing patient privacy risks with derived benefits, HCOs can utilize different strategies to address the risk/benefit equation: (a) encrypt data in motion and at rest, (b) develop a contractual agreement with partners regarding data retention, transfer, encryption, transformation, and ownership, (c) do not share data with third parties, (d) accept risk in the existing arrangement. Digital transformation of HCOs will require consideration of strategies (a) and (b).

The NIST Privacy Framework structure is analogous to the Cybersecurity Framework and makes it convenient to develop a crosswalk between the two. The document represented in the following link crosswalks Core subcategories (objectives) between the NIST Privacy and Security Frameworks (NIST 2021). Like its cybersecurity counterpart, the NIST Privacy Framework comprises three parts: Core, Profiles, and Implementation Tiers. The Core includes functions, categories, and subcategories which provide functions and desired outcomes regarding Privacy. HCOs generate Profiles by utilizing Core details to develop desired privacy activities. Implementation Tiers indicate whether HCOs have adequate structure in place to manage their desired privacy risks.

The following citation contains a link to crosswalks between (a) NIST Privacy Framework v1 and NIST SP 800-53 r5 (controls) and (b) NIST Cybersecurity Framework and NIST SP 800-53 r5 (NIST 2020).

HITRUST

In addition to NIST, HITRUST has also developed a privacy framework that combines information from different privacy laws and standards including state, federal, and international regulations into a comprehensive security and privacy framework – HITRUST CSF. The Framework includes information from Fair Information Practice Principles (FIPPs), European Union's General Data Protection Regulation (GDPR applicable to organizations that target or collect data related to people in the EU), and the California Consumer Privacy Act (CCPA). The HITRUST assessment process looks at privacy programs in conjunction with security mitigation and risk management programs.

HCOs that have invested in HITRUST CSF for security certification may wish to consider privacy controls as part of a program to manage organizational risk due to ePHI security and privacy.

Privacy Program: Ethical Considerations

The following ethical considerations for HCO privacy programs have been enunciated by Rob Frieden, VP and CIO, of a mid-west Health System (Frieden 2022):

1. Privacy Officer should report to the Board – Audit and Compliance Committee.
2. Payment-driven reasons lead to excessive data capture, regardless of the reason for visit. Data collection should be necessary but not excessive and follow HIPAA's "minimum necessary" rule.
3. Patient data should not be stored for a period longer than necessary to fulfill the purpose for which it is used. Patient data retention should follow policies defined by the healthcare entity and federal organizations.
4. Patients should be made aware of how their data can be used through Notice of Privacy Practices – which should be closely followed.
5. Privacy compliance programs should investigate all complaints using pre-approved standards and report their findings regardless of the responsible party.
6. Upon notification of privacy violation(s) and subsequent investigation, all findings should be reported to the patient including the privacy violation, resolution status if found, or a statement that the complaint was unfounded.
7. HCO employees should be empowered to report their discovery regarding privacy violations. For example, if IT personnel are unaware of the end date, in a third-party contract to transmit de-identified data, then the transmission may continue beyond the contract. However, if the responsible IT employee notices no subsequent acknowledgment from the third party, then they should speak up. This questioning will inevitably lead to stopping the transmission.
8. HCOs must implement a comprehensive audit program within the EHR with proactive reviews of attempted or actual privacy violations including flagging VIPs. This may require integrating audit logs from multiple systems and sources that support the HCO's EHR efforts.

9. HCO should be aware of how aggregated patient data sold to third parties is used and/or sold and for what purpose. For instance, a log should be maintained of all data aggregated or sold to third parties with regular audits to ensure data is being used as per the original agreement.
10. Ensure the workforce is knowledgeable regarding HIPAA Privacy fundamentals and ethical privacy policies implemented by the organization.

Technical Considerations

Introduction

Technical considerations focus on cloud computing, client devices, and network segmentation with the goal of enabling digital transformation and improving cybersecurity of ePHI systems. The topics include the advantages and disadvantages of cloud computing services and configurations, types of client devices, and network configuration and management services. For a comprehensive discussion on designing and managing networks, HCOs are referred to a vast array of resources, including consulting organizations, that specialize in these services.

Cloud Computing

According to the National Institute of Standards and Technology (NIST)

> cloud computing is a model for enabling convenient, on-demand network access to a shared pool of configurable computing resources (e.g., networks, servers, storage, applications, and services) that can be rapidly provisioned and released with minimal management effort or service provider interaction.

> **(NIST CSRC 2021)**

The modernization of healthcare systems, and transition to EHRs, was supported by on-premises computing to process applications and store data. The transition to cloud computing began with the commercialization of the internet and increased adoption of EHRs. HCO management realized that on-premises servers, storage, and application systems were difficult and expensive to scale, manage, and secure to accommodate the expanding requirements of digital data. The cost of scalability, coupled with increases in cyberthreats, incentivized HCO managements to consider software as a service (SaaS) – a cloud computing platform offering.

In addition to facilitating transitions from legacy environments, the availability of big data on the cloud, coupled with AI technologies, has enabled aggregators to analyze and leverage data for PHM and transition HCOs towards CDS.

Cloud systems generally offer the following advantages:

- Higher availability due to redundant infrastructure.
- Improved performance due to customer ability to locate their service close to users.
- Improved responsiveness in terms to access to additional resources and transitioning to an agile organization.
- Improved security due to encryption and 24-hour monitoring and response systems.
- Improved scalability due to shared infrastructure (public cloud).
- Increased cost savings due to avoidance of capital expenditures and paying for required computing resources.
- Increased portability since cloud services are internet-based.
- Access to AI and ML platforms including tool sets.
- Data backup and storage.

Cloud vendors offer services in several configurations. The three commonly used configurations are Infrastructure as a Service (IaaS), Platform as a Service (PaaS), and Software as a Service (SaaS). In addition, the demands of big data have made Data as a Service (DaaS) a sought-after cloud offering. "As a service" refers to the way IT assets are supported in cloud offerings.

Cloud Service Offerings

Cloud services are defined by the OSI layers supported by vendors. While cloud-based service offerings continue to expand, the commonly offered services are described below.

Infrastructure as a Service (IaaS): IaaS provides access to a cloud-based computing infrastructure which includes networking, storage, servers, virtualization, and operating system. In this configuration, HCO-IT teams are responsible for managing applications, data, middleware, and operating systems. This option is good for HCOs that would rather rent than purchase and maintain their computing infrastructure.

Examples of *IaaS* vendors: Amazon Web Services (AWS), Google Cloud, IBM Cloud, and Microsoft Azure.

Platform as a Service (PaaS): PaaS provides access to a cloud-based development platform which includes networking, storage, servers, virtualization, operating system, middleware, and runtime software. In this configuration, HCO-IT teams are responsible for managing applications and data. This option is good for HCOs that wish to create in-house solutions to address specialty requirements and optimize operational workflows. It is a low-risk way of adopting new technologies.

Examples of *PaaS* vendors: AWS Elastic Beanstalk, Google App Engine, Red Hat OpenShift on IBM Cloud, and Microsoft Windows Azure.

Software as a Service (SaaS): SaaS provides access to cloud-based software applications. This option is popular among HIS vendors and is fast becoming a low-cost, scalable, secure solution for HCOs to license and implement software applications.

Examples of *SaaS* vendors: Google Drive, Dropbox (cloud file storage), Microsoft Office 365 (productivity), Salesforce (CRM), Oracle Cerner (HIS), and Epic (HIS for independent medical groups), and Meditech (HIS).

Data as a Service provides access to cloud-based storage, integration, and processing services. The primary benefits of *Data as a Service* solutions are data aggregation and tools to extract information from organization-wide data. This service is useful for HCOs that utilize a combination of on-premises and cloud systems, each with its own data structure and reporting solutions.

Use Cases: the following examples offer different ways in which DaaS can help HCOs: (a) patient dashboards for comprehensive access to data, (b) disaster preparedness, (c) data analytics, (d) HINs/HIEs to combine data from member organizations for an enhanced review of population and public health initiatives.

Examples of *Data as a Service* vendors: Amazon AWS, Gartner, McKinsey, and MS Azure.

Cloud Configurations

Cloud services can be offered using different cloud configurations. The most common cloud configurations are public, private, community, and hybrid. It is important for HCOs to understand the advantages and disadvantages of each configuration in the context of security and costs.

The Cloud Security Alliance (CSA) (CSA n.d.) is an organization dedicated to raising security awareness of cloud computing. It may be useful for HCOs to participate in CSA to better comprehend cloud computing and related security as they can continue their digital transformation journey.

Cloud configurations offer the following advantages and disadvantages for HCOs.

Public Cloud: provides computing resources via a multi-tenant configuration around resource sharing among multiple customers. While public clouds sacrifice control and security of customer data, they provide significant benefits in terms of increased scalability, lower costs, geographical dispersion, and faster access to newer technologies.

Examples of vendors that offer public clouds: AWS, Microsoft Azure, Google Cloud, and IBM.

Private Cloud: dedicates computing resources to a single customer. Private clouds can be created using a physical infrastructure or virtual configuration. Under the physical infrastructure configuration hardware and software resources are dedicated, configured, and hosted on-premises or off-premises. Virtual private clouds can be created by cloud vendors on public cloud infrastructure – essentially a cloud within a cloud. Private clouds provide increased control over security and privacy configurations, customizability, and organizational control but may require capital expenditure. HCOs can also consider private clouds for big data storage and analytics.

Examples of vendors that support private clouds: AWS, Microsoft Azure, Google Cloud, and IBM.

Community Cloud: this serves communities with similar applications, security, compliance, and computing requirements. These clouds are especially useful for heavily regulated industries such as healthcare and finance. Private clouds can be segmented to support several organizations within the same industry. These clouds can be configured to offer security and privacy at the level desired by HCOs while realizing cost savings. Community clouds are more expensive than public clouds.

Examples of vendors that support community clouds: AWS, Microsoft Azure, Google Cloud, and IBM.

Hybrid Cloud: this configuration comprises multiple cloud infrastructures which are integrated into a single environment using integration or orchestration. HCOs should consider this configuration to protect ePHI in a private cloud and SaaS applications in a public cloud which are designed to work seamlessly with one another. Since private clouds follow cloud configuration requirements, HCOs can incorporate private and public clouds in their computing strategy based on data security and privacy requirements. Hybrid clouds provide HCOs the flexibility to select the optimal cloud environment for individual applications and big data analytics for optimal security, performance, and cost-effectiveness.

Examples of vendors that support hybrid clouds: AWS, Microsoft Azure, Google Cloud, and IBM.

Recommendation

Since most HCOs utilize SaaS solutions for EHRs including supporting databases, it is important to validate the cloud type utilized by vendors for applications and databases. While public clouds are the most viable and cost-effective solution, they can be vulnerable to large-scale, high-volume cyberattacks that impact sizable patient information through a singular SaaS application. Because of this, it is important for HCO-IT teams to get visibility into the cloud technical environment, including tools used and access.

Client Devices

User devices that allow users to access network resources are termed clients. HCOs that use on-premises infrastructure for legacy applications predominantly use thick clients such as desktop computers and laptops. On the other hand, HCOs that have transitioned to cloud-based EHRs increasingly use mobile client devices such as laptops, tablets, and smartphones, and thin clients to support a variety of workflows within and outside HCO physical boundaries. Cloud services can be accessed using thin clients or browser-based devices. Client device management must be an integral component of a well-architected network platform that considers security and operational costs of client devices.

Categories

Client devices can be divided into three categories based on their level of functional independence of a central server – thick clients, thin clients, and zero clients. In addition, organizations can deploy thin client devices through desktop virtualization. There are three options to enable virtual desktops: Virtual Desktop Infrastructure (VDI), Desktop as a Service (DaaS), and Remote Desktop Services (RDS). We will describe VDI and DaaS solutions since RDS is a variant of VDI. Desktop virtualization has emerged as a cost-effective and scalable client solution – for the entire HCO or select areas such as remote care providers.

In the era of cloud computing and increasing cyber threats, HCOs must assess existing client devices on their networks based on cost of acquisition and maintenance, application/workflow requirements, and security. This analysis must consider patients, employees, and care provider requirements. The following discussion offers advantages and disadvantages of each category.

Thick Clients: these devices provide a high level of functional independence such as running programs, databases, customizability, and accessing resources over the internet. Thick clients, such as personal computers and laptops, can support high multimedia performance and, if needed, operate independently of central servers. However, expanding networks, transitions to SaaS cloud computing, and impending security threats require HCOs to reassess thick clients for overall effectiveness. Since thick clients are fully functioning computers, they are vulnerable to cyberattacks via network servers or client devices. In addition to security vulnerabilities, these clients are expensive to purchase, deploy, replace, and manage – including network-wide deployments of device-level software upgrades and antivirus programs.

Examples of companies that offer thick clients: Apple, HP, and Lenovo.

Thin Clients: these devices are used to access programs and databases stored on a central server as opposed to local drives. Thin clients have a CPU, storage, memory, and operating system. Usefulness of these devices is generally restricted to applications accessible through on-premises or cloud applications. Thin client devices are (a) more cost-effective than thick clients due to lower acquisition and deployment costs, (b) more secure since they are controlled by a central server, and (c) easy to deploy and manage. However, thin clients are generally limited in their flexibility and support of high multimedia performance. It is important to understand workflow requirements prior to deploying these devices.

Examples of companies that offer thin clients: VMware, HP, and Dell/ Wyse.

Zero Clients: these devices connect to central servers, on-premises, or cloud, to access applications and data. Zero clients have no local storage, operating system, or CPU. They use a chip to decode PC over IP (PCoIP) and act as terminals to central servers for delivering applications and data to end users. These devices are very secure since they have no "intelligence." Zero clients tend to support single remote display protocols, which makes it important for HCOs to determine compatibility with application providers.

Examples of companies that offer Zero clients: VMware, HP, Dell/Wyse, IGEL, LG, Pano Logic, and NComputing.

Virtual Desktop Infrastructure (VDI): A VDI deployment uses virtual machines through on-premises servers to organize and manage virtual desktops. It can be deployed on PCs, thin client devices, smartphones, or tablets at minimal cost and is useful for remote work while meeting security requirements. VDI configuration is supported by HCO-IT teams that are responsible for the deployment, management, and upgrade of the hardware infrastructure.

Examples of companies that offer VDI management software: Amazon WorkSpaces, Microsoft Azure, Citrix Workspace, VMware Horizon Cloud, and Red Hat Virtualization.

Desktop as a service (DaaS): DaaS is enabled by cloud service providers and supports SaaS, legacy applications, and Windows-based virtual desktops. DaaS supports any device through an internet connection via a web browser or an application downloaded to a device such as laptop, desktop, smartphone, tablet, or thin client. This flexibility of supporting a multitude of devices and ease of deploying a virtual desktop makes this an ideal solution for home health workers and other remote service providers that play a significant role in digital healthcare models. DaaS is a cost-effective, secure, and scalable virtualization solution that is configured and managed by third-party vendors.

Examples of companies that offer VDI management software: Amazon WorkSpaces, Microsoft Azure, Citrix Workspace, VMware Horizon Cloud, and Red Hat Virtualization.

Recommendation

Since most of the HCO application and data infrastructure has transitioned to the cloud, organizations should consider utilizing virtual desktops to ensure scalable, secure, and cost-effective endpoint connections. HCOs can begin this transition by supporting remote service providers and mobile care providers.

Network Configuration and Management Services

Network Architecture – Flat vs. Segmented

Flat Networks: Flat network designs have been predominantly used in HCO-IT networks. These configurations offer fast, reliable, and convenient connectivity across devices, applications, and data sets, but they introduce vulnerabilities across the entire network, including mission-critical systems, in the event of a cyberattack.

Network Segmentation: NIST defines network segmentation as

> splitting a network into sub-networks, for example, by creating separate areas on the network which are protected by firewalls configured to reject unnecessary traffic. Network segmentation minimizes the harm of malware and other threats by isolating it to a limited part of the network.

Network segmentation can limit access to mission-critical applications and their vulnerability to cyberattacks and malware. Sub-networks should be audited periodically to ensure they are meeting evolving HCO needs.

Designing Segmented Networks

1. Restrict access to third parties. Statistics from multiple cyber breaches point to lax third-party systems that act as a gateway to mission-critical systems and PHI data.
2. Balance the needs of legitimate users with additional security layers to prevent cyberattacks.
3. Constantly monitor network performance to ensure no gaps or vulnerabilities in network infrastructure.
4. Regularly audit and update to accommodate new users and business needs.
5. Inventory assets on the HCO network such as IoT devices, client devices, databases, servers, and medical devices. Assign importance level and data sensitivity to each device type and organize according to the extent and sensitivity of EHI stored.

Recommendation

HCO-IT team should segment their network to limit damage to mission-critical applications and PHI. For example, moving third parties and vulnerable IoT biomedical devices on separate sub-networks can protect HCO-wide ePHI from cyberattacks that originate from infected third-party systems or biomedical devices connected to the EHR.

Managing Networks

For a comprehensive cyber security risk management program, it is important to establish security methods and techniques outlined in this chapter, staying in contact with governmental resources and implementing a program that continuously monitors, assesses, and redesigns the network.

Several applications can assist in-house IT teams to manage network health. For example, SIEM systems help manage security events through collection and analysis of log data from network devices such as modems, routers, switches, servers, client devices, and printers. Analysts can use SIEM tools to identify deviations from normal activity, manage security incidents, detect, and respond to cyber threats.

HCOs that do not possess in-house expertise or resources to implement and utilize SIEM tools, can outsource management of network security systems to managed security service providers to support any of the following services depending on their needs: managing firewalls (through continuous monitoring network traffic, establishing patterns, and triggers), intrusion detection (protects all network devices and systems), virtual private network (to shield HCO operations), vulnerability scanning (on all network devices), and anti-malware services to protect an organization's network.

Key Takeaways

1. Cybersecurity risks have significantly increased due to EHR adoption, prevalence of distributed digital systems, and PHI.
2. Cyberterrorists have understood the monetary value of ePHI on the dark Web and HCO reliance on EHRs for patient care.
3. Besides network servers, third parties, IoT-based medical devices, business associates, and smaller healthcare systems pose a great cybersecurity risk to connected healthcare organizations.
4. Frameworks include desired objectives and outcomes to design and implement a comprehensive cybersecurity risk management program. HCOs can use the NIST or HITRUST Frameworks depending on their needs. HITRUST Frameworks offers third-party certification programs that can be useful.
5. HCOs that process credit card payments for consumers must comply with the PCI DSS Framework.
6. Resources and guidelines have been included to meet organizational risk management objectives – either through a framework or individually.
7. HIPAA Privacy is reliant on the security of EHI – especially ePHI. However, HCO operational factors can significantly impact breach of

patient data. For example, transfer of or sale of patient data for non-treatment, payment, or operations.

8. While the 21st Century Cures Act (Cures Act), Information Blocking (IB), and USCDI are focused on data transparency and exchange for B2C (HCOs to patients) and B2B (HCOs to HCOs), privacy considerations must be built into interoperability and transparency.

9. Privacy Frameworks by NIST and HITRUST have been discussed. The NIST Framework describes privacy considerations due to security breaches and HCO operational considerations.

10. Ethical considerations for privacy programs are enumerated by the VP and CIO of a mid-west health system.

11. Technical considerations such as cloud computing, client devices, network configuration, and management have been discussed keeping security and the transition towards digital health. In addition, the following recommendations are provided regarding cloud computing and client devices.
    – HCO and IT vendors who use third-party cloud services must ensure visibility into the tools used to manage cloud offerings. Examining access controls must be a key part of this visibility.
    – HCOs should consider virtual desktops as part of their client device solution. As part of this transition, HCOs should begin by supporting remote service providers and mobile care providers.

References

AMA. 2022. *Patient Survey Shows Unresolved Tension Over Health Data Privacy.* July 25. https://www.ama-assn.org/press-center/press-releases/patient-survey -shows-unresolved-tension-over-health-data-privacy.

Approov. 2021. "'Knight Ink Research Report: Playing with FHIR: Hacking and Securing FHIR APIs'-Summary of Findings." *approov.* October 13. https:// approov.io/for/playing-with-fhir/.

CISA. 2021. *Analysis Report (AR21-013A).* January 14. https://www.cisa.gov/uscert/ ncas/analysis-reports/ar21-013a.

———. n.d. *Cyber Hygiene Services.* Accessed November 2022. https://www.cisa .gov/cyber-hygiene-services.

———. n.d. *Known Exploited Vulnerabilities Catalog.* Accessed November 2022. https://www.cisa.gov/known-exploited-vulnerabilities-catalog.

CRS. 2022. *H.R.8152-American data Privacy & Protection Act.* June 21. https://www .congress.gov/bill/117th-congress/house-bill/8152.

CSA. n.d. *Cloud Security Alliance.* Accessed November 2022. https://cloudsecurityal liance.org.

FBI. 2022. "Cyber Criminals Targeting Healthcare Payment Processors, Costing Victims Millions in Losses." *American Hospital Association*. September 14. https://www.aha.org/cybersecurity-government-intelligence-reports/2022-09-14 -aha-fbi-pin-tlp-white-cyber-criminals?utm_source=newsletter&utm_medium =email&utm_campaign=aha-today.

———. 2022a. "Unpatched and Outdated Medical Devices Provide Cyber Attack Opportunities." *American Hospital Association*. September 12. https://www .aha.org/cybersecurity-government-intelligence-reports/2022-09-12-fbi-pin-tlp -white-unpatched-and-outdated.

FDA. 2022. "Cybersecurity." *FDA*. November 15. https://www.fda.gov/medical -devices/digital-health-center-excellence/cybersecurity.

Frieden, Rob. 2022. Interview by Rajiv Kapur. *VP & CIO*.

FTC. 2022. *FTC Sues Kochava for Selling Data that Tracks People at Reproductive Health Clinics, Places of Worship, and Other Sensitive Locations*. August 29. https://www.ftc.gov/news-events/news/press-releases/2022/08/ftc-sues-kochava -selling-data-tracks-people-reproductive-health-clinics-places-worship-other.

HCPLAN. 2021. "Health Care Payment Learning & Action Network: Adoption of Alternative Payment Models in Commercial, Medicaid, Medicare Advantage, and Traditional Medicare Programs." *Health Care Payment Learning & Action Network*. December 15. https://hcp-lan.org/apm-measurement-effort/2020-2021 -apm/#1638982499890-78a9577c-d60c.

———. 2017. "The APM Framework." *Health Care Payment Learning & Action Network*. http://hcp-lan.org/workproducts/apm-framework-onepager.pdf.

HHS. 2022. "HHS Threat Brief: Electronic Health Records." *Health Care Innovation*. February 17. https://www.hhs.gov/sites/default/files/2022-02-17-1300-emr-in -healthcare-tlpwhite.pdf.

HHS OCR. n.d. *Breach Portal*. Accessed September 2, 2022. https://ocrportal.hhs .gov/ocr/breach/breach_report.jsf.

———. 2016. "HIPAA Security Rule Crosswalk to NIST Cybersecurity Framework." *HHS*. February. https://www.hhs.gov/sites/default/files/nist-csf-to-hipaa-security -rule-crosswalk-02-22-2016-final.pdf.

HITRUST. n.d. *HITRUST CSF*. Accessed November 2022. https://hitrustalliance.net/ certification/hitrust-csf/.

ISA. n.d. *International Society of Automation*. Accessed November 2022. https:// www.isa.org/standards-and-publications/isa-standards/isa-iec-62443-series-of -standards.

ISACA. n.d. *COBIT*. Accessed November 2022. https://www.isaca.org/resources/ cobit/cobit-5#sort=relevancy.

ISO. n.d. *ISO/IEC 27001*. Accessed November 2022. https://www.iso.org/isoiec -27001-information-security.html.

Mahendru, Puja. 2022. "The State of Ransomware in Healthcare 2022." *Sophos News*. June 1. https://news.sophos.com/en-us/2022/06/01/the-state-of-ransom- ware-in-healthcare-2022/.

Marron, Jeffrey A. 2022. "Implementing the Health Insurance Portability and Accountability Act(HIPAA) Security Rule." *NIST*. July. https://doi.org/10.6028/ NIST.SP.800-66r2.ipd.

NDNB. n.d. *SOC 2 Framework Introduction and Overview.* Accessed November 2022. https://socreports.com/white-papers/soc-2/soc-2-framework-introduction -and-overview.

NIST CSRC. 2021. *Cloud Computing.* December 10. https://csrc.nist.gov/Projects/ cloud-computing.

———. 2020. "Security and Privacy Controls for Information Systems and Organizations: NIST Publishes SP 800-53, Revision 5." *CSRC.* December 9. https://csrc.nist.gov/News/2020/sp-800-53-revision-5-published.

NIST. 2018. *Framework for Improving Critical Infrastructure Cybersecurity.* April 16. https://doi.org/10.6028/NIST.CSWP.04162018.

NIST. 2021. *Cybersecurity Framework Crosswalk.* April 23. https://www.nist.gov/pri-vacy-framework/resource-repository/browse/crosswalks/cybersecurity-frame-work-crosswalk.

———. 2020. *NIST Privacy Framework and Cybersecurity Framework to NIST Special Publication 800-53, Revision 5 Crosswalk.* December 10. https://nvl-pubs.nist.gov/nistpubs/SpecialPublications/NIST.SP.800-53r5.pdf.

ONC. 2022. *Information Blocking Claims: By the Numbers.* October. https://www .healthit.gov/data/quickstats/information-blocking-claims-numbers.

PCI SSC. n.d. *PCI Security Standards Council.* Accessed November 2022. https:// www.pcisecuritystandards.org.

Wider, Janette. 2022. "Advocate Aurora Health Data Breach Could Impact Up to 3 Million Patients." *HC Innovation Group.* October 21. https://www.hcinnova-tiongroup.com/cybersecurity/data- breaches/news/21284747/advocate-aurora-h ealth-data-breach-could-impact-up-to-3-million-patients/.

WORK TRANSFORMATION

Section III includes chapters on Work Transformation Methods, Tools, and Techniques, Design Principles for Digital Transformation (DT), and an Assessment Framework designed to assess the state of HCO readiness for DT. This section is an amalgamation of methods, tools, principles, and frameworks. For example, the chapters on work transformation discuss ways to design and implement digital platforms and information technology for effective use, the chapter on design principles offers a collection of methods and principles discussed throughout the book, and the Assessment Framework includes objectives to assess the state of HCO readiness for DT efforts.

Chapters 11 and 12 discuss work transformation methods through process improvement (PI) and DT efforts including tools and techniques to enable HCOs to undergo successful DT efforts. Work transformation methods help to blend technological systems in work processes and require PI efforts to be implemented in increasing levels of scope and complexity. In addition, DT should be implemented in phases starting with a pilot(s) that serves as proof of concept for clinical and management acceptance. The scope of subsequent phases is defined by the business and digital health strategies of HCOs.

Chapter 13 offers design principles for key DT systems. HCOs considering DT efforts are advised to review these principles prior to assessing their readiness using the framework offered in Chapter 14. This framework can be customized by HCOs and used to generate a gap analysis that can be remediated to ensure readiness for DT efforts.

DOI: 10.4324/9781003366584-13

Chapter 11

Work Transformation of HCOs

Introduction

Healthcare organizations (HCOs) are a collection of subsystems that inter-face with one another to achieve a goal. These subsystems comprise clinical, support, billing, and administrative departments and functional processes that are regulated by federal and state organizations and influenced by payer plans. The subsystems work together to support ambulatory care, inpatient care, emergency care, operating rooms, ancillary services, allied health, support services, and patient billing. Information systems representing the myriad of subsystems are either provided by multiple vendors or a single healthcare information technology (IT) vendor.

The HITECH Act and meaningful use (MU) compliance requirements transitioned HCOs from different vendor-developed "best of breed" infor-mation systems to single vendor-based EHR systems. EHR vendors support a clinically integrated solution including patient billing, supply chain, and general financial systems. These vendors provide user interfaces and navi-gational tools to access, communicate, and document data. Care providers, including physicians and nurses, use EHRs to access electronic health infor-mation (EHI), communicate with care providers, and document patient diag-nosis, findings, and treatment information. EHR vendors also support patient portals that provide patients access to their EHI and other desired services.

To accommodate COVID-19 requirements for virtual access, leading EHR vendors have integrated their system with telehealth platforms to offer multi-modality communication options such as video, voice, email, and text, between patients and providers. In addition, several telehealth platforms sup-port remote patient monitoring for at-home care. The integration of telehealth platforms into EHRs supports digital health models using work transformation methods such as Lean Six Sigma (LSS), and human factors engineering (HFE) that align technological innovations to care provider requirements.

The work transformation chapter is the integrator of advanced IT systems, applications, EHRs, and telehealth platforms including DHPs. It presents methodologies and principles to transform different modalities into innovative care models. These methodologies include increasing levels of process improvement (PI) efforts and phases of digital transformation (DT). We will discuss *inter-relationships* between digital platforms, advanced IT systems, and work redesign methodologies, to enable digital transformation of HCOs.

The chapter begins with the *Quadruple Aim*, a framework developed by the Institute of Healthcare Improvement (IHI) to improve the state of healthcare.

Quadruple Aim – Four Strategies for Improving Healthcare

Quadruple Aim, a framework for improving healthcare, was developed and revised by the Institute of Healthcare Improvement. This framework has been widely adopted by the US Department of Health and Human Services (HHS) and the Centers for Medicare and Medicaid Services (CMS). It recommends four strategies to improve healthcare outcomes. These strategies are driven by key outcome metrics such as satisfaction, costs, and outcomes and form the cornerstone of measuring DT efforts in HCOs. *Quadruple Aim* includes the following:

1. Enhancing the patient experience – includes improving access to care and involving patients in their healthcare decision-making which leads to improved patient experience and positive clinical outcomes. This is a necessary component of value-based care payment arrangements including Accountable Care Organizations (ACOs) and Medicare Shared Savings Program (MSSP).
2. Reducing costs – according to the CMS, US national health expenditure grew 2.7% to $4.3 trillion in 2021 and accounted for 18.3% of the GDP; national health spending is expected to grow at an average annual rate of 5.4% for 2019–28 and to reach $6.2 trillion by 2028 (CMS 2022). These cost increases must be controlled and reduced.
3. Improving healthcare outcomes – includes managing population health such as life expectancy, suicide rate, chronic diseases, obesity rate, and rate of avoidable deaths.
4. Improving the clinician and staff experience – it is important that healthcare DT efforts include care providers, clinicians, and support staff in addition to patients.

Case for Digital Transformation of HCOs

Most HCOs have continued their emphasis on optimizing EHR functionality by streamlining the UI and conforming to provider navigation requirements and associated workflows which require PI efforts and human factors engineering techniques. However, leading health systems have integrated virtual care models with brick-and-mortar care settings to digitally transform a broad range of clinical services ranging from primary care to chronic disease management for severely ill patients and hospital-at-home care models for patients requiring acute care.

Digitally transformed care models are used to manage patient populations that are part of risk-based reimbursement arrangements. The goal is to manage patient care through wellness programs, access to EHI, medication management, multi-modality access to care providers, early detection and treatment of diseases, and cost-effective management of chronic diseases.

These cases illustrate that access and cost reduction incentives such as providing primary care access, supporting multiple entities, extending care markets, and risk-driven alternative payment models (APMs) will be likely drivers of HCO DT efforts. HCOs are increasingly transitioning to risk-based payment strategies by switching from FFS to APMs such as MSSP and ACOs. The change in care models is directly impacted by risk assumption levels. For example, low-risk payment models generally do not impact the extent of DT as compared to fully capitated payment models that require increased patient engagement with emphasis on wellness programs, access to primary care that can diagnose and treat diseases during the early stages of onset, and effective chronic disease management.

The Health Care Payment Learning & Action Network (HCP LAN) in partnership with America's Health Insurance Plans (AHIP) conducts a survey to assess the nationwide adoption of APMs. Their 2021 Measurement Effort included results from the 2019 and 2020 measurement years. Key survey findings saw an increase in the adoption of APMs: from 38.2% of healthcare payments representing 72.5% of covered lives in 2019 to 40.9% of healthcare payments, representing 80.2% of covered lives in 2020. Survey results for Medicare Advantage, Medicaid, and commercial payers all showed increased adoption (HCP LAN 2021).

The above statistics indicate a shift toward value-based APMs. There is widespread recognition throughout the healthcare ecosystem that the balance between cost of healthcare and quality of life in the current healthcare system must be altered such that quality of life is improved at reduced care costs. While this transition appears counterintuitive, it is precisely what is needed in our healthcare system. Quality specialists have long understood that simplification of work processes not only reduces errors while improving quality but also lowers the cost of operations. This is the reason public and private payers are shifting payment to value-based reimbursement models. These models focus on managing risks through population health stratification, wellness programs, and chronic disease management which require providers to develop innovative care models to improve outcomes while reducing costs.

Recent M&As have consolidated the number of independent DHPs but compelling benefits continue to incentivize nontraditional providers of care such as payers, employers, and independent DHPs to provide telehealth-enabled patient services.

Healthcare reimbursement models are increasingly transitioning toward APMs and value-based alliances. These alliances are being driven by traditional and nontraditional providers of care. With payers reducing FFS payments, it is important for HCOs to participate in risk-based reimbursement models that require managing member lives in a cost-efficient and care-effective manner. This participation requires HCOs to utilize digital health models with the following understanding:

- Risk-based contracts, including bundled payments, can be used to support various aspects of patient care. This requires a focus on primary care, care coordination through team-based care, and elimination of unnecessary tests/procedures. These risk-based arrangements are supported through big data aggregation, predictive analytics, and AI.
- HCOs participating in value-based reimbursement programs use PHM to implement chronic disease management, wellness care, proactive disease management, care coordinated networks including different care provider specialties, and patient-centered medical home (PCMH).
- Data consolidation from virtual visits, remote monitoring devices, wearables, EHRs, employment information, socioeconomic status, etc. use AI, ML, and data analytics to compare the effectiveness of treatments, identify device safety problems, assist with diagnoses, and analyze patterns of patient diseases.
- HFE techniques for user-intuitive interface and "frictionless" provider and patient experience. This includes data collected from a variety of sources, consolidated, and presented in a contextually relevant "pane." For example, patient data collected from a variety of health apps, including patient-generated health data, can be aggregated, and presented to providers through Apple Health. Relevant information can also be incorporated into the patient EHR.

As healthcare practitioners are acutely aware, digital transformation requires experience with IT systems, digital platforms, and work transformation methods. It is difficult to design AI-enabled digital care models without requisite IT capability levels and work transformation methods that align user requirements with redesigned care models.

Since IT is a key requirement for effective digital transformation, this chapter includes a classification of IT capability levels and their requirements for different operational complexities of work transformation. In addition to IT CLs, this chapter discusses work transformation methods ranging from process improvement levels to digital transformation phases, similarities and differences between PI and DT efforts, key considerations for PI projects, and examples/case studies of HCOs that have integrated digital technology in patient care models.

Classification of Information Technology Capability Levels (IT CLs)

IT CLs Required to Support Different Levels of Work Transformation

IT plays a key role in healthcare systems and design of work processes. This role continues to increase as advantages through cloud computing, digital platforms, big data, and AI provide competitive advantage to HCOs through improved patient outreach, engagement, and outcomes. Therefore, to be successful, healthcare work redesign efforts must actively consider IT systems and their modifications in change strategies. This is increasingly important in digital transformation efforts where team collaboration care models are used to leverage telehealth and DHPs.

The following classification is designed to provide HCOs a tool to generate the capability level of their IT function – including the state of information systems and the quality of their technology team. This classification tool can help HCOs understand whether their IT CL requires to be upgraded to support desired work transformation efforts. This classification system can be used in conjunction with the Assessment Framework, a self-assessment tool that can guide HCOs to generate and remediate gaps to prepare for digital transformation efforts (refer to Chapter 14).

The IT CLs are derived from Chapters 7, 8, 9, and 10. The following nine categories help classify IT into capability levels that can support increasing levels of scope and complexity of work transformation efforts:

IT Categories

1. Senior management support
2. IT management
3. Project management
4. System functional capabilities and user satisfaction
5. DHPs
6. Big data and AI analytics
7. Interoperability
8. Security and privacy of EHI
9. Technical considerations for improved security and IT systems

The following summary provides an overview of each IT CL and its ability to support various levels and complexities of work transformation efforts. Refer to Table 11.1 for a discussion of each of the nine categories and their application to the four CLs.

IT CL1: Comply with Federal Mandates

Implement minimum technological requirements under federal mandates – billing, registration, and ancillary systems. IT relies on third parties to handle IT requirements, including security, and does not leverage data for clinical, financial, or administrative decision support.

Management considers IT a mandatory expense for business and federal mandates, and there is minimal emphasis on workflow optimization. In addition, user committees are established for information dissemination but are not empowered to prioritize IT projects and participate in system design and implementation.

CL1 is the minimum requirement to conduct *functional PI* projects, depending on the function being considered for improvement. IT CL1 is inadequate to support any phase of digital transformation.

IT CL2: Comprehensive Internal IT Systems – Capable of Supporting Cross-functional PI Efforts

IT CL2 implements the core IT infrastructure to support in-house operations (EHR, ERP, and patient billing solutions) using vendor-developed systems and recommended workflows. The IT department works with security vendors to protect confidential information (e.g., firewalls, spam/phishing filters, endpoint encryption) but lacks advanced technologies for effective intrusion, detection, and response strategies for new virus signatures (or virus definitions) and cyberattacks.

HCO-IT uses third-party consultants to implement security solutions. They can utilize managed security service providers of security information and event management (SIEM) systems for continuous monitoring of IT systems.

HCO collects patient data generated by in-house systems which is aggregated and analyzed to meet regulatory requirements and internal quality measures. IT relies on third parties for risk management analytics. HCO does not consider IT an integral part of its core business.

IT CL2 is the minimum requirement to conduct *cross-functional PI* projects that can range from low-impact to medium-impact efforts across the HCO.

Management supports HCO-wide user committees to provide input in system design and implementation. There is minimal emphasis on acquiring the necessary technical expertise for advanced technologies since IT is not considered a source of business advantage. IT CL2 is inadequate to support digital transformation efforts.

IT CL3: Advanced IT Systems Including Digital Technologies – Capable of Supporting Organization-wide PI Efforts and Level 1 DTs

In addition to vendor-developed systems, IT CL3 deploys advanced technologies and analytics to support population health management, patient portals, telehealth, and consumer engagement. They realize limited success from strategic initiatives due to inadequate workflow redesign and implementation.

PMO leverages a structured SDLC framework primarily using Waterfall methodologies. PM does not emphasize quantitative measures to define the success of projects.

IT implements advanced information security risk mitigation strategies. They utilize third-party security consultants for affirmation of their security strategies. If needed, HCO-IT can contract with third-party managed security service providers of security in SIEM systems.

Data is collected and used, mostly retrospectively, to improve patient safety and quality. IT relies on third parties for risk management analytics and implement advanced technologies such as remote monitoring and at-home care models. DHPs, especially telehealth systems, are supported but not integral to HCOs' business strategy.

Management supports HCO-wide decision-oriented user committees to prioritize and guide project implementation efforts and invests in technical expertise required for DT. However, management is unwilling to take technology-based risks without a compelling business objective.

IT CL3 is minimally required to support the *pilot and startup phases of HCO DT efforts.*

IT CL4: Advanced IT Systems and Technical Team – Capable of Supporting Any Level of Change in HCOs

HCO management considers technology as a key enabler of clinical excellence and business strategy. It supports HCO-wide decision-oriented user committees, IT capital requests, in-house IT expertise, and implementation techniques that engage users in system design and implementation.

IT CL4 department and systems are leaders in healthcare technology. In addition to the systems/technologies deployed in CL3, they transform traditional work models through digital technologies. PMO utilizes a combination of Waterfall and Agile methodologies and focuses on workflow optimization when implementing IT systems. PM emphasizes complying with desired outcome measures prior to successful project completion.

IT department is considered a leader in data interoperability with external systems such as telehealth, RPM, DTx, intelligent wearables, and EHRs. It works with EHR vendor(s) to implement innovative solutions. The department has expertise in digital device data aggregation and presentation to providers for diagnosis and treatment.

HCOs that use IT CL4 utilize AI algorithms for analytics (for PHM and value-based care), CDS, speech recognition, and image recognition in conjunction with a clinically integrated SCM system. They optimize provider workflows by introducing intelligent systems in the EHR including customizing care plans that coordinate and drive patient care.

IT CL4 departments use risk management frameworks to implement cybersecurity and privacy risk mitigation plan including system backups and restore, cloud computing, network segmentation, VDI, and DaaS clients. They benefit from third-party services such as 24/7 network monitoring through managed security service providers and event management systems. IT CL4 can support *all scope and complexities of HCO DT efforts.*

NOTE: HCOs interested in assessing their overall readiness for DT efforts can use the Assessment Framework offered in Chapter 14.

Table 11.1　IT Categories and CLs

Category		CL1	CL2	CL3	CL4
HCO Management	**1**	Independent care providers or small long-term care facilities. IT expense is considered for business and federal mandates. Minimal emphasis on (a) user committees to participate in system design and implementation (b) acquiring technical expertise.	Management supports IT to meet clinical, financial, administrative, and security needs. It does not consider IT integral to its core business. Management supports HCO-wide user committees to provide input in system design and implementation. There is minimal emphasis on acquiring the necessary technological solutions for DT.	Management a. Supports IT systems across the HCO b. Empowers user committees to guide IT projects c. Supports select IT leadership roles across the HCO d. Understands the role of PI and LSS but does not link it to effectiveness of IT systems e. Supports limited user involvement in system design f. Supports IT and digital technologies g. Invests in select technologies such as platforms, interoperability, data analytics, advanced security systems, and select technical expertise. Management is risk averse and unwilling to invest in digital systems unless dictated by business needs.	Management a. Supports IT systems across the HCO b. Empowers user committees to guide IT projects c. Supports IT leadership roles across the HCO d. Understands the role of PI in the effective performance of IT systems e. Supports user involvement in system design f. Considers IT and digital technologies as enablers of competitive advantage g. Invests in necessary technologies such as platforms, interoperability, data analytics, advanced security systems, and technical expertise for effective DT. Management is unafraid to be on the leading edge of advanced technology.

(Continued)

Table 11.1 (Continued)

	Category	CL1	CL2	CL3	CL4
2	IT Management	Reliance on IT vendors to design and implement IT systems. Use third parties for compliance with HIPAA security and technical infrastructure.	Reliance on IT vendors to design and implement IT systems. HCO-IT department provides application support. Use third parties for compliance with HIPAA security and technical infrastructure.	IT implements advanced functional, technical, and security systems principally with the help of vendors. It relies on vendors for configuring and implementing HIS. IT team customizes system navigation by using vendor utilities to support user workflows. IT team can support select data exchange, aggregation, and analytics but cannot support system customization efforts.	IT team is adept at blending advanced technologies with user requirements. In-house IT team works with vendors and PI experts to design and implement IT systems including specialty workflows. The principal focus of the IT function is user satisfaction (care providers and patients) by improving productivity and desired outcomes. IT team supports data exchange, aggregation, analytics, and develops advanced functional systems.
3	Project Management Office (PMO)	No PMO. Project management is provided by IT vendor. Minimal emphasis on workflow optimization. Depending on the department, scope, and complexity, IT can support *functional PI* projects.	PMO uses the "waterfall" configuration to implement the system development life cycle (SDLC) methodology. Implementation is guided by vendor best practice recommendations including workflow redesign. Due to automation of core HCO functions, IT can support *cross-functional PIs of low and medium impact levels across most organizational systems.*	PMO uses the sequential "waterfall" configuration to implement the SDLC project methodology. It sporadically uses iterative "agile" methods and involves functional users in system design to reduce project risk. IT can support PI efforts of all levels and select DT phases.	PMO works with functional users, vendors, and IT team to manage the project. It utilizes SDLC project management methodology in a sequential "waterfall" configuration and "agile" methods to increase user participation and reduce project risk. Successful project implementations include compliance with outcome measures desired from the project. HCO-IT can support all levels of PI efforts and phases of DT initiatives.

(Continued)

Table 11.1 (Continued)

	Category	CL1	CL2	CL3	CL4
4	Functional Systems User Satisfaction	Vendor-developed IT systems that meet federal mandates – ancillaries, registration, and billing systems – are implemented. Utilize vendor-developed interfaces to transfer data across information systems.	IT vendor-developed ancillary systems, EHR, ERP, and revenue cycle solutions – including data exchanges across multi-vendor systems. Utilize structural level of exchange to package and exchange data across HL7 compatible systems as defined by HIMSS levels (refer to Chapter 9).	In addition to a comprehensive suite of application systems, HCOs leverage advanced digital technologies. They aggregate and analyze data *retroactively from internal and external sources* to improve patient care. Utilize structural and semantic data exchange levels (HIMSS definition). Care providers are reasonably satisfied with system usability, and IT training and support.	In addition to CL3, HCOs *proactively* analyze and utilize, information from *internal and external sources* to enhance patient satisfaction and outcomes. Principally utilize semantic level data exchange that includes defining data format to enable use by receiving systems (HIMSS definition). Care providers and patients are satisfied by the overall system usability, and IT training and support.
5	DHPs	Rely on proprietary, turnkey telehealth platforms that support virtual care for primary and related care services. Telehealth and HIS vendors integrate minimal patient data across their systems.	Rely on proprietary, turnkey telehealth platforms that support virtual care for primary care and other diseases offered by the HCO. Telehealth, other digital solution providers, and HIS vendors integrate patient data across their systems to generate preliminary digital solutions.	Understand and implement different types and configurations of DHPs, including telehealth solutions, RPMs, DTx, intelligent devices, and PGHD for at-home care. IT can support DT pilots and startup phases which include integrating telehealth and digital platforms in HIS to operationalize digital health.	Understand and implement different types and configurations of DHPs including telehealth solutions, RPMs, DTx, intelligent devices, and PGHD for at-home and hospital-at-home care. IT can support all phases of DT.

(Continued)

Table 11.1 (Continued)

Category		CL1	CL2	CL3	CL4
Big Data and AI Analytics	9	Big data is not generated from internal and external systems.	Digital data is generated from internal EHR and external EHI (through HIEs). Analytics is performed for retroactive decision-making. Minimal emphasis on AI models.	Generate big data and utilize vendor-developed advanced analytics to retroactively generate clinical, financial, and administrative decision support. IT relies on external solution providers for data aggregation, analytics, presentation, and AI models.	Generate big data and utilize vendor- and in-house-developed advanced analytics. IT can implement innovative AI solutions such as CDS, image AI algorithms, and medical speech recognition to work seamlessly with EHRs and PACS/RIS systems. It can implement intelligent SCM and billing systems and expertise to aggregate and present information to providers from a variety of digital sources.
Interoperability	7	Participate in local, state, or regional HIEs for EHI exchange and value add offerings. IT can enable data exchange at HIMSS levels 1 and 2.	Participate in local, state, regional, or national HIEs for EHI exchange and value add offerings. IT can enable data exchange at HIMSS levels 1 and 2.	Participate in local, state, regional, or national HIEs for EHI exchange and select value add offerings. IT can enable data exchange at HIMSS level 3. This helps with PHM and other analytical solutions.	Participate in local, state, regional, or national HIEs for EHI exchange and select value add offerings. IT can enable data exchange at HIMSS level 3. This helps with PHM and other analytical solutions.

(Continued)

Table 11.1 (Continued)

Category	CL1	CL2	CL3	CL4
Cybersecurity & Privacy Controls Compliance (8)	Use third-party consultants to implement security and privacy solutions required by software vendors and federal mandates.	Using third-party consultants to implement security and privacy solutions to secure PHI and other confidential data within the HCO. May utilize intrusion detection and response systems by MSSPs.	Implement security and privacy solutions to secure PHI and other confidential data within and external to the HCO. May utilize third-party security consultants to implement these systems. Work collaboratively with government resources such as the FBI and CISA, to stay abreast of security breaches and protection protocols. Utilize intrusion detection and response systems offered by MSSPs for cyber protection.	Implement security and privacy solutions to secure PHI and other confidential data within and external to the HCO. Integrate cybersecurity and privacy frameworks with the overall HCO risk management strategy. Work collaboratively with government resources such as the FBI and CISA, to stay abreast of security breaches and protection protocols. Utilize AI models to detect cyberthreats and breaches with immediate response.
Technical Infrastructure for cybersecurity Infrastructure (6)	Technical infrastructure supports vendor requirements. May utilize cloud computing as part of vendor SaaS offerings. Most client devices are multi-functional PCs prone to cyber attacks.	Use standard technology and shared infrastructure. On-premises or cloud computing is dictated by software vendor requirements. Not focused on network segmentation to secure ePHI from cyberattacks. Use a combination of thick and thin client devices to reduce the risk of cyberthreats.	Use cloud computing for scalability, but software vendor requirements may dictate on-premises solutions. Implement network segments to isolate high-risk access sources from ePHI in case of cyberattacks. Utilize a combination of thick, thin, and DaaS client devices for lower costs, improved device management and reduced risk of cyberthreats.	Use cloud computing for scalability, data aggregation and analytics. Implement, and continuously improve, network segments to isolate high-risk access sources from ePHI in case of cyberattacks. Principally use virtual desktops through a combination of VDI and DaaS client devices for lower costs, improved device management and reduced risk of cyberthreats.

Work Transformation Levels

As stated in Chapter 6, a variety of digital platforms proliferate the health-care landscape due to care requirements and a vast array of venture capital investments. These platforms have several different owner/operator con-figurations – independent, payers, businesses, and retailers. However, for these platforms to successfully support patients across the care continuum, they must work with HCOs to support asynchronous and synchronous work models. This integration requires HCOs to digitally transform care models in order to seamlessly generate a longitudinal patient record.

Healthcare work transformation efforts should actively consider IT sys-tems. This is increasingly important in DT efforts where team collaboration care models are used to leverage telehealth and DHPs. These hybrid care models must be carefully designed and implemented.

Successful work transformation efforts require transforming the culture of HCOs through evolutionary change management. This requires implement-ing PIs of increasing scope and complexity prior to embarking on digital health efforts.

There are key requirements for PI efforts that enable the cultural trans-formation of HCOs. These requirements will be highlighted in this chapter. However, engaging functional users in the analysis and design of informa-tion systems is key to a successful transformation, therefore,

HCOs should utilize agile methodologies for system design and project management. Agile is an iterative framework that permits users to design, prototype, test, and inform prior to implementation.

Finally, while culture, people, legacy, and technology (digital platforms and in-house capability) are important in transforming HCOs, the most important factor in successful DT efforts is the vision and support of senior leadership.

HCO work transformation efforts are divided into two categories: *PI and DT.* These categories are further divided into increasing levels of scope and operational complexity. Implementing work transformation projects that involve core operations without prior experience in process improvements can lead to user frustration and project failure. *PI* efforts incorporate work redesign, spatial optimization, and IT systems and are divided into three levels – *functional, cross-functional, and organization-wide processes. DT* efforts incorporate work redesign, spatial optimization, advanced digital technologies, and IT systems and are divided into multiple phases starting with the pilot phase and transitioning to phases that utilize increasingly complex technologies and care protocols. The following discussion on PI levels and DT phases offers implementation strategies for successful work transformation.

Process Improvement Levels

PI levels are briefly discussed in Table 11.2. A detailed discussion follows later in this chapter. As represented in Table 11.2, the scope and complexity of processes is represented by three levels of PI efforts – functional processes, cross-functional processes, and organization-wide processes. Since cross-functional processes (processes that involve multiple departments and cost centers) are prevalent in HCOs and range in operational complexity, they are divided by their impact levels: low, medium, and high, where impact levels are determined by the ability of these projects to improve core operations and help transform HCO culture to transition through process changes.

Each PI project must define quantitative metrics based on benchmarks and desired outcomes. Examples of desired outcomes can include cost reduction, operational streamlining through reduction of process steps, care provider satisfaction, improved outcomes, and number of active patient users of patient portal. Projects that meet desired outcomes are considered a success.

1. Functional PI projects are conducted in individual departments to improve operational efficiency and effectiveness. Improvements in support departmental functions can impact departments across the HCO. For example, *improvements in IT response time can positively impact all departments using the IT system.*
2. Cross-functional PI projects are conducted to improve the efficiencies and effectiveness of systems that comprise cross-functional processes of varying scope and complexities. These projects are classified, based on their scope, complexity, and ability to influence organizational culture to accept process modifications and disruptions: *low impact, medium impact*, and *high impact*.

■ *Low-impact* cross-functional PI projects engage select departments and are not complex in their joint operations. For example, *reduce patient wait time for scheduled provider visits.*

- *Medium-impact* cross-functional PI projects engage several departments. The impact of these projects is a function of the scope and complexity of processes being improved. For example, *improving patient turnaround time (TAT) in the ERs* can fall in this category since ER visits generally involve physicians ordering lab tests, x-rays, and other exams, and consulting specialists which span multiple departments. Therefore, improving patient TAT in ERs can also impact "external systems" such as ancillary departments, acute care units, and speciality operations.
- *High-impact* cross-functional PI projects engage a majority of HCO clinical departments that impact patient and provider satisfaction. These efforts can influence organizational culture to handle disruptive transitions and can be predecessors to DT. For example, *improving patient care processes across a broad spectrum of areas including patient ER admission, emergency surgery, ICU admission, transfer to general surgical unit, and discharge process* to lower TAT can improve patient satisfaction, outcomes, and length of stay.

3. Organization-wide PI projects are designed to improve HCO patient care services and include direct care, indirect care, and support processes including IT, biomedical devices, supplies, and billing. These projects can be initiated as part of a work transformation effort to improve patient care areas from a provider and patient perspective across the HCO. Organization-wide improvement efforts can be initiated in conjunction with HCO-wide HIS upgrades that include major enhancements.

Table 11.2 Work Transformation – PI Levels

Scope and Complexity of Processes		Description
Functional Processes		PI efforts conducted in individual departments. Improvements in individual departments (e.g., support departments) can impact departments across HCOs.
Cross-functional Processes	Low impact level	PI conducted for processes that impact select departments. These projects generally have limited impact on other departments.
	Medium impact level	PI conducted for processes that span several departments. These efforts can restructure departments and functional roles. Organizational impact of these efforts depends on the scope and complexity of processes under study and the departments involved.
	High impact level	PI efforts engage a majority of clinical and support departments that impact patient outcomes. These efforts can restructure departments and functional roles. If implemented correctly, they can help HCOs effectively manage the transformation resulting from DTs.
Organization-wide Processes		PI efforts designed to improve core operations across the HCO. These projects are designed to improve house-wide patient care services including direct care, indirect care, and support processes. The scope and complexity of these efforts impacts HCO culture to manage complex transformation efforts.

Key Considerations for Process Improvement Projects

The following considerations have been designed for PI projects but also apply to DT projects. Refer to the section on *PI and DT in HCOs – Similarities and Differences* to transition between these work transformation efforts.

1. Senior leadership involvement: organizational Board of Directors and senior leadership actively support a culture of LSS and continuous PI efforts by engaging with employees and managers.
2. Management involvement: management at all levels supports LSS and ongoing PI efforts. They support desired changes, ensure transparent

communication regarding system status, and encourage ongoing measurement of outcome metrics to identify outstanding gaps with desired outcomes and develop remediation strategies.

3. Functional user involvement: HCO PI efforts rely on modifications to information systems and functional processes; therefore, system analysis and redesign are accomplished by the active involvement of functional users. Prior to implementing functional and process changes, users approve redesigned systems.

4. Continuous PI: HCO supports ongoing review and PI efforts post-implementation. This prevents transformed systems from reverting to their original state – either due to stress, lack of employee buy-in, or lack of management attention.

5. Metrics and benchmarks: LSS/PI projects are metric-driven to monitor progress toward desired outcomes which are driven by internal and external benchmarks. Metrics and outcomes are established prior to system analysis and design and include the following traits: (a) quantifiable, (b) ratio-based (e.g., output/time, patient satisfaction), (c) readily available data to generate metric results, (d) ongoing monitoring to measure progress.

6. Project documentation: project charters and project outcomes are documented to establish a formal culture that assists during change management: (a) problem definition and scope, (b) project goals and objectives, (c) project duration, (d) team composition including project manager, (e) project plan including implementation techniques and communication strategies, (f) metrics and benchmarks to meet desired goals and objectives, (g) tools and techniques used such as electronic dashboards, (h) current functional processes, related IT systems and gaps, (i) proposed functional processes and IT systems, (j) post-implementation outcomes, and (k) revised policies and procedures.

7. Process prioritizations: Inefficiencies that impact care provider roles are prioritized for process improvement efforts.

8. Process standardizations: Operations that support care provider needs are standardized. For example, patient admission/scheduling, diagnostics (labs, imaging), pharmacy, patient *handoffs* across functional areas, and patient discharge.

9. Tools and techniques: LSS techniques are adapted to the complexities and variations in healthcare processes. Information systems are appropriately considered in the design and implementation of current and proposed workflows.

10. "Change management" culture: The HCO transitions to effectively handle changes resulting from PI efforts of increasing scope and operational

complexity. This process enables users to trust management and IT to proactively address issues that result from workflow disruptions. Key components to an effective change management culture are *management/IT commitment, user engagement,* and a *metrics-driven* culture for PI projects.

Digital Transformation Phases

DT projects utilize in-house IT systems and advanced digital technologies, to transform HCO care models. These projects utilize agile methodologies, including LSS tools, and PI techniques, during the analysis and design stage of the SDLC.

Deployment strategies for digital health are dictated by the clinical and business interests of HCOs and their digital vision. HCOs that offer limited services and wish to digitize select operations can implement DT through pilots that can be expanded to operationalize their digital health vision. However, in most cases, digital health strategies need to be deployed in multiple phases. This book recommends a three-phase deployment approach preceded by a pilot phase that may include several pilots.

Table 11.3 further illustrates the different phases in which each phase builds on the technological and process requirements of its predecessor phase(s).

Pilot Phase: designed to address key operational problems and roadblocks that significantly impact patient care. Digital pilots serve as "proof of concept." Successful outcomes from the pilot project(s) form the foundation for a plan to implement a multi-phase digital transformation of HCOs. This phase requires IT CL3 or greater.

Example: an HCO learns from its implementation of telehealth systems to handle the COVID-19 pandemic and whether they can be extended to improve patient care in other areas.

Startup Phase: derived by expanding the scope of the pilot phase. The startup phase utilizes work transformation methods to embed advanced digital technologies in revised care models. This phase requires IT CL3 or greater to support transition to value-based models, and digitally transform HCO care models using vendor platforms that support data APIs and digital complements. HCOs can also use the startup phase to construct key service offerings for patients via a digital front door.

Example: a health system offers a comprehensive suite of services and specialties and elects to implement the following solution during the startup phase: expand the use of telehealth for primary and urgent care to handle COVID-19 emergencies, digital integration of primary care, urgent care, pediatric care, behavioral health, and heart health with traditional brick-and-mortar care to extend services to rural facilities and CAHs, and offer patients access to multi-channel care modalities.

Growth Phase: extends operationalization of the HCO digital health strategy using technical and process complexities that integrate virtual, onsite, clinic, intelligent devices, and home care. The growth phase supports goals and objectives of the HCO that includes a transition to value-based reimbursement models. This phase requires IT CL4 to digitally transform HCO care models. DHPs selected in these efforts support the data and functions of APIs for partner extensions and third-party complements to encourage innovation in AI analytics, software, and hardware. This phase drives innovative service offerings for patients to form a comprehensive digital front door.

Continuing with the example from the startup phase, in the growth phase the health system may expand its digital transformation of ICU care and chronic disease management to support care for diabetes, cancer, MSK, and COPD including at-home care using advanced monitors. This model requires the integration of intelligent devices such as biometric sensors, RPMs, digital therapeutics, PGHD, and smart wearables. The goal is to use this configuration to monitor patient conditions, aggregate machine-generated data, and present it to providers for diagnosis and treatment using apps such as Apple Health (using SMART on FHIR standard). This phase also incorporates complements and other DHPs such as ambient medical speech recognition, AI models for CDS, and image AI models to support provider productivity and workflow.

Mature Phase: completes operationalization of the HCO digital health strategy that integrates virtual, onsite, clinics, intelligent devices, and home care. This phase continuously evolves digital technology and workflows associated with providers and patients. In addition to supporting the HCO digital health goals, this phase standardizes digital offerings to support external entities.

Continuing with the previous example – during the mature DT phase, the health system will achieve its digital health vision. This can include in-house designed, configured, and implemented models such as acute care for hospital-at-home care, ICU care, and multi-disciplinary support for remote access. HCOs also continue their pursuit of digital solutions including in-house development of CDS, AI analytics, and hardware solutions, through affiliates or in partnership with third parties. Depending on their digital requirements, these HCOs may own and operate DHPs and other digital solutions while offering them for sale. This phase encourages their collaboration with other HCOs and care providers to develop innovative care models that address complex operational challenges.

Table 11.3   Phases of DT

	Scope and Complexity of Digital Engagement	Intelligent Devices/ Complements	Hybrid Care Models	Patient Engagement	Provider Usability
Pilot Phase	Digital pilots are designed to address key operational problems and roadblocks that impact patient care. They serve as proof of concept for organization-wide DT efforts.	This phase requires IT CL3, or greater, to digitally transform HCO care models using *innovation platforms* for data exchange and analytics.	This phase utilizes work transformation methods to embed advanced digital technologies in multi-modality care models.	HCOs may implement a pilot that supports key patient services via a digital front door.	Digital technologies are integrated into provider workflows (as dictated by the pilot).
Startup Phase	Generated by expanding the scope of the pilot phase. This phase can support the transition toward value-based models.	This phase requires IT CL3, or greater, to digitally transform HCO care models using *innovation platforms* for data exchange and analytics.	This phase utilizes work transformation methods to embed advanced digital technologies in multi-modality care models including at-home care.	HCOs should use this phase to construct key service offerings for patients via a digital front door.	Digital technologies are integrated into provider workflows.

(Continued)

Table 11.3 (Continued)

	Scope and Complexity of Digital Engagement	Intelligent Devices/ Complements	Hybrid Care Models	Patient Engagement	Provider Usability
Growth Phase	Further operationalizes the HCO digital health strategy using technical and process methods that integrate virtual, onsite, clinic, intelligent devices, and home care. This phase supports the HCO digital health goals and objectives including a transition to fully capitated value-based models.	Requires IT CL4 to digitally transform HCO care models. DHPs selected in these efforts encourage third-party and partner innovation in AI analytics, and software, hardware, and service complements.	Supports hybrid care models that leverage virtual, brick-and-mortar, at-home care, and home health visits. This phase supports complex digital modalities such as intelligent medical devices in home care models to monitor, diagnose, and treat patients.	This phase drives innovative service offerings for patients to form a comprehensive digital front door.	Digital technologies utilized across the HCO are integrated to support desired provider workflows. Patient information collected remotely, or onsite, is presented to providers to ensure a seamless experience.

(Continued)

Table 11.3 (Continued)

	Scope and Complexity of Digital Engagement	Intelligent Devices/ Complements	Hybrid Care Models	Patient Engagement	Provider Usability
Mature Phase	Completes operationalization of the HCO digital health strategy using technical and process complexities that integrate virtual, onsite, clinic, and home care. During this phase the IT organization focuses on customization to better meet HCO needs and standardization to support digital offerings for external entities. HCOs may own and operate digital solutions to support their needs while offering them for sale to other providers to care.	Requires IT CL4 to digitally transform HCO care models. DHPs selected in these efforts encourage third-party and partner innovation in AI analytics, and software, hardware, and service complements.	The HCO completes its transformation according to its digital health vision. This can include in-house designed, configured, and implemented models such as acute care for hospital-at-home care, ICU care, and multi-disciplinary support for remote access.	This phase continues to further integrate innovative care models to further engage patients in their care and support value-based models.	In addition to the prior phases, the focus in this phase transitions to in-house development of digital solutions to support clinical decisions, and workflows.

Transitioning from PI to DT

Figure 11.1 indicates the relationship between different PI levels and transitioning to DT. As the figure indicates, change management culture is the link to the transition from PI efforts of different scope and complexity levels to DT phases. This requires HCOs to conduct cross-functional PI projects of increasing impact levels.

Once high-impact PI projects, including cross-functional and organization-wide, have been successfully implemented, HCOs can begin their digital health journey by developing a strategic vision. This can be followed

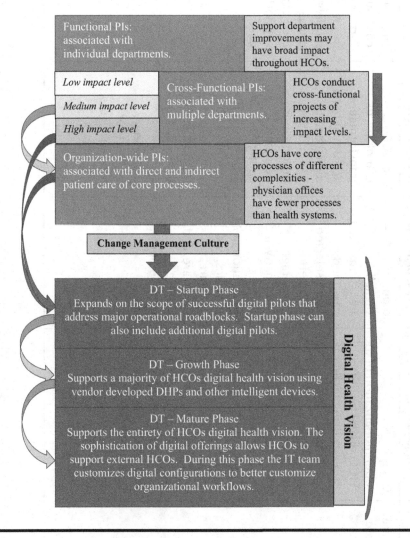

Figure 11.1 HCO work transformation levels – from process improvement (PI) to digital transformation (DT).

by a DT pilot that addresses a complex operational problem relating to a key interaction. HCOs may elect to conduct multiple DT pilots to remove bottlenecks from different key interactions within the HCO. Examples of key interactions are patient/primary care encounters, providing specialty care, and supporting chronically sick patients.

DT phases should be dictated by HCO business strategies and digital health requirements. However, as Figure 11.1 indicates, the *startup* DT phase expands on the scope of successful digital pilots that address major operational roadblocks designed to implement a portion of HCOs digital health vision. The *growth* DT phase further operationalizes the HCO digital health vision with the goal to support internal HCO needs using DHPs, brick-and-mortar care, intelligent devices, and home care. The *mature* DT phase, in addition to operationalizing the HCO digital health strategy, continues to innovate as needs arise. The sophistication of digital offerings allows HCOs to support external HCOs.

Process Improvements (PI) and Digital Transformation (DT) in HCOs – Similarities and Differences

1. **Emphasis on Patients:** While PI and DT efforts focus on redesigning system and workflows to meet the requirements of users namely care providers, ancillary, financial, and administrative users, DT also focuses on engaging HCO members, patients, and home caregivers.
2. **Disruption Level:** While PI efforts focus on streamlining and optimizing care within existing modalities, DTs disrupt existing healthcare processes by combining remote, in-person, and machine-generated care modalities.
3. **Cost Restructuring:** PI efforts focus on improving system usability and user satisfaction with minimal impact on cost reduction. On the other hand, while DT efforts also focus on improving system usability, they leverage decentralized multi-disciplinary care teams to restructure care models and lower costs as a result. For example, a pilot study at Brigham and Women's Hospital indicated the potential to lower costs and other outcomes for hospital at-home care for patients requiring hospital admission. The results demonstrated a 38% reduction in costs for home care with patients spending a smaller proportion of the day sedentary or lying down and were readmitted less frequently within 30 days (Bridger 2019).

4. **Intelligent Machines:** PI efforts utilize biomedical and other intelligent devices in brick-and-mortar care settings such as clinics and hospitals. On the other hand, DT efforts leverage intelligent biometric monitors, smart wearables, and digital therapeutics for continuous patient monitoring and data generation away from traditional care settings.
5. **AI Analytics:** DT results in large data sets that can be used for clinical decision support (CDS) and AI analytics to support PHM, precision medicine, and image recognition AI algorithms.

IT CLs and Work Transformation Levels

The IT CL classification (refer to Table 11.1) is based on categories that have been discussed in Chapters 7 to 10. This classification provides a relationship between various levels of PI/DT efforts and the IT CLs required to accomplish these efforts.

Table 11.4 illustrates IT CLs required for different levels of work transformation. For example, functional PIs minimally require IT CL1 or CL2 depending on the functional area, and extent of improvement; *low- and medium-impact* cross-functional PIs require IT CL2 or higher, whereas *high-impact* cross-functional and organization-wide PI efforts require IT CL3 or higher. When transitioning to DT, increased IT CLs are required to support the functional, data interoperability, and data analytics requirements of these efforts: *pilot and startup phases* of DT projects require IT CL3 or higher, whereas *higher phases* require IT CL4.

Table 11.4 Work Transformation Levels and IT CLs

Work Transformation Levels	IT CLs			
	CL1	*CL2*	*CL3*	*CL4*
Functional PIs	√	√	⟶	
Cross-Functional PIs	N/A	√	√	⟶
Organization-wide PIs	N/A	N/A	√	⟶
DT – Pilot Phase and Startup Phase	N/A	N/A	√	⟶
DT – Growth Phase	N/A	N/A	N/A	√
DT – Mature Phase	N/A	N/A	N/A	√

Figure 11.2 illustrates the relationship between business strategy, work transformation, and IT systems. PI and DT efforts that impact organizational change management culture should be part of the HCO business strategy. This figure illustrates that while PI projects primarily leverage information systems that support brick-and-mortar operations, DT efforts require advanced digital systems, including telehealth, big data, and analytics to support hybrid, decentralized, and team-based care models. It also illustrates the impact of increasing phases of digital transformation on patient engagement in their healthcare.

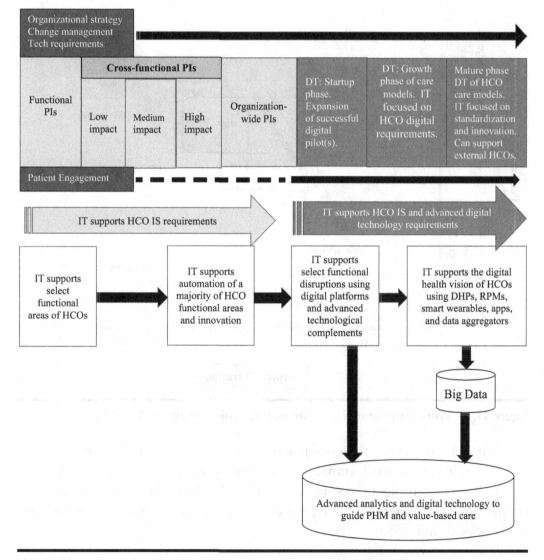

Figure 11.2 Organizational strategy, IT, and work transformation.

Figure 11.3 illustrates the correlation between the scope of projects and duration.

While functional PI projects can be completed in relatively short time periods, depending on the scope of change, the time taken to implement cross-functional projects increases with their impact level (defined by the scope and complexity of change). Organization-wide PI projects are broad in scope, complexity, and impact levels and can take significant time to stabilize in HCOs. On the other hand, DT projects of similar scope as PI efforts generally take longer to implement due to the extent of process design and change.

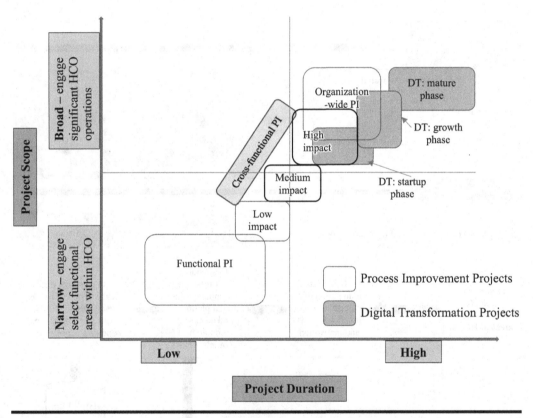

Figure 11.3 Work transformation – correlating project scope and duration.

Figure 11.4 illustrates the correlation between the extent of change affected by different work transformation levels and project risk. As the figure illustrates, project risks increase with DT efforts due to the extent of change involved. Therefore, DT projects should be preceded by well-defined goals prior to initiation.

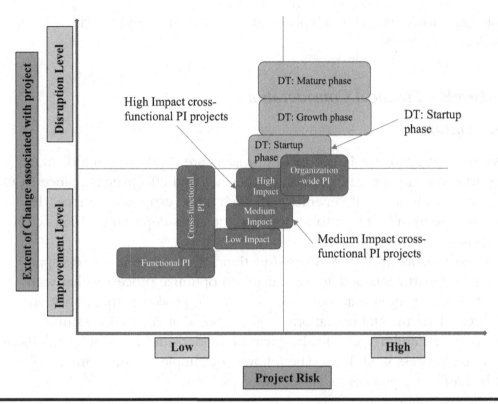

Figure 11.4   Work transformation projects – correlating levels of change and risk.

A few points of note from Figure 11.4: (a) PI efforts generally carry a lower risk when compared to DT, (b) the *growth phase* of DT projects while potentially smaller in scope than organization-wide PI targets digital disruption, which increases implementation risk, (c) while the change associated with DT is greater than PI efforts, they do not necessarily introduce proportional risk. The assumption in these observations is that HCOs utilize structured planning and work transformation methods to instill a change management culture that acclimatizes users to transition through DT disruptions.

Work Transformation Projects – Practical Considerations and Examples

The following section discusses process improvement levels and Digital Transformation phases from an implementation perspective. This section includes a detailed description of PI levels and DT phases, leadership involvement, project design principles, tools, techniques, and IT CLs, potential problems and roadblocks, outcomes, metrics and benchmarking, and case examples.

PI Levels – Practical Considerations

Description

Departmental projects: Functional PI projects are conducted in individual departments to improve operational efficiency and effectiveness. Since HCO departments functionally interact with each other, especially support departments, care must be taken to understand the cross-departmental impact of proposed changes.

Cross-functional projects: Cross-functional improvement projects span multiple departments and are conducted to optimize processes that work together to accomplish an outcome. As a result, processes that transition different departmental operations require special attention: for example, timely "alerts and triggers" for busy care providers and efficient "handoffs" to optimize process workflows. The following example illustrates the number of handoffs in a process for hospitalized patients:

- *Physician orders tests.*
- *Phlebotomist comes to the patient's room to collect specimens.*
- *Lab technician conducts tests.*
- *Tests resulted and approved by technician.*
- *Test results appear in the EHR.*
- *Physician receives an email or text notification regarding the new test result.*
- *Physician reviews the results.*
- *Physician orders medication in EHR.*
- *Follows up with the nurse regarding the new medication.*
- *Pharmacist sees the new medication in the pharmacy system.*
- *Pharmacist generates unit doses.*
- *Pharmacy technician brings medication to the unit and places it in the automated medication dispensing (AMD) system.*
- *Nurse withdraws medications and administers to the patient.*

Addressing the *handoffs* and *triggers* in this process through effective automation and workflow design can optimize turnaround time, improve patient care, and reduce patient length of stay.

Cross-functional PI efforts require active participation from impacted departments. These changes should be continuously monitored in case individual departments decide to change a process that is part of the cross-functional process change. These projects are divided into three levels based on scope, complexity, and organizational impact: *low, medium, and high.* The following examples regarding supply chain management and patient care systems illustrate the different cross-functional levels.

Supply chain management, including disposable, non-disposable supplies, and medications, can be classified in several ways depending on problem areas and organizational needs. Supply chain improvement projects that involve the optimization of non-critical supplies for multiple departments can be classified as *low impact*; projects that involve optimizing supplies for urgent care, procedure rooms, and clinical departments can be classified as *medium impact*; and projects that involve optimizing organization-wide supplies, including physician offices, and pharmacy can be classified as *high impact.*

Similarly, patient care improvement projects can be classified based on the number, scope, and complexity of impacted patient care departments. Consider the following patient care examples – *low impact*: projects that seek to improve turnaround time for lab test results involve few departments; *medium impact*: projects that seek to improve patient TAT in the ER involve multiple departments from registration to discharge, care providers, physician consults, pharmacy, diagnostic, and other clinical departments; *high impact*: projects that aim to reduce *patient length of stay in a hospital* engage a majority of departments, including housekeeping, registration, nursing units, ancillaries, allied health, transportation, discharge planning, and follow-up.

Organization-wide projects: engage most HCO departments and can take extended time and effort with uncertain outcomes. Due to this, organization-wide projects are generally initiated as part of (a) new IT system implementation that supports services and workflows across the organization, (b) comprehensive IT system upgrade including enhancements to key functional areas across the organization; (c) comprehensive review as part of an acquisition by another organization.

Leadership Involvement

Departmental PI projects: should be supported by departmental management. These projects may need senior management sponsorship for changes in support departments, which can impact a cross section of other departments.

Cross-functional and organization-wide PI projects: should be managed under the sponsorship of senior executive responsible for the impacted departments. These projects should be driven by the strategic goals and objectives of the HCO.

Design Principles

- Project teams must follow the *Key Considerations for PI Projects* elaborated in this chapter.
- Functional PI efforts should document the impact of their process improvements on other departments.
- *High-impact* and *organization-wide* PI projects may incorporate digital technology to meet organizational goals and objectives.
- PI projects should be documented and maintained using version control. These documents should also include departments impacted by, but not involved in, the project.
- Successfully implemented *high-impact* PI projects help to transition HCO culture toward change acceptance. They can be precursors to DT efforts that can lead to functional disruptions.

Tools and Techniques

- PI projects should utilize agile methodologies (Lean and related tools), depending on their scope and complexity, for rapid and iterative design. Agile methodologies include *design thinking* that modifies processes for improved user experience and outcomes.
- Projects should include monitoring techniques, such as managing daily improvement (MDI) boards, to assist with continuous PIs. Continuous monitoring and adjustments ensure post-implementation HCO compliance with established benchmarks.

Potential Problems/Roadblocks

Departmental projects

- Departmental PI efforts that impact other functional areas should be undertaken after consultation with impacted departments.

Cross-functional and organization-wide projects

- Cross-functional and organization-wide projects can alter functional boundaries (changing functions performed by departments) and functional roles/responsibilities within departments (changing responsibilities for existing roles). Structural changes require significant management intervention to be successful which can over time develop a culture that accepts process disruptions.

Outcomes, Metrics, and Benchmarking

- Project charter for cross-functional and organization-wide PI projects should be approved by the project sponsor and representatives from involved departments.
- Projects are considered *successful* when post-implementation improvements comply with pre-established metrics and benchmarks.
- Establishing Metrics: it is important to establish the correct metrics to monitor PI projects. These can be derived from qualitative critical success factors (CSFs) that represent organizational goals and objectives. Progress toward CSFs can be measured through quantitative metrics namely key performance indicators (KPIs). The following discussion elaborates on these metrics:
- **CSFs:** for projects whose goals and objectives are defined by multiple CSFs, care should be taken to define the relationship. For example, a project with goals of improving patient outcomes and lowering the cost of care may create conflicting KPIs. In this situation, a relationship between improving patient outcomes and lowering costs must be established prior to defining KPIs.

  Examples of CSFs: *improve patient engagement, improve nurse retention, improve physician satisfaction, improve staff retention rate, reduce patient length of stay in hospital, reduce cost of care provision, and improve patient outcomes.*
- **KPIs:** One or more KPIs can be used to indicate progress toward CSFs. High-impact PI efforts can incorporate KPIs at the organizational and departmental levels to assess progress toward CSFs. Each KPI should be accompanied by *best practice* benchmarks that define measures to achieve CSFs. KPIs should be developed while keeping in mind the ease with which data required for the measures can be automated.

  Examples of KPIs to *Improve Patient Engagement*: The CSF of *improve patient engagement* can be tracked through the following KPIs:

patient satisfaction with portal service offerings, percentage of patients who use the portal for at least one hour/week, and percentage of patients who use telehealth services through the portal.

Examples of KPIs to *Improve Nurse Retention*: The CSF of *improving nurse retention* can be tracked through the following KPIs: *satisfaction with management, satisfaction with EHR, hours spent documentation in EHR per shift, and market competitive salaries.*

If structured correctly, well-configured CSFs, KPIs, and benchmarks can transform organizational culture toward effective change management.

Examples of Departmental Projects

IT-Related PIs

- Add fields to a departmental screen to streamline provider workflow.
- Consolidate information from multiple screens into one screen to streamline provider workflow.
- Remove computer access of employees, who have terminated employment, in a timely manner.
- Improve IT response time (e.g., 3 secs to 1 sec) to positively impact automated functional areas.
- Reduce IT downtime (e.g., from 1% to 0.5%) to positively impact automated functional areas.
- Improve IT help desk service level agreement (SLA) compliance:
  - Response time: answer 90% of incoming calls within the third ring.
  - Turnaround time: resolve 80% of calls on the day of the call.
  - User complaints: update users on the status of their request within an hour of issue resolution or discovery of complications. The average compliance for this SLA is 90%.

Examples of Cross-functional PI Projects

1. Ride-share capabilities integrated into EHR
   - An example of a *low-impact* cross-functional PI project is linking Lyft Ride Share Capabilities into the Epic EHR; and Uber partnership with Cerner to give patient rides for non-emergency appointments.
   - Based on the patient's socioeconomic status, rides are arranged when scheduling appointments, and followed up with rides at

patient discharge. This helps patients get to their appointments and back home after the visit without needing to do anything else. Lyft data shows that using the service can help reduce missed appointments by 27% (Landi 2020).

2. Patient Appointment Scheduling Process with Physician Clinic
   - Goal: increase convenience for patients to schedule and modify appointments with physicians. This example represents cross-functional PI with *low impact*.
   - Current Process: Patient calls physician's office for an appointment or emails a request through patient portal → scheduling clerk/ nurse checks physician schedule and communicates open slots to patient → patient selects open day/time slot → the process is repeated for appointment modifications.
   - Proposed Process: Physician calendar accessible online through patient portal → patient logs into online patient portal → patient accesses physician availability and schedules appointment → if necessary, patient logs into portal to change appointment date/time based on physician availability.

3. Patient Turnaround Time (TAT) at Physician Clinic
   - Goal: Reduce turnaround time for patient treatment. This example represents cross-functional PI with *low-medium impact* depending on the structure of the physician clinic and ancillary departments.
   - Assumption: this scenario assumes that patient symptoms and prior history do not mandate an in-person follow-up visit.

Figure 11.5 represents a clinic-based process in which the patient arrives at the clinic for their scheduled appointment with the provider and is discharged with physician orders to get lab tests and chest rays. The *in-person* process is well defined but can be improved to reduce patient waiting time and care provider time using the EHR.

■ Post Visit: The patient travels to lab and imaging centers to get a blood draw and chest rays.
   - Current Process: Lab results and x-ray reports are sent to the physician's office via mail or secure email. The patient is instructed to come back for a follow-up. The process in Figure 11.5 is repeated.
   - Proposed Process: Lab results and x-ray reports are interfaced with the physician's EHR and the patient portal. Post-visit care is conducted via portal, email, and phone.

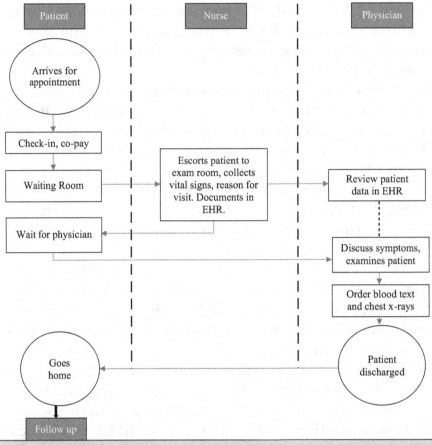

Figure 11.5   Flow chart representing patient workflow at physician clinic.

Examples of Organization-wide PI

Replacing and Upgrading Existing IT System

■ HCOs that replace departmental legacy systems with an integrated HIS including EHR and supporting modules, engage the entire HCO in order to achieve the desired project goals and objectives from system implementation. This results in an organization-wide work redesign and PI effort.

- IT upgrades and functional enhancements that impact a majority of HCO functionality require that HCOs address this as an organization-wide work redesign and PI effort. While this extends the time to upgrade the IT, the resulting effort optimizes key processes across the healthcare organization.
- As this chapter has emphasized, a structured approach to project management is critical to the successful implementation of HCO-wide PI efforts.

DT Phases – Practical Considerations

Description

Digital transformation projects should be led by functional leaders and comprise representatives from functional areas, IT, work design (including user experience and spatial design), and project management. Project teams should utilize agile methodologies (lean and related PI tools) for iterative improvements. IT CLs should be able to guide and support project teams through advanced DHPs, telehealth, and digital systems. Project teams will likely integrate digital technologies as part of their workflow to develop hybrid models that operate in *virtual* and *in-person* environments.

Depending on the size and scope of healthcare organizations, DT should be implemented in phases that support a comprehensive digital health strategy, starting from the ***pilot phase(s)*** which serve as proof of concept and expanded to generate the ***startup phase***. The startup phase builds on the proof of concept to further embed advanced digital technologies in revised care models. The ***growth phase*** further operationalizes the HCO digital health strategy using technical and process complexities that integrate virtual, onsite, clinic, and home care. It supports the internal goals and objectives of the HCO and supports a comprehensive transition to value-based models. Finally, the ***mature phase*** completes the operationalization of the HCO digital health strategy. This phase innovates the use of digital technology to improve patient outcomes while reducing costs. In addition to supporting the internal goals and objectives of the HCO, this phase standardizes digital offerings to support external entities.

Leadership Involvement

- These projects must be sponsored and overseen by senior HCO management and driven by the strategic goals and objectives of the organization.

■ Management must be educated on advanced digital platforms, and their ability to transform the HCO, prior to initiating transformation efforts.
■ Project teams should be led by functional experts who are well versed in the clinical, financial, and support systems being considered for restructuring and potential disruption.

Digital Platforms

■ Digital platforms play a key role in DT efforts. Venture capital investments have accelerated the growth of DHPs which have altered the landscape for the provision of healthcare services. The landscape continues to evolve with M&As consolidating the number of platforms available in the healthcare ecosystem. As expected in the world of platforms and demand economies of scale, M&As target platforms that offer different services. Therefore, the consolidated world of third-party owned and operated DHPs is moving toward an increasing array of remote and at-home services.
■ These platforms are intelligent in architecture since they support third-party developers (for more information on DHPs, refer to chapter 3).
■ HCOs can participate as buyers and/or sellers to leverage core platform offerings and exchange data and/or functionality with the digital platform. The clinical complexity of hybrid work models may necessitate increased HCO engagement in DHPs through partial ownership and management (for more information on HCO participation levels in DHPs refer to chapter 5).

Design Principles

■ Project teams must follow the *Key Considerations for PI Projects* elaborated in this chapter. These considerations are also applicable to DT projects.
■ DT projects include a project charter approved by senior management. The project charter should include well-defined problem statements, scope, CSFs, KPIs, associated benchmarks, tools, and techniques to be utilized, and approved by senior management. Projects are considered a *success* when post-implementation measures comply with established benchmarks.
■ Advanced digital technology projects potentially restructure and redefine existing functional boundaries. Upon implementation, resultant processes and systems should be continuously monitored and refined.

Potential Problems/Roadblocks

- DT efforts can impact a significant portion of the HCO. Hence, these projects should not be undertaken unless the HCO has previously implemented, and learned from, high-impact PI efforts.
- Traditional departmental boundaries and roles can be impacted and disrupted.
- DT impacts organizational cultural norms and takes time to implement and stabilize.

Outcomes, Metrics, and Benchmarking

- As we have mentioned DT efforts assist with requirements for value-based care such as population health management, patient engagement, wellness programs, automated case management, and proactive disease management. These and other goals should be reflected while defining DT CSFs.
- DT KPIs can be developed using methods described for PI projects.

DT Example: Transitioning from In-Person Care to Virtual Care Model

Patient Turnaround Time – Using the Digital Front Door

Figure 11.6 represents the revised patient care process using the *digital front door*. It has been redesigned using digital technologies (refer to Figure 11.5, for comparison).

DT Example: A Case Study Using Mercy Virtual Platform

An example that vividly illustrates the impact of a pilot and phased approach to digital transformation is illustrated in the following case study from Mercy Virtual Care Center.

This Center manages chronic diseases in which the sickest patients (5%) are responsible for 50–60% of expenditures. The program focused on the sickest patient population and started with a pilot of 50 patients in 2015, to apply higher intensity care and improve outcomes. These patients were equipped with biometric monitoring, daily surveys, and real-time virtual access to providers. As part of this care, staff trained patients in self-care to avoid acute care facilities.

Upon meeting its desired outcomes, the pilot was expanded to include additional high-risk patients. This required the incorporation of advanced

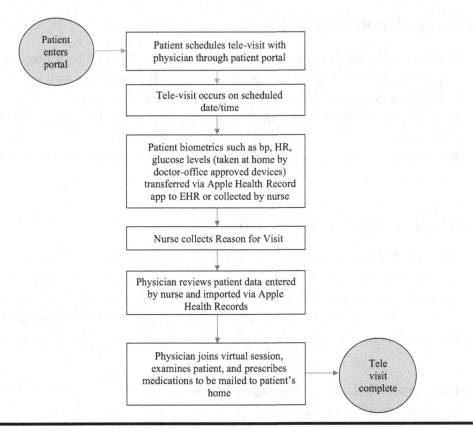

Figure 11.6   Proposed flow chart using telehealth and digital front door.

technologies and work methods to support the care team. In 2020, Mercy Virtual selected Myia Health's cloud-based RPM platform to accomplish four strategies without the need to expand the care team.

The *first strategy* was to risk-stratify the patient population using ML models to better match patient needs with the care provided. The *second strategy* was to leverage synchronous messaging, as opposed to real-time video communication, by using Myia Health's "closed-loop" asynchronous messaging. In this the care team receives alerts if messages are not read by patients within a defined timeframe. The *third strategy* focused on reducing the volume of false alerts which was accomplished by presenting a panel of patients sorted by acuity. The definition of "false alerts" was continuously refined using provider feedback on whether an alert caused a change in care. The *fourth strategy* was to develop a panel to allow clinicians to review teamwork priorities, assign patients to "priority patients," and control the care process.

From the initial pilot of 50 patients in 2015 this program has expanded to include 4,474 patients by October 2022. While operating expense has reduced from over $750 to less than $300 per patient per month, the patient satisfaction score has stayed at NPS 86. In addition, the program has reduced patient inpatient admissions by 50% resulting in significant savings. For example, an average hospitalization for a CHF admission is approximately $14,000 (Siwicki 2023).

Lessons Learned: digital transformation efforts require an innovative blend of technology, work transformation, and people to be successful. They can be extremely effective in improving patient outcomes, increasing satisfaction, and reducing costs. However, they are most effective when employing a phased approach, starting with a pilot. Metrics must also be used to measure the effectiveness of these efforts.

Digital Health: HCOs

Introduction

A comprehensive strategy for DT of HCOs requires DHPs that support a comprehensive array of clinical and administrative services, provided by HCOs. However, existing DHPs are configured to provide services for select patient conditions. Therefore, DT of a health system requires DHPs that are uniquely configured and implemented to support their digital health strategy.

Several US-based healthcare organizations have implemented comprehensive digital health strategies that are integrated within their traditional offerings. This has proven to be effective during the COVID-19 pandemic and will continue to enhance their systems post-COVID. The following case examples illustrate HCOs that have successfully "transformed" their organizations by using virtual models to extend and improve patient care while coordinating virtual and physical care through a team-based approach.

Since HCO DT efforts are evolving continuously, it is difficult to classify digital health-supported care levels captured in a snapshot. However, the following examples of HCOs that incorporate digital platforms in their care models illustrate the range of services being offered by HCOs across the US. They can be used by HCOs to generate ideas for their digital health vision.

- **Mercy Health's Virtual Program:** *Mercy Virtual* provides care to patients across Mercy's four states in rural and urban hospitals alike. To support comprehensive services, the Mercy Virtual platform works in conjunction with the traditional Mercy healthcare model making Mercy a hybrid company that uses both traditional and platform patient care models. It supports a range of services such as mental health, acute care, stroke, sepsis detection and treatment protocol, ICU support, hospitalist support, pediatric care, nurse on call, centralized telemetry (EKGs and pulse oximeters) and consultations from specialists in oncology, neurology, cardiology, sleep medicine, etc. (Mercy n.d.).

- **Kaiser Permanente:** KP's digital transformation has been informed by patient needs and care provider workflows supported by IT solutions, redesigned physical architecture, and digital platforms. KP uses digital technologies designed to complement its EHR, patient portal, and telehealth platforms. It supports most of its service offerings through advanced digital platforms. KP has implemented hospital-at-home programs for patients with complex diseases who can receive high-quality acute care in their home (Arora, Dyer and Kochan 2020).

- **Avera Health:** Avera eCare by Aquiline is a telehealth platform designed by Avera Health and supports healthcare systems, rural hospitals, OP clinics, long-term care facilities, assisted living, and schools across 32 states. The platform is a collaboration of specialty care providers and includes a broad range of service lines including Behavioral Health, Correctional Health, Emergency Services, Hospitalist, ICU, Pharmacy, School Health, Specialty Clinic, and Senior Care. The design of the platform includes telemedicine equipment in central and remote locations and collaboration between remote specialists and onsite care providers. It also includes equipment to collect data to assist with care management (Avel eCare n.d.).

- **Cleveland Clinic – Digital Technology to Disrupt the State of Patient Care**
  Cleveland Clinic has developed and/or manages platforms around the Epic MyChart platform to focus on the following functionalities:
  a. Patient Portal: Cleveland Clinic provides patients comprehensive mobile access to their health data such as allergies, conditions, immunizations, lab results, medications, procedures, vitals, and more, and a way to manage appointments, message their physicians, and more.
  b. Apple Health Records: Cleveland Clinic makes patient data available via the Apple Health Records app which gives patients increased

control over managing their health including aggregating their health data from multiple sources such as smartwatches and smartphone apps. Apple Health Records also allows patients to share their medical information with relevant stakeholders including family caregivers and other healthcare providers (Heath 2018).

c. Virtual Visits: Cleveland Clinic promotes their telemedicine platform for virtual visits which provides patients 24/7 access to a healthcare provider from anywhere. Virtual visits can be on-demand or scheduled. On-demand visits can be used for problems such as allergies, asthma, back strains, sprains, bronchitis, common cold, COVID-19 screening, flu, minor burns or lacerations, painful urination, pink eye, rashes, sinus infections, and upper respiratory illness. Scheduled visits are with a patient's PCP or specialist and are used as follow-up visits, before and after surgery, pregnancy and infant well-checks, pre-visit information sessions, medication reviews, genetic counseling, infectious disease visits before traveling, and more (Cleveland Clinic n.d.).

Key Takeaways

In addition to introducing work transformation concepts such as PI and DT, this chapter discusses LSS methods which are elaborated in chapter 12. This chapter also utilizes concepts and methods related to digital health platforms and IT systems.

1. The Quadruple Aim framework for making healthcare better developed, and revised, by the Institute of Healthcare Improvement (IHI) includes the following strategies: (a) enhancing the patient experience, (b) reducing costs, (c) improving healthcare outcomes, (d) improving the clinician and staff experience. These strategies are well supported by DHPs, Agile Framework, and lean methodologies.

2. Work transformation efforts require appropriate IT CLs. A methodology has been developed to help HCOs assess their IT CL to undertake work transformation initiatives. This methodology consists of four IT CLs and is derived from the information discussed in Chapters 7 to 10.

3. Work transformation efforts have been divided into process improvement levels and phases of digital transformation. PI efforts are subdivided into the following levels: functional, cross-functional – low impact, medium impact, and high impact (based on the potential

impact on organizational boundaries and functional roles), and organization-wide. DT projects are divided into phases, beginning with a *pilot* phase, and progressing to *startup, growth*, and *mature* phases. Each phase builds on prior efforts with the goal to operationalize HCO's digital health strategy.

4. Similarities and differences between PI and DT efforts have been enumerated. A key difference between the two is the emphasis on increasing patient engagement during DT efforts.

5. Key considerations for PI projects have been presented to assist HCOs in work transformation efforts.

6. Figure 11.2 indicates the amalgamation between strategy, IT CLs, and work transformation. In addition, Figure 11.3 indicates that DT projects take longer to implement due to the changes introduced in existing processes. Figure 11.4 illustrates increased risks associated with DT efforts. These risks can be managed through prior PI implementations that include *high-impact* projects.

7. A detailed description of process improvement levels and digital transformation phases, supplemented by examples, is included for practical consideration and implementation in HCOs.

References

Arora, Anubhav, Barbara Dyer, and Thomas A. Kochan. 2020. "A Case Study of Integrating Technology and Work Systems at Kaiser Permanente's Health Hubs." *MIT Work of the Future*. November 24.

Avel eCare. n.d. Accessed December 2022. https://www.avelecare.com.

Bridger, Haley. 2019. *Home Hospital Model Reduces Cost by 38%, Study Says*. December 16. https://news.harvard.edu/gazette/story/2019/12/home-hospital -model-reduces-costs-by-38-improves-care/.

Cleveland Clinic. n.d. *Virtual Visits*. Accessed January 2023. https://my.cleveland-clinic.org/online-services/virtual-visits.

CMS. 2022. "NHE Fact Sheet." *CMS*. December 14. https://www.cms.gov/research -statistics-data-and-systems/statistics-trends-and-reports/nationalhealthexpend-data/nhe-fact-sheet.

HCP LAN. 2021. "2020 & 2021 Measurement Efforts." *HCP-LAN*. December 15. https://hcp-lan.org/apm-measurement-effort/2020-2021-apm/.

Heath, Sara. 2018. "Cleveland Clinic Taps Apple Health Records for Patient Portal Data." *TechTarget/Patient Engagement HIT*. July 6. https://patientengagementhit .com/news/cleveland-clinic-taps-apple-health-records-for-patient-portal-data.

Landi, Heather. 2020. "Lyft Deepens its Healthcare Ties with Epic Integration." *Fierce Healthcare*. October 8. https://www.fiercehealthcare.com/tech/lyft-deepens-its-healthcare-ties-epic-integration.

Mercy. n.d. *About*. Accessed January 2023. https://www.mercyvirtual.net/about/#.

Siwicki, Bill. 2023. *Mercy Virtual Care Center: A Deep Dive into a Virtual Hospital*. January 3. https://www.healthcareitnews.com/news/mercy-virtual-care-center-deep-dive-virtual-hospital.

Chapter 12

Work Transformation Tools, Techniques, and Methodologies

Introduction

Work redesign originated from time and motion studies in Industrial Engineering. These studies include streamlining and standardizing work processes to improve worker productivity, customer satisfaction, and reduce costs and have over the years been adapted to work processes in healthcare systems. These enhancements include Lean methodologies which incorporate tools such as process flowcharts, Value Stream Mapping (VSM), Root Cause Analysis (RCA), and A3 thinking.

Most work redesign tools and techniques have been developed to improve manufacturing operations. These tools have been adapted to healthcare operations. However, analysts using these tools must understand the inherent variability in healthcare processes. For example, "patient-facing" and "hospital-facing" processes have inherent variabilities. While it is intuitive to understand reasons for significant variability in patient-facing processes (processes or services received by patients), hospital-facing processes (back-office processes such as planning, forecasting, and purchasing materials) are also subject to variability due to provider requirements, orders, patient diagnosis, and resource utilization. Therefore, hospital-facing processes must also be included in workflow analysis and PI efforts. The goal of healthcare PI efforts should be to identify all processes that contribute to operational bottlenecks and roadblocks, reduce variability, and eliminate non-value-add activities.

Chapter 12 discusses Lean tools and techniques which have been used to improve healthcare processes. HCOs are familiar with tools and techniques used to analyze sentinel events and system problems such as Root Cause Analysis (RCA), Failure Mode and Effects Analysis (FMEA), and workflow charts. For additional details, readers can refer to information published by federal organizations, journal articles, university research, and a variety of books on this topic. In addition to variabilities in healthcare processes, work redesign techniques should consider the role of information systems.

To enable digital transformation of HCOs, analysts must consider the differences between process improvement (PI) and digital transformation (DT) efforts. For example, PI efforts focus on improving in-house systems, whereas digital transformation involves using advanced technologies to enhance in-house systems and disrupt existing operational models. This requires an understanding of advanced digital technologies and working knowledge of Lean tools. Digital transformation efforts focus on reducing friction in patient engagement systems in addition to optimizing care provider workflows.

Work transformation methods enable the effective design and implementation of IT systems which include using human factors engineering (HFE) methodologies such as UI and UX. System usability and overall user experience (UX) are achieved by applying design thinking methods. While project management and HFE methods are discussed in Chapter 8, a summary of these concepts is included at the end of this chapter.

Impact of Lean Methodology on Healthcare Processes

Prior to reviewing Lean tools and techniques that are applicable to healthcare, it is useful to consider the areas of non-value-add activities identified by Taiichi Ohno of Toyota, the originator of Lean principles. He described seven areas of waste in manufacturing which were amended to add an eighth waste. The following wastes (NEJM Catalyst 2018), which can be identified through process and system reviews, are explained using healthcare examples.

1. Reduce wait/idle time – healthcare examples: (a) patients idle in waiting areas and exam rooms, (b) healthcare personnel waiting for physician orders, (c) idle laboratory and diagnostic equipment.

2. Minimize inventory – healthcare examples: (a) duplicate diagnostic equipment, (b) nursing unit staff "hoarding" supplies leading to increased expense, storage cost, spoilage, and loss, (c) purchasing bulk supplies to negotiate lower prices but increasing storage costs, materials handling, and wastage.

3. Eradicate defects to improve care quality – healthcare examples: (a) medication errors due to improper EHR design or care provider error, (b) surgical errors due to lack of checks and balances, (c) allergic reactions due to poorly maintained allergies list.

4. Decrease movement of workers, patients, supplies, and equipment – healthcare examples related to patient flow: (a) poor spatial design necessitating the excessive transfer of patients, supplies, and equipment, (b) poor signage confusing patients and delaying treatment, (c) materials management department located in distant areas of the healthcare facility for receiving bulk supplies and equipment, without travel considerations to patient care areas.

5. Prevent injuries and reduce motion – healthcare examples: (a) excessive supply inventory in central areas resulting in non-ergonomic layouts and workplace injuries, (b) excessive walking for care providers due to hospital architecture, (c) injuries due to improper patient transfer between beds, wheelchairs, and other modalities.

6. Minimize overproduction – healthcare examples: (a) extending hospital length of stay due to inefficient processes, (b) over-utilization of resources such as duplicate lab tests due to lack of longitudinal patient information, (c) medication wastage.

7. Remove waste from over-processing – healthcare examples: (a) entering same patient data in multiple systems due to poor system design and lack of data exchange across subsystems, (b) excessive tests ordered than clinically necessary.

8. Identify waste and untapped human potential – healthcare examples: inefficiently designed information systems that waste care provider time through (a) excessive navigation, (b) information clutter, (c) excessive care documentation, (d) poorly designed documentation tools.

Lean Six Sigma (LSS)

DT results in innovative care models using advanced digital technologies. This requires work restructuring to be accepted by care providers, patients, and payers. While the strive for operational excellence has expanded the use of Lean for continuous process improvement in traditional healthcare systems, its tools have become increasingly relevant in the DT of HCOs.

The Lean approach in healthcare was derived from the Toyota Production System with a focus on reducing space, defects, steps, people, and cost. On the other hand, Six Sigma was derived from statistical quality control to improve operational quality by reducing process variations.

However, since Lean and Six Sigma are used concurrently in most organizations, work transformation tools are designated as Lean Six Sigma (LSS). In this model, Lean focuses on eliminating waste, and streamlining workflows, while Six Sigma focuses on improving quality by reducing process variations.

The LSS approach in healthcare considers non-value-add resources (processes and operations) for the end customer to be "waste." A variety of LSS tools aid in addressing specific problems in healthcare.

DMAIC Methodology

In order to improve organizational processes, LSS tools and techniques are used in conjunction with DMAIC, a data-driven methodology that follows a phased approach for process improvements. The following description of DMAIC, *Define, Measure, Analyze, Improve, and Control*, indicates how these phases can be applied to solve healthcare problem areas.

Define phase includes a project charter which includes stakeholders, outlines project goals including user requirements, project plan, and cost/benefit analysis. This phase also defines metrics and desired benchmarks to assess progress through process improvements. For additional information, refer to Chapter 11.

Measure phase includes generating process flow charts and value stream maps to record activities and bottlenecks to achieve desired results. This phase also includes baseline values for metrics decided in the *Define phase*. For example, in order to reduce wait time for patients to be seen by physician post ER triage, the metric would be *time for patients to be seen by physician post ER triage*. Benchmarks for acceptable wait times based on the severity of patient condition could be derived from patient surveys or best practices. Key in this phase is the identification of data collection sources and methods that enable automated collection.

Analyze phase includes techniques to understand the reasons for process problem areas. In this phase the PI team can use tools such as *Root Cause*

Analysis (RCA) to identify reasons for process problems and *Failure Mode and Effects Analysis* (FMEA) to identify possible process failures. These tools are commonly used in analyzing healthcare problems and have been described in the following section on Lean Health Tools.

Improve phase involves eliminating root causes. For example, let us assume that the root cause of patient backlog in ERs waiting for inpatient beds is identified as a lack of timely communication post patient discharge between nursing units and housekeeping. This problem can be addressed by a page to the housekeeping supervisor as soon as a patient is discharged in the computer system. Once housekeeping cleans the room, they can enter room cleaned status in the computer system triggering a page to the nursing unit supervisor to communicate that the room is ready for the next patient. In this scenario the metrics could be the *time between patient discharge in system and bed availability notification to ER*, and *number of patients backlogged in ERs*.

Control phase involves ensuring that process improvements are made permanent once the project is complete. This requires using dashboards that display ongoing metric outcomes, continuous process improvement and process performance, 5S to organize the workplace for efficiency and effectiveness, and poka yoke for mistake proofing to reduce errors at the onset of the process. *For example, a common problem in healthcare begins during patient registration when an existing patient comes in with a name change. If the clerk enters the patient's stated name without confirming a potential name change, the registration system will generate a new patient record with no prior history. If unchecked during care provision, this error can impact the quality and cost of patient care. Poka yoke offers a solution. A patient-facing camera on the clerk's workspace scans the patient and highlights her/his name in the registration system. This helps the clerk greet the patient by name. In case of a name change, patients can request an edit to the patient record. This process is analogous to smartphone appointment check-ins which require patient facial recognition scans to access the portal. Upon access, the application can ask the patient if there has been a name change since the previous visit prior to confirming patient check-in.*

Lean Health Tools

DMAIC serves as a framework for LSS by introducing a data-driven methodology. This approach is important at all levels, scope, and complexities of work transformation, ranging from process improvements to digital disruptions. Without this framework it is difficult for HCOs to understand change management including ways to transition from current to proposed states – and maintain the new state. The DMAIC framework can be used in conjunction with the SDLC project management methodology discussed in chapter 7.

Several LSS tools are utilized to identify sub-optimal healthcare processes and propose solutions. *It is necessary that HCOs familiarize themselves with commonly used Lean tools, including how best to utilize them in different change management efforts within their organization.* A culture of continuous process improvement and change management requires managers to understand and support LSS by developing a working knowledge of Lean tools and methodologies and their applicability in digital transformation efforts.

While a number of LSS tools and techniques have been developed over the years, commonly used tools in LSS healthcare are *workflow charts, VSM, RCA, A3 thinking (based on Deming's PDCA principles), PDCA (Plan-Do-Check-Act), Kaizen Events (rapid improvement events, RIE), 5S, Poka Yoke, Visual Management Systems (VMS), Kanban, and FMEA (Failure Mode and Effects Analysis).*

As illustrated through the DMAIC methodology, these tools are used in conjunction to define, measure, analyze, improve, and control healthcare processes.

Description of Tools

Workflow Charts

are the most common types of business process maps as they most closely resemble what the Gilbreths introduced almost a century ago. Process charts diagram the steps required for a process. These charts are applicable during patient care situations, including emergency rooms, operating rooms, imaging, laboratories, and pharmacies. There are different representation methodologies for workflows such as process flowcharts and swim lane diagrams.

Process flowcharts document tasks and activities associated with *current functional processes* in a structured representation. They use a business process model that illustrates the sequence of tasks included in a process and is developed using Business Process Model and Notation (BPMN). Developing a graphical representation of business processes indicates problem areas (gaps) which can be rectified or removed. Once gaps have been remediated, *desired workflows* are developed for the functional processes being analyzed. The following steps are recommended for optimal outcomes using flowcharts.

1. To the extent possible *key interactions* (core activities in a particular healthcare setting) should be studied for bottlenecks and roadblocks. Removing these bottlenecks/roadblocks from work processes will result in desired outcomes.
2. Examples of key interactions: physician/patient interaction for patient care; provider/provider interaction for care coordination, EHR documentation (ease of documentation and navigation by physicians), and patient portal usage (access to EHI and functions to support an omnichannel patient experience).
3. The interaction, and associated processes, under consideration should be carefully defined to capture all functional and cross-functional tasks.
4. Flowcharts representing *current* and *proposed* processes associated with *key interaction(s)* should be developed. Swim lanes can be used to represent cross-functional departments. *Current* flowcharts should represent inefficiencies and roadblocks.
5. *Current* workflows should be followed by flowcharts representing *proposed* workflows. These flowcharts should represent improvement(s) in desired outcomes whether they are associated with provider satisfaction, patient satisfaction, lowering costs, increasing revenues, or increasing interactions.

Common BPM Notations

○ A circle represents an *event*, anything that happens during a process. For example, the start and end of a process represent the trigger and end events.

▢ A rectangle represents *tasks* associated with a process. It is the most common symbol used in a process flowchart.

◇ A diamond represents a *gateway* – process flow. It is commonly associated with forking the process based on decisions made in the workflow.

⇨ An arrow represents *flow* – the path of a process flow.

Figure 12.1 represents the current state of scheduling appointments through front-office staff. While the staff uses an automated scheduling system, the physician's schedule is controlled by the physician's assistant. Figure 12.2 represents a proposed state of scheduling where the patient has access to

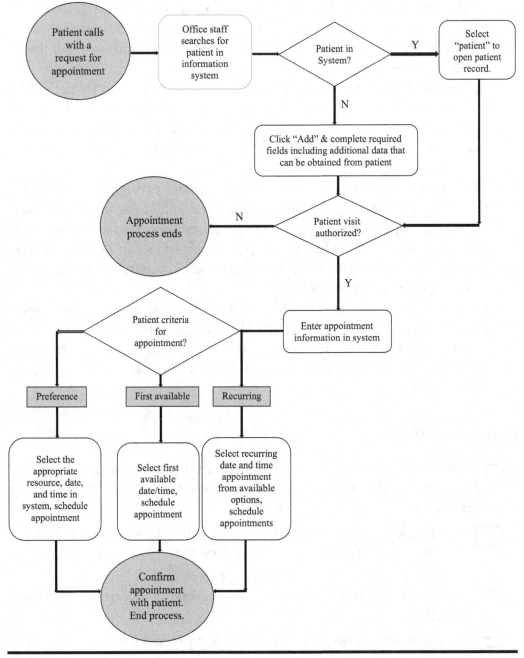

Figure 12.1 Scheduling appointment through front-office staff (current).

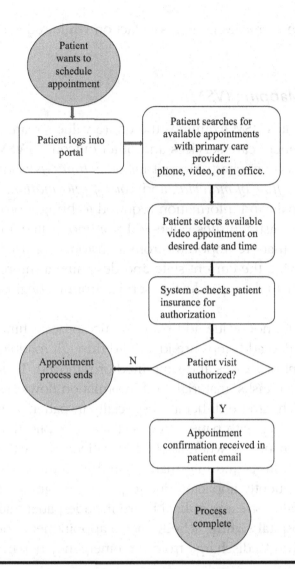

Figure 12.2 Patient scheduling appointment through portal (proposed).

the provider's schedule. In addition, the physician has adopted telehealth modalities for patient convenience such as phone and video in addition to in-office appointments. The patient can quickly select available appointments based on their preferred date/time and modality. Appointments can also be conveniently canceled.

The physician scheduling system is also linked to insurance providers to automate the process of authorization prior to confirming a patient appointment.

This workflow redesign represents the power of disrupting the existing status quo using information systems, telehealth, and operational changes such as providing patients access to physician schedules.

This disruption increases patient satisfaction while reducing front-office expenses.

Value Stream Mapping (VSM)

As its name indicates VSM examines the entire value stream associated with providing patient care services and other outcomes. VSM is broader in scope than workflow charts since it includes *times associated with each step in the process, flow of material*, and *flow of information*. VSM analyzes the flow of materials and information required to bring a product or service to a customer and distinguishes value-add from non-value-add steps. Value refers to activities that are important from a customer or user perspective. It assists in analyzing the current state and designing a future state for the series of events that take a product or service from its beginning through the customer.

VSM can identify non-value-add steps, reduce process time, and improve processes. Non-value-add steps are identified through roadblocks and complexities in current processes and simplified or removed. This requires collecting details about tasks, material, and information flows associated with each process which can be difficult – especially in patient care processes where care levels vary with patient needs. These complications tend to make VSM tools time-consuming when applied to patient care activities. However, the combination of tasks and information can be useful since care provider workflows are frequently impacted due to poorly designed information flows.

Examples of value streams in healthcare include patient admission to discharge in a hospital setting; scheduling to appointment completion in a clinic setting; arrival to discharge from the emergency department.

Steps to Creating a Value-Stream Map

1. Determine the product or services HCOs wish to map.
2. Select a team of process experts from cross-functional areas that contribute to the process being studied. This team should be familiar with how the current system works. Add human factors, IT, and other tech experts. Include a facilitator such as a manager over the cross-functional areas, work redesign expert, or an independent consultant familiar with the tool and its execution.
3. Identify the process steps or tasks performed. This can be done through process flowchart(s) which form the preamble to VSM diagram(s).

4. Add information flows to process steps that provide added information, such as informing each process what to do next and when to do it.
5. Gather critical data for each process such as inventory items held for each process, cycle time, transfer time, number of people needed to perform each step, number of products that must be scrapped, pack size, batch size, etc.
6. Create a timeline for process and inventory times and use it to calculate total Lean time.
7. Generate current state map (CSM).
8. Identify eight wastes of Lean (discussed previously).
9. Generate a future state map (FSM) that reduces wastes.
10. Implement findings.
11. To ensure continuous process improvement, the initial state or CSM transitions to FSM which then becomes CSM, and the process improvement cycle continues.

VSM Symbols: commonly used symbols of value-stream mapping toolsets track the supply chain and information which means using Kanban symbols, process box, databox, etc. These symbols can be found in Lean books, VSM software tools, and technical articles.

Root Cause Analysis

RCA can be conducted to understand the cause of any level and severity of problems experienced in care settings. However, HCOs commonly conduct RCA to understand the root cause of sentinel events. It is an important toolset within the LSS methodology since it can be used in the *analysis* phase of DMAIC – Define, Measure, Analyze, Improve, and Control. RCA is a collective term that includes a variety of tools and techniques used to uncover the core issue responsible for problems. RCA tools can be used independently, or simultaneously, for a range of problem identification and resolution techniques, from general problem-solving to RCA. While some tools use statistical analysis others require Boolean logic or drilling deeper to determine the root cause of problems. The following tools are commonly used to conduct RCA.

1. **5 Whys Analysis:** this tool is rooted in asking 5 "Whys" to identify the root cause of the problem. Care should be taken to avoid going too deep into causes otherwise the results can be spurious. This tool helps to analyze the results of a Pareto Chart.

2. **Pareto Chart:** is a bar chart that separates trivial from significant problems by ranking them in decreasing order of occurrence. This focuses Lean teams to better direct their improvement efforts to significant problems. The 5 Whys Analysis subsequently helps identify the root cause of these problems.

3. **Failure Mode and Effects Analysis:** is a management tool to identify and address *potential* problems or failures, analyze risk levels, and assess their causes and effects on the system or process. This tool is widely used in healthcare settings since it assists in preemptive error prevention, an essential component of quality patient care.

   According to the abstract from "Failure mode and effects analysis for proactive healthcare risk evaluation: A systematic literature review" by Hu-Chen Liu, Li-Jun Zhang, Ye-Jia Ping, and Liang Wang, "a review of 158 journal papers published over the period of 1998 to 2018 were extracted and reviewed. These publications were classified into four categories (i.e., healthcare process, hospital management, hospital informatization, and medical equipment and production) according to healthcare issues to be solved and analyzed regarding the applicable fields and the utilized FMEA methods." They conclude that their research "supports academics and practitioners in effectively adopting the FMEA tool to proactively reduce healthcare risks and increase patient safety, and provides an insight into its state-of-the-art."

   ■ While both FMEA and RCA are structured tools, RCA addresses problems after they occur.

   ■ CMS through its Quality Assessment and Performance Improvement organization provides the following overview of the steps of FMEA.
      – Select a process to analyze.
      – Charter and select team facilitator and team members.
      – Describe the process (use process flowcharts).
      – Identify what could go wrong during each step of the process.
      – Pick which problems to work on eliminating (based on seriousness of outcome (severity) and how often the mistake is likely to occur (probability)).
      – Design and implement changes to reduce or prevent problems.
      – Measure the success of process changes.

   ■ Each of the seven steps identified above has been enumerated in CMS's QAPI website (CMS, n.d.). Templates structuring the FMEA process have been developed by several organizations for use in healthcare.

4. **Fault Tree Diagram:** uses Boolean logic to determine the cause of problems for undesirable events. In this diagram all causes are written down as branches of a tree that starts with the problem.

5. **Fishbone Diagram:** is like the Fault Tree Diagram, since it divides the causes for each problem into different categories such as *processes*, *machines*, *materials*, and *personnel*. The diagrammatic representation resembles a fishbone.

6. **Scatter Plot Diagram:** plots two different variables such as problem and cause, in the x- and y-axis of a graph. The cause most highly correlated with a problem becomes the one that should be addressed prior to others. The assumption in this tool is the availability of quantitative data to represent the problem and associated cause(s).

A3 Lean thinking

A3 process is a structured problem-solving and continuous improvement technique. This systematic approach documents current state problems, proposed recommendations, and improvement plans. A3 is also known as SPS – "Systematic Problem Solving." The process is based on the principles of Edward Deming's PDCA (Plan-Do-Check-Act).

The following steps highlight the process associated with A3.

1. Identify Problem: problem identification is an important component of this analysis. Problems need to be clearly identified and preference given to problems that occur frequently and impede effective patient care, equipment utilization, or caregiver productivity.

2. Understand Current System: it is best to observe and document work processes using diagrams that show how work is being done currently. Process workflow charts can be utilized to do this. Quantify the magnitude of problem, for example, the gap between the time required for care providers to complete a patient visit versus the time allocated for patient appointments.

3. Establish Target/Goals: Goals and targets are critical to the success of A3 and other Lean efforts. While these are established after analyzing a non-optimal system to identify problems and their causes, additional details, identified during the RCA, could influence changes in goals and targets.

4. Root Cause Analysis: in this step the root causes of the problems observed in the previous step are ascertained. To accomplish this, start

with a list of the main problems and then ask "why" until the root cause for each problem becomes evident. Refer to the previous discussion on Root Cause Analysis in this section.

5. Countermeasures: are changes to work processes that will help to remove the causes contributing to the identified problem(s). Countermeasures should lead to a clear understanding of how the established goal will be achieved. In the A3 report, target state should be a diagram (analogous to the representation used to illustrate the current situation) that illustrates how the proposed processes will work.

6. Implementation Plan: includes the list of actions to implement countermeasures and achieve the target state. This plan includes individual(s) responsible for each task and due date. Additional items such as implementation costs may also be added.

7. Follow-up Plan: this plan ensures the implementation plan was properly executed, target state was realized, and expected results were achieved. It is important to include best practice benchmarks used to measure project success. This should be used as the framework for continuous process improvement.

PDCA

(Plan-Do-Check-Act) is a four-step model for change management. It is also referred to as Deming cycle. The PDCA cycle should be used in continuous improvement mode. This tool should be used when initiating a new improvement project or developing a new or improved process, or service design in healthcare.

- **Plan:** plan a change based on work transformation or reengineering opportunities.
- **Do:** Pilot or prototype the change and test.
- **Check:** Review and analyze results including lessons learned.
- **Act:** If change is not acceptable, then revise the plan and redo the PDCA cycle. If change is acceptable, then move it to a broader scale.

Kaizen events

Kaizen events, also known as rapid improvement events (RIEs), bring together a cross-functional team of key participants to analyze and solve a problem in a compressed timeframe, generally, four to five days. Teams utilize other Lean tools as part of their improvement effort. These events can analyze one-time events, recurring events, and initiatives involving hundreds of events throughout the healthcare organization. RIEs can be applied to patient care areas, pharmacies, operating suites, and emergency departments.

5S

5S of Lean is a methodology to ensure a clean, orderly, and safe working environment that promotes reliable work practices. It is used in pharmacies, nursing units, and surgical departments. This technique works in conjunction with VSM to demonstrate operational improvements in healthcare organizations.

- Sort – eliminate essential supplies, medications, tools, and instrumentation from non-essential materials.
- Set – arrange and identify supplies, medications, and instruments for ease of use.
- Shine – clean the work area.
- Standardize – schedule regular cleaning and organization of the work area to maintain its organization.
- Sustain – make the previous 4Ss a requirement and a habit for all employees.

Kanban

Kanban helps synchronize material and information flow of disconnected processes to enable Just in Time (JIT) production. The *pull system* controls the flow of resources through a system by replacing only what has been consumed or requested. Kanban uses signals or visual controls to trigger material and information movement. Most inventory systems attempt to achieve a level of proficiency with *pull system*. In healthcare, Kanban sets quantitative limits on wait times for supplies and people. Supply chain advancements, such as RFID labels on supply packages and readers, facilitate requirements tracking and replenishment. For example, the Kanban-inspired two-bin system has been used to manage supplies on nursing units in healthcare institutions. VSM studies identify roadblocks and wait times that are generated by the *push system* in which resources are delivered on assumptions of patient (or patient floor) needs. Streamlining roadblocks reduces wait times and generates an efficient continuous process or *pull system*.

Poka Yoke

Poka Yoke or mistake proofing is an effective technique that is built into a process to prevent or eliminate errors. Refer to example on poka yoke in the previous discussion on DMAIC methodology.

Visual Management Systems

Visual Management Systems are useful for streamlining processes. Applications include visual planning boards, "a communication tool that provides at-a-glance information about current process performance, both quantitative and qualitative data, to help clinical staff coordinate and guide their daily work and monitor ongoing improvement projects. Data displayed on the board help teams track key metrics" (IHI n.d.). These visual data displays are typically accompanied by daily communication processes such as huddles. *Examples of visual planning boards – track the status of flow of lab specimens, and graphical display of patient safety trends serve as visual reminders of performance.*

Human Factors Engineering (HFE): Digital Transformation Considerations

In healthcare the role of information systems and digital technologies in process design requires a discussion of computer design to optimize user experience. Organizational strategies and goals dictate healthcare operations that drive information system design and experience. Most HCOs utilize vendor-developed information systems that must be reconfigured to accommodate user preferences. However, technological advancements generally require restructuring existing processes to achieve desired outcomes.

HFE tools and techniques can be used in healthcare to optimize user experience with information systems and help to minimize errors when users interact with information systems. Therefore, systems must be designed while considering care provider and other healthcare professional interaction requirements. Without this interactive understanding most information systems can become a frustrating experience for care providers. In healthcare this is particularly true for care providers such as physicians and nurses.

The following discussion presents a summary of these concepts. Refer to Chapter 8 for additional details.

UI and UX

To be effective, an application's design must incorporate design concepts to optimize user interface (UI) and user experience (UX). The goal of UI is anything a user may interact with to use a digital product or service, whereas UX, as defined by Don Norman, encompasses all aspects of the end-user's interaction with the company, its services, and products. As a general rule, UI design principles and design thinking strongly influence the UX of information systems.

UI/UX considerations for EHRs: a computerized provider order entry application, within an EHR, designed with an excellent user interface may lead to poor user experience if providers have difficulty finding and ordering certain tests and procedures.

UI/UX considerations for Digital Technologies: The difference between UI and UX becomes pronounced when care providers are dealing with data and AI analytics. With remote patient care, especially at-home care, supplemented by remote monitoring and other digital devices with well-designed UI, patient data transferred to EHRs for physician review and analysis requires an understanding of provider requirements, otherwise, aggregated data may not meet provider needs resulting in a poor UX. Another example that illustrates the difference between UI and UX can be well-designed AI tools (good UI) that are not appropriately integrated in provider workflow (poor UX).

In clinical healthcare, the two classes of users with different EHR requirements are care providers and patients. Therefore, in the world of patient care, UX must be designed and architected separately for care providers and patients. In addition, system design must accommodate UX requirements by care provider specialty and preferences.

Project Management

Healthcare work transformation projects rely on effective project management. While work redesign tools are critical to effective process improvement and digital disruption efforts in healthcare organizations, these must be coordinated through project management. Work transformation comprises three key components: *people, process, and technology.*

Project management methodologies are key facilitators of work transformation tools, LSS and HFE, for effective work transformation. HCOs generally implement new technologies or upgrades via two methodologies: (a) "waterfall" methodology where technology design and implementation are sequential processes; (b) "agile" methodology where technology design and implementation are iterative, dictated by problems or roadblocks identified by users. These are discussed in detail in Chapter 8.

Healthcare Adoption

Agile is recommended to transform healthcare operations including core process improvements and digital transformations. This methodology involves many of the steps identified in the Waterfall approach with an emphasis on utilizing multi-disciplinary teams that understand different aspects of the functions being studied. In this approach, prototypes and pilots are utilized to validate system concepts. These tools encourage innovation and ownership by educating users on available technologies, training users on the optimal use of workflow tools, and incorporating spatial constraints including changes introduced by telehealth. This methodology does not provide well-defined completion timelines, but the resulting digital disruption is far more acceptable to users. The time taken for final technology adoption is more aggressive than the Waterfall approach.

Key Takeaways

1. This chapter presents tools, techniques, and frameworks required to implement process improvement and digital transformation efforts in healthcare organizations.
2. The chapter focuses on popularly used LSS/continuous process improvement, human factors engineering, and project management tools and techniques in HCOs. Organizations that would like access to additional details regarding these tools, and techniques can review references and recommended readings included in this chapter. In addition, there is ample information available on the Internet.

3. It is advisable for HCOs to utilize LSS tools for PI efforts prior to digital transformation projects. Utilizing LSS tools provides analysts the experience to decide on appropriate tools for different work transformation efforts.
4. Prior to initiating digital transformation efforts HCOs must document their desired scope based on the needs and desires of their patients, clinicians, and payors.
5. Finally, if HCOs are unsure of the next steps regarding digital transformation tools, they should contact appropriate consulting professionals.

References

CMS. n.d. *Guidance for Performing Failure Mode and Effects Analysis.* Accessed November 2022. https://www.cms.gov/Medicare/Provider-Enrollment-and -Certification/QApi/downloads/GuidanceForFMEA.pdf.

IHI. n.d. Visual Management Board. Accessed December 2022. https://www. ihi.org/resources/Pages/Tools/Visual-Management-Board.aspx.

NEJM Catalyst. 2018, April 27. *What is Lean Healthcare?* Accessed November 2022. https://catalyst.nejm.org/doi/full/10.1056/CAT.18.0193.

Recommended Readings

AHRQ. n.d. *Value Stream Mapping.* Accessed September 2022. https://digital.ahrq .gov/health-it-tools-and-resources/evaluation-resources/workflow-assessment -health-it-toolkit/all-workflow-tools/value-stream-mapping.

ASQ. n.d. *Quality Tools.* Accessed September 2022. https://asq.org/quality-resources /quality-tools.

Baltzen, Paige. 2022. *Business Driven Technology.* New York, NY: McGraw Hill Education.

Kanbanize. n.d. *Lean Management.* Accessed January 2023. https://kanbanize.com/ lean-management.

Schonberger, Richard J. 2018. "Reconstituting Lean in Healthcare: From Waste Elimination Toward 'Queue-Less' Patient-Focused Care." *Business Horizons* *61*(61): 13–22.

Sobek II, Durward K., and Michael Lang. 2010. "Lean Healthcare: Current State and Future Directions." Edited by A Johnson and J. Miller. *Proceedings of the 2010 Industrial Engineering Research Conference*, Cancun, Mexico.

Chapter 13

Design Principles for Digital Transformation

Introduction

Traditional HCO care models are presented in brick-and-mortar settings and home healthcare, whereas digital health models break down location and distance barriers and offer several modalities for the provision and receiving of care – telehealth, home healthcare, at-home intelligent monitors, and brick-and-mortar settings are used to develop hybrid workflows across multidisciplinary teams.

Digital considerations predominantly lead to the design and development of hybrid models that comprise the following modalities:

- Brick-and-mortar care – hospital and clinic based, including portable clinics.
- Telehealth – video visits, phone communication, secure emails SMS, and text.
- Home healthcare – care providers traveling to patient home.
- Intelligent device monitors – biometric monitors, remote monitors, digital therapeutics, smart wearables, health apps, and complementary systems (Apple Health Record).

The above care models can offer an omnichannel patient experience and improve patient engagement but rely on several unknowns which increase implementation risks. The risks, along with initial capital expenditure and

DOI: 10.4324/9781003366584-16

organizational reluctance, are the major reasons for the slow adoption of digital health models in HCOs.

Three major systems that work together for the successful transformation of HCOs are: *Digital Health Platforms*, *Advanced IT systems*, and *Work Transformation Methods*. These systems must be led and coordinated by *Leadership* and *Project Management* to achieve desired results. Table 13.1 represents design principles that should be considered by HCOs prior to digital transformation. Each design principle is associated with a reference to the chapter from which it was derived. Understanding these principles will also help HCOs apply the Assessment Framework presented in Chapter 14.

Deriving the Design Principles

Design principles for Table 13.1 have been derived from Chapters 2-6 on digital health platforms, and Chapters 11-12 on work transformation. Design principles for information technology have been derived from Chapters 7–10 and guidelines to assess IT capability levels developed in Chapter 11.

Design Principles for Digital Transformation of HCOs

Table 13.1 highlights design principles associated with the major systems and support systems required for digital transformation. The three major systems, DHPs, IT systems, and work transformation, are supported by leadership and project management. Table 13.1 includes these five systems each supported by several principles. Each principle is associated with a relationship to digital transformation and includes a reference to the chapter from which it is derived. These principles are a compilation of analysis and observations made throughout the book and form the foundation for digital transformation of HCOs.

Table 13.1 Design Principles for Digital Transformation

No.	Principles	Relationship to Digital Transformation	Chapter Reference
A. Leadership commitment			
1	Develop a digital health strategy to plan HCO's digital transformation	HCOs must define their strategic vision for digital health, along with desired outcomes, prior to initiating a digital transformation (DT) effort. In addition, HCOs must recommend a digital pilot (or multiple pilots). Successful pilot(s) form a springboard for the phased implementation of the digital health vision.	Refer to Chapter 6 for defining a strategic vision and Chapter 11 for DT implementation phases
2	Use of pilots	Digital pilots designed to address operational problems and roadblocks that generate improvement feedback for subsequent DT efforts and serve as proof of concept. In addition to addressing problems, removing roadblocks, and generating desirable outcomes, successful pilots lead to expansions that define the scope of the startup phase (Phase one) of HCO DT efforts.	Refer to Chapter 11
3	Desired outcomes	HCO digital health goals and objectives must drive desired outcomes for DT efforts. These outcomes must be supported by quantitative metrics and benchmarks and used to influence system design and implementation.	Refer to Chapter 11
4	Executive support	DT efforts disrupt existing care models. It is important that senior management, including the board of directors, sponsor DT efforts including the costs, benefits, and risks associated with these disruptions.	Refer to Chapter 7
5	Mid management support	The change introduced by DT is best managed by middle and line management. Therefore, it is critical for them to be supporters of DT efforts.	Refer Chapter 7

(Continued)

Table 13.1 (Continued)

No.	Principles	Relationship to Digital Transformation	Chapter Reference
6	Transition from FFS to Value-based reimbursement strategies	DT efforts are critical in enabling HCO transition from FFS to value-based care models that incorporate PHM and risk management. In these models, patient care shifts to wellness and proactive care management which can be designed through DHPs, telehealth, and DT.	Refer to Chapter 11
7	Active user engagement	Expertise from functional users is critical during system analysis and design. Prototypes engage functional users in digital care models that are significantly transformative.	Refer to Chapter 7
8	IT leadership in key areas	In addition to the CIO, IT leadership roles such as CMIO, CNIO, CTO, CDO, and CISO are necessary to communicate and design the functional interests of clinical areas in DT efforts. HCOs can combine IT leadership roles with the understanding that resulting roles provide functional expertise for desired DT outcomes.	Refer to Chapter 7
9	Digital transformation office	DT efforts should be led by an organization's strategic business plan along with an understanding of advanced digital technologies, organizational information systems, and workflow transformation methodologies. These efforts are enabled by a digital transformation office (DTO) that includes project management and other transformation specialists. The DTO should be led by the Chief Digital Transformation Officer (CDTO) with working knowledge of the organization's culture, business goals, care models, and advance digital platforms. The CDTO should work under the CEO's leadership with direction from the board of directors.	Refer to Chapter 7

(Continued)

Table 13.1 (Continued)

No.	Principles	Relationship to Digital Transformation	Chapter Reference
10	Empower user functional committees	User functional committees should be empowered to prioritize and implement IT projects. DT efforts must be presented to these committees for review and input.	Refer to Chapter 7
B. Project Management			
1	Project management office (PMO)	PMO must be familiar with HCO work transformation efforts. PMO personnel must be familiar with LSS and HFE techniques. PMO should utilize a project charter that includes metrics that indicate progress towards desired outcomes, benchmarks, scope, time, and budget constraints.	Refer to Chapter 7
2	SDLC framework and methodologies	PMO should possess working knowledge of "waterfall" and "agile" methods and use them effectively to increase user participation and reduce project risk. The "agile" methodology encourages innovation and ownership by educating SMEs on DHPs and digital technologies, optimal use of workflow tools, and spatial considerations introduced by telehealth. The iterative "agile" approach encourages user participation through prototypes to validate system design and meet user expectations.	Refer to Chapter 7
3	Subject matter experts (SMEs)	PMO can utilize SMEs from within their department or functional areas (preferable). Costs related to SME participation should be approved prior to initiating DT efforts.	Refer to Chapter 7

(Continued)

Table 13.1 (Continued)

No.	Principles	Relationship to Digital Transformation	Chapter Reference
C. Digital Health Platforms			
1	DHPs	DHPs, including telehealth platforms, are critical components of digital health and should be understood prior to selection and implementation.	Refer to Chapter 3
2	DHP categories	Understand the various categories of DHPs – *transaction, exchange, innovation, and integration platforms* – based on their ability to provide different forms of value to their ecosystem participants.	Refer to Chapter 3
3	DHP governance	HCOs can use the following criteria to analyze DHP governance philosophies and ensure compatibility with HCO technical, functional, and ethical requirements: a) Impact of M&As on DHP architecture and functional offerings b) "Openness" to users c) "Openness" to partners and third-party developers d) Cybersecurity methodology and breach history e) Protecting patient data privacy f) Validating AI models g) Regulatory compliance	Refer to Chapter 5

(Continued)

Table 13.1 (Continued)

No.	Principles	Relationship to Digital Transformation	Chapter Reference
4	DHP participation levels	HCOs can participate on DHPs as a) Buyers of products and services offered by independent DHPs: This can include acquiring turnkey services such as primary care, urgent care, specialty care, and chronic disease management or utilizing telehealth solutions. Regardless, HCOs should understand the level of innovation encouraged on the platform and adaptability to their care models. b) Sellers of products and services on DHPs: HCOs can sell products and services such as supplies, CDS, and image AI models on platforms. c) Owners of DHPs: requires understanding healthcare platform architecture, categories, and configuration. d) Managers/Operators of DHPs: requires understanding management strategies for platforms. e) Combinations of (a)–(d) options. Each participation level has its advantages and disadvantages that should be considered as part of the HCO digital strategy. HCOs generally limit their participation on independent DHPs to buyers (and sellers) of platform products and service offerings. They may increase their involvement by owning and managing DHPs, to meet their expanding needs as they progress towards mature phases of DT.	Refer to Chapter 5

(Continued)

Table 13.1 (Continued)

No.	Principles	Relationship to Digital Transformation	Chapter Reference
5	Ownership and operation of DHPs	HCOs that wish to own and/or manage DHPs should consider the following: a) IT has the expertise to develop and support data and functional APIs. b) HCO marketing develops ways to attract consumers to the platform. c) HR develops platform governance policies that strike a balance between "openness," quality, privacy, and ethical use. d) R&D focuses on external producers.	Refer to Chapter 5
6	Configurations of telehealth platforms	HCOs must implement telehealth platform configurations that provide competitive advantage in the upcoming world of digital health, PHM, and value-based care. Telehealth platform configurations can be classified based on the following criteria: (a) turnkey services, (b) flexible solutions ranging from services to telehealth technologies, (c) innovation offerings from third parties, (d) telecommunication solutions, and (e) marketplace services.	Refer to Chapter 4
7	Configurations of DHP complements that support at-home patient care	HCOs should ensure that medical devices, RPMs, digital therapeutics, smart wearables, public agencies, and PGHD can interoperate with their telehealth solution. The resultant information should be aggregated and analyzed either within HCO EHRs or exported to complements such as Apple Health Records for patient care and engagement.	Refer to Chapters 4 and 6

(Continued)

Table 13.1 (Continued)

No.	Principles	Relationship to Digital Transformation	Chapter Reference
D. Information Technology			
1	HCO management support of IT systems	Management support of IT systems should include the following: • Empowers user committees to guide IT projects. • Supports IT leadership roles across the HCO. • Understands the role of PI in the effective performance of IT systems. • Supports active user involvement in system design. • Considers IT and digital technologies as investments for competitive advantage. • Supports project efforts through adequate capital and operational fundings.	Refer to Chapter 7
2	IT management	IT management is adept at blending advanced technologies with user requirements. In-house teams work with IT vendors and PI experts to design and implement IT systems including supporting specialty workflows.	Refer to Chapter 7
3	PMO	Discussed in B.1	
4	Ensure EHR usability for care providers	Since digital transformation efforts utilize care models and information that either originate from or terminate in EHRs, it is important to design systems that optimize EHR usability for providers.	Refer to Chapter 8

(Continued)

Table 13.1 (Continued)

No.	Principles	Relationship to Digital Transformation	Chapter Reference
5	Convert EHRs into "intelligent" systems	The overarching goal of "intelligent EHRs" is to ensure that the system acts as an integrator of patient care across decentralized, multi-disciplinary care teams while proactively assisting in the patient care process. This can be accomplished through evidence-based care plans that incorporate SDOH and can be used across healthcare facilities. These care plans also alert care providers in case of changes in patient conditions. This will likely require EHRs to transition from a vendor-developed solution to innovation platforms that support the evolving needs of HCOs.	Refer to Chapter 8
6	Implement AI models	HCOs should consider AI tools and DHPs to enhance provider productivity and provide intelligent virtual assistance. These include CDS, image AI algorithms, and analytics that are integrated in provider workflows.	Refer to Chapters 8 and 9
7	Utilize HFE	DT generally includes multiple care modalities, and teams that monitor, aggregate, and analyze patient information. This makes it important to utilize HFE methodologies such as design thinking and UI design principles to implement information systems that optimize overall user experience (UX). This involves designing user requirements around digital health requirements.	Refer to Chapter 8

(Continued)

Table 13.1 (Continued)

No.	Principles	Relationship to Digital Transformation	Chapter Reference
8	Implement a digital front door for patients	The *digital front door* offers a single sign on for a patient portal through different medium such as laptops, mobile phones, and tablets to access multiple application systems such as medication refills, self-scheduling, telehealth communication with providers, wellness programs, and compliance programs such as PT. A component of the *digital front door* is the ability to export patient health data from different applications, and platforms to external systems such as Apple Health Records for aggregation and analytics.	Refer to Chapter 8
9	Applicability of AI models	HCOs and EHR vendors should validate the applicability of AI models to HCO patient population and confirm the absence of bias in these models.	Refer to Chapter 9
10	Use FDA guidelines	HCOs and EHR vendors should use FDA guidelines to determine whether CDS and other AI models qualify as a device. For example, AI models that detect life-threatening diseases such as stroke or sepsis qualify as a device subject to FDA approval. AI models that are classified as non-device CDSs require transparency including patient-specific training information.	Refer to Chapter 9
11	Data exchange levels	Implement data exchange at HIMSS levels 3 and 4. HIMSS level 3 ensures semantic data exchange level by formatting data through standardized and coded data set to enable the use of transmitted data by receiving systems. This level of exchange helps PHM and risk-based contracting. Level 4 includes participation in HIEs and promotes interoperability which is key to DT.	Refer to Chapter 9

(Continued)

Table 13.1 (Continued)

No.	Principles	Relationship to Digital Transformation	Chapter Reference
12	Cybersecurity compliance	Implement a cybersecurity compliance program by utilizing a risk management framework such as NIST and HITRUST. These frameworks include desired objectives, customized to HCO risk management strategies. Objectives are implemented using standards and guidelines. In addition to frameworks, HCOs can use governmental resources to develop a cybersecurity program. An effective cybersecurity program is mandatory prior to initiating DT.	Refer to Chapter 10
13	Ethical privacy compliance program	Utilize a framework that considers privacy compromises related to system, product, and service operations with data and cybersecurity. Data can exist in digital, paper, and voice format. In addition to frameworks, HCOs should consider incorporating the ethical privacy compliance program in Chapter 10.	Refer to Chapter 10
14	Cybersecurity insurance	HCOs should purchase a cyber insurance policy to protect against loss of revenue. These policies can be obtained by brokers who coordinate with multiple insurance companies to provide the desired coverage. Insurance companies require HCO response to detailed questions regarding their state of cybersecurity readiness prior to acceptance. This can also help HCOs implement a cybersecurity compliance strategy.	Refer to Chapter 10

(Continued)

Table 13.1 (Continued)

No.	Principles	Relationship to Digital Transformation	Chapter Reference
15	Technical infrastructure for cybersecurity	HCOs should consider the following advancements in technology to enable DT while reducing IT expenses. These include: • Cloud computing for scalability, data aggregation, and analytics. • Continuous monitoring of organizational network systems. • Segment networks to isolate high-risk sources from ePHI. • Use virtual desktops through a combination of VDI and DaaS client devices for lower costs, improved device management, and reduced risk of cyberthreats.	Refer to Chapter 10
E. Work Transformation Methods			
1	LSS/PI – methodology and tools	HCOs should utilize the LSS/DMAIC structured, and data-centered methodology to implement work transformation efforts. There are several tools and techniques that can be used to support different PI and DT projects. Commonly used methodologies, tools, and techniques are process flowcharts, Value Stream Mapping (VSM), Root Cause Analysis (RCA), and Failure Mode and Effects Analysis (FMEA). These are supported by A3, PDCA, Kaizen, 5S, Poka Yoke, and other tools to conduct PI and DT projects.	Refer to Chapter 12

(Continued)

Table 13.1 (Continued)

No.	Principles	Relationship to Digital Transformation	Chapter Reference
2	PI efforts	LSS/PI should be accepted by the HCO and continue post implementation of PI efforts. It is recommended that HCOs implement PI projects of different functional complexities and scope including *cross-functional PI efforts* involving multiple departments, and *organization-wide PI efforts* involving functional processes across the HCO. PI efforts must include *current workflows* that reflect the processes under study. This is necessary to ensure that *proposed workflows* do not omit any processes and bottlenecks can be eliminated.	Refer to Chapter 11
3	Digital transformation efforts	Implement digital health strategy in HCOs using multiple phases of DT. This includes implementing digital pilot(s) followed by startup, growth, and mature phase for implementing DT. Chapter 11 describes DT phases that can be used by HCOs to implement their digital health vision. DT efforts focus on optimizing both patients and care provider process flows. This is because DT is focused on bringing technology closer to consumers and is key to patient engagement, reducing costs, and improving outcomes.	Refer to Chapter 11
4	Transform HCO culture towards effective change management	HCOs can cultivate a change management culture through their own LSS/PI experiences of undergoing PI and DT projects of increasing scope and complexity. Projects should document goals and objectives, supported by metrics and benchmarks, that must be achieved for them to be classified a success.	Refer to Chapter 11

Chapter 14

Assessment Framework: Readiness for Digital Transformation

Framework Introduction

This Framework has been designed to assess the readiness of HCOs for digital transformation (DT) efforts. The Framework consists of the three principal requirements of digital transformation that form the foundation of this book: Digital Health Platforms, IT systems, and Work Transformation methods which include leadership and project management requirements. The requirements are divided into ten categories, each represented by a table. Each table consists of subcategories which include desired objectives that should be achieved in order to be prepared for digital transformation. Desired objectives can be achieved through different tools, techniques, and methodologies depending on the size, scope, and digital health goals of HCOs.

The following table numbers and categories contain the subcategories and desired objectives that comprise the Assessment Framework:

Table 14.1: Understanding Digital Health Platforms
Table 14.2: DHP Strategies
Table 14.3: Telehealth and DHPs
Table 14.4: DHP Usage
Table 14.5: Managing IT Systems
Table 14.6: Usability of EHRs and IT Systems

DOI: 10.4324/9781003366584-17

Understanding the Framework

Readers are advised to understand the Framework including categories, subcategories, and desired objectives. It is difficult to accurately score each objective without understanding its applicability in the context of digital transformation. The following section explains the scoring system and ways of using the Framework in preparation for digital transformation. Figure 14.1 explains the process of utilizing the Framework and offers a stepwise approach for generating the gap analysis.

Who Should Conduct the Assessment?

A DT Steering Committee (DTSC) should be formed to plan the digital health strategy and oversee the DT effort. The DTSC should invite functional experts (FEs) to lead select subcategories and join the Committee. The DTSC should review the DT design principles in Chapter 13 and the categories, subcategories, and objectives in the Assessment Framework. Once the Framework has been understood, the DTSC can initiate the process of customizing the Framework to HCO business objectives and digital health strategy (refer to Figure 14.1).

Customizing the Framework

HCOs may wish to utilize the Framework as it is configured; however, some may decide to customize it to better reflect the scope of their service offerings and digital health goals. Framework customization can include eliminating, adding, or modifying categories, subcategories, and objectives. HCOs should be careful to not eliminate, add, or modify objectives without understanding their impact on the state of DT readiness. Scoring can begin once the Framework has been approved by the DTSC. This process results in a gap analysis and remediation plan (refer to Figure 14.1).

Scoring Criteria

Each objective should be rated on a scale of 1–4. Rating levels are based on the following criteria:

Level 1: minimal compliance with objective (<25% of the time)

Level 2: compliance with objective approximately 50% of the time

Level 3: compliance with objective a majority of the time (approximately 75% of the time)

Level 4: 100% compliance with objective

For each objective, a *score of 3 is considered acceptable* in terms of readiness for DT. However, the DTSC may decide that all or select objectives must receive a score of 4 in order to be prepared for DT. These decisions form the criteria for generating the gap analysis.

Each subcategory comprises "homogeneous" requirements (objectives). This homogeneity makes it possible to subtotal scores. However, while subcategory objectives are related, each may not hold the same weight (importance) in indicating HCO readiness for digital transformation. Therefore, subcategory subtotals should only be used as indicators if they are perfect.

Gap Analysis

Figure 14.1 enumerates the process for utilizing the Framework. Once the DTSC has scored all objectives in the Framework, it can initiate the process of generating the gap analysis. We will illustrate this method using an example.

Example

Hospital A's DTSC, after developing a digital health strategy, and reviewing Table 14.2 of the framework, decides that each objective with a score less than 3 will be assigned to the gap matrix.

The DTSC assigns the following scores to each of the seven objectives in Table 14.2 subcategory B.1: **B.1.1** = 4, **B.1.2** = 2, **B.1.3** = 4, **B.1.4** = 2, **B.1.5** = 3, **B.1.6** = 3, **B.1.7** = 4.

Since the subtotal for B.1 is less than perfect (22 out of a possible 28), the DTSC reviews each objective and assigns objectives B.1.2 and B.1.4 to the gap matrix for remediation.

Remediation Plan

Once the gap analysis is generated for all subcategories, a remediation plan should be developed for each objective included in the gap matrix. After the gaps have been remediated, the Assessment Framework Tables can be re-scored to assess HCO readiness for DT efforts.

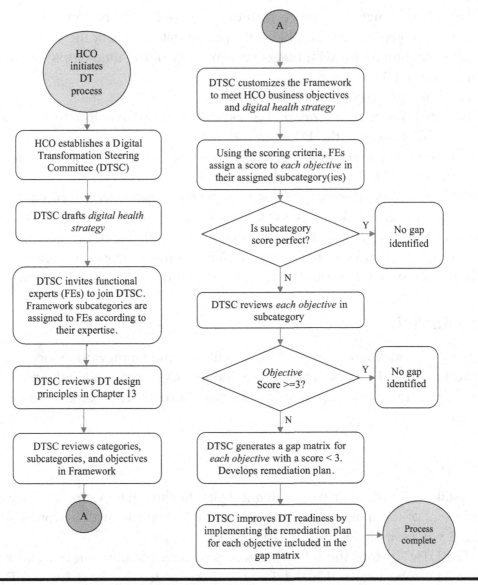

Figure 14.1 Process for Utilizing the Digital Transformation (DT) Readiness Assessment Framework.

Digital Transformation Readiness Framework

The Assessment Framework comprises categories, subcategories, and objectives. Each category in the Framework comprises subcategories which are described briefly including their relationship to digital transformation. In addition, each subcategory comprises multiple objectives some of which have been discussed with examples.

DHP Assessment

Understanding Digital Health Platforms

NOTE: HCOs should assess this subcategory regardless of whether they have implemented, or plan on implementing, telehealth, and DHPs.

Table 14.1 assesses HCO understanding of digital health platforms – including e-commerce.

- ■ A.1 – Understanding DHPs

Subcategory A.1 helps to assess knowledge of e-commerce and DHPs. While regulatory controls, payment systems, and specialties make telehealth and other DHPs different in their configurations than e-commerce platforms, it is important to understand the underlying principles of platforms to help select the DHP that is best equipped to meet the current and future needs of HCOs.

Examples

Objective 1 assesses HCO understanding of demand economies that are fundamental drivers of digital platforms as opposed to supply-side economies that drive traditional businesses.

Objective 2 assesses HCO understanding of "core interactions" which are central to the design of platforms. For example, in healthcare, common core interactions are between care providers and patients, and between care providers.

Objective 3 assesses HCO understanding of the importance of APIs – in e-commerce and digital health platforms.

Objective 6 assesses HCO understanding of the different categories of telehealth solutions and DHPs – marketplace, data exchange, innovation, and integration platforms. Each of these categories offers different levels of services and value to consumers.

Table 14.1   Understanding Digital Health Platforms

	Assessment Questionnaire: Understanding Digital Health Platforms (Refer to Chapters 2, 3)	Score
A.1	**Understanding Digital Platforms, DHPs, and Telehealth**	1–4
1	Understand fundamentals of e-commerce platforms (non-healthcare) and differences with traditional businesses.	
2	Understand core interactions in e-commerce platforms.	
3	Understand API economy.	
4	Understand similarities and differences between e-commerce platforms and DHPs.	
5	Understand relationship between DHPs and consumerism.	
6	Understand differences between marketplace platforms, data exchange platforms (HIEs), innovation, and integration platforms that encourage complements from third parties and partners.	
7	Understand differences between participating and owning/operating DHPs.	
8	Understand advantages and disadvantages of public and private APIs.	
9	Understand circumstances under which to use different types of DHPs: transaction, exchange, innovation, and integration.	
	Subtotal	

DHP Strategies

NOTE: HCOs should assess this subcategory regardless of whether they have implemented, or plan on implementing, telehealth and DHPs.

Table 14.2 assesses HCO understanding of ways to implement telehealth and DHPs (refer to Chapter 5). This table comprises the following subcategories:

- B.1 – Digital Health Strategies
- B.2 – DHP Governance Criteria

Subcategory B.1 objective 1 assesses HCO progress with developing, a digital health strategy prior to employing a phased digital transformation approach.

Table 14.2 DHP Strategies

	Assessment Questionnaire: DHP Strategies (Refer to Chapters 3, 4, 6)	Score
B.1	**Digital Health Strategies**	**1–4**
1	Develop digital health strategy to improve patient access, increase services, redefine, and extend markets. Depending on scope, it is preferable to use a phased implementation approach.	
2	Incorporate DHPs, IT systems, and work transformation methods to generate multiple care modalities that support patient services across the care continuum.	
3	Establish alliances and partnerships with HCOs, independent DHPs, payers, and employers.	
4	Generate metrics and benchmarks to assess the impact of DHPs and digital health.	
5	Utilize an integrated telehealth solution including AI models, DHPs, and intelligent devices to accommodate HCO's digital health requirements.	
6	Use digital healthcare models to support *care provider* workflows.	
7	Use *digital front door* to support patient engagement.	
	Subtotal	
B.2	**DHP Governance Criteria**	**1–4**
	NOTE: HCOs should use the following criteria to assess governance of each DHP/telehealth platform that is part of their digital health strategy.	
1	Assess the impact of M&As on DHP architecture and functional offerings.	
2	Assess DHP "openness" to users – ease of accessing, viewing, editing, and appending patient data on platform (potential impact on patient privacy).	
3	Assess DHP "openness" to partners and third-party complement developers, dictated by the APIs offered, including DHP review and approval process of third-party hardware and software complements (potential impact on security of patient data and quality of third-party solutions).	
4	Assess preparedness and third-party certification for cybersecurity.	
5	Assess strategies to protect the privacy of patient data.	

(*Continued*)

Table 14.2 (Continued)

	Assessment Questionnaire: DHP Strategies (Refer to Chapters 3, 4, 6)	Score
6	Assess whether AI models are validated for the absence of bias and provide information in terms of the purpose, training data used, and outcomes.	
7	Assess compliance with regulatory requirements, for example, HIPAA and Cures Act.	
	Subtotal	

Subcategory B.2 presents seven governance criteria that are recommended for HCO consideration to assess DHP and telehealth platforms that are being considered (or in production) to operationalize their digital health vision.

Telehealth and DHPs

NOTE: HCOs should assess this subcategory regardless of whether they have implemented, or plan on implementing, telehealth, and DHPs.

Table 14.3 comprises the following subcategories:

- C.1 – Utilizing Telehealth Platforms in HCO
- C.2 – Telehealth and DHP Complements
- C.3 – Specialty DHPs

It is important to assess the understanding of DHPs, how HCOs are currently using, or plan on using, telehealth platforms, and specialty DHPs to support their digital health vision.

C.1 assesses the effectiveness of existing, or potential, telehealth platforms in HCOs. For example, an HCO that scores the Subcategory at 15/16, indicates that the existing (or new) telehealth platform(s) will be useful in extending service offerings.

C.2 assesses the effectiveness of telehealth and DHP complements (existing or new) to improve patient services.

C.3 helps HCOs assess the state of specialty platforms and their deployment effectiveness in the HCO. These platforms are designed to increase provider productivity, intelligent virtual assistance, and workflow integration.

Table 14.3 Telehealth and DHPs

	Assessment Questionnaire: Telehealth and DHPs (Refer to Chapters 3, 4, 5)	Score
C.1	**Utilizing Telehealth Platforms**	**1–4**
1	Utilize telehealth platform(s) to improve accessibility to HCO patient services.	
2	Utilize telehealth platform(s) to enable patient services in addition to those currently offered by HCOs. For example, chronic disease management through at-home care using biometrics and intelligent devices.	
3	Utilize telehealth platform(s) to enable alliances and partnerships with HCOs, payers, employers, and independent DHPs.	
4	Utilize telehealth platform(s) to enable value-based arrangements with HCOs, payers, employers, and independent DHPs.	
5	Ensure telehealth platform(s) is integrated in HCO care models to meet digital health requirements.	
	Subtotal	
C.2	**Telehealth and DHP Complements**	**1–4**
	NOTE: This section assesses software and hardware complements and their potential benefits.	
1	Utilize DHPs such as IoT-based remote patient monitors, DTx, and smart wearables, to support telehealth platforms.	
2	Optimize telehealth and complementary DHPs to generate a *digital front door* attractive to members/patients. For example, telehealth platforms that provide care provider access through video, phone, and email, wellness platforms such as mental health, and specialty portals such as physical therapy. Ability to export aggregate patient data to HCO EHR.	
3	Optimize telehealth and complementary DHPs to support a distributed care model, using hybrid modalities. This configuration accommodates patients and care teams that include primary care providers, specialists, NPs, nurses, pharmacists, and allied health professionals.	
4	Assess whether EHR vendor utilizes APIs to convert their apps to platforms (e.g., SMART on FHIR APIs). The platform can offer complements through a marketplace to help HCOs implement AI systems that offer optimum value.	

(Continued)

Table 14.3   (Continued)

	Assessment Questionnaire: Telehealth and DHPs (Refer to Chapters 3, 4, 5)	Score
5	Assess the variety and quality of partner extensions and third-party complements to meet HCO digital health requirements.	
	Subtotal	
C.3	**Specialty DHPs**	**1–4**
	NOTE: HCOs can rate the following three objectives using the bullet DHPs as guides. HCOs can also use other DHPs to score these objectives.	
1	AI systems support provider productivity	
	• Medical speech recognition.	
	• EHR platforms.	
2	AI systems provide virtual clinical assistance	
	• CDS available through EHR platform, or marketplaces.	
	• Image AI algorithms available through marketplaces enabled through PACS/RIS or speech recognition platforms.	
3	Specialty platforms are appropriately integrated in provider workflow.	
	Subtotal	

DHP Usage (optional)

NOTE: This subcategory should be assessed by HCOs that currently own/operate DHPs and/or use multiple telehealth platforms.

- D.1 – HCO Ownership and/or Management of DHPs
- D.2 – Configurations of Telehealth Platforms on which HCO Is Participating – or Plan on Participating

Table 14.4 assesses HCOs understanding of their telehealth solutions including usage.

D.1 presents strategies that should be followed in cases where HCOs own and manage DHPs and telehealth solutions.

Table 14.4 DHP Usage

	Assessment Questionnaire: Optional DHP Considerations (Refer to Chapters 3, 4, 6)	Score
D.1	**HCO Ownership and/or Management of DHPs**	**1–4**
	NOTE: These questions must be completed by HCOs that own and/or manage DHPs (refer to Chapter 5).	
1	IT supports external alliances and partnerships by offering APIs to third-party developers and partners.	
2	Marketing understands requirements of platform producers and consumers to help design key system features that attract consumers and patients to the platform.	
3	Human resources develop and maintain platform governance policies, regarding openness, quality, privacy, and ethical use.	
4	R&D refocuses attention on external producers of the platform including HIEs, data management, and functional extensions.	
	Subtotal	
D.2	**Configurations of Existing Telehealth Platforms on which HCO Is Participating – or Plan on Participating (refer to Chapter 4)**	**1–4**
	NOTE: Scoring should be based on whether the existing configuration of telehealth systems is adequate to meet HCO digital health requirements. HCOs that are using multiple telehealth systems should assess their satisfaction with each solution and collective telehealth solutions.	
1	Turnkey solutions that provide patient services including telehealth systems, providers, data exchanges, and *third-party data complements*.	
2	Telehealth system supports a range of services for HCOs – from turnkey solutions to telehealth platforms that support HCO EHR and providers. Supports *third-party data complements*.	
3	Telehealth system supports a range of services for HCOs – from turnkey solutions to telehealth platforms that support HCO EHR, specialty applications, and providers. Supports *third-party data and functional complements*.	
4	Telecommunication technologies, data exchange, and *third-party data complements*. System can be embedded in HCO EHR and specialty applications to support provider workflows.	
5	Digital marketplace for patient care, purchasing supplies, renting equipment, staffing, etc.	
6	Impact of collective telehealth solutions on digital health.	
	Subtotal	

D.2 assesses telehealth configuration options and their applicability to HCO digital health strategy. For example, HCOs that are using multiple telehealth systems should assess their satisfaction with each solution, including their overall impact on digital health.

IT Assessment

Managing IT Systems

Table 14.5 assesses HCO management of IT systems which includes the following subcategories:

- E.1 – Management Considers IT Integral to Business Strategy
- E.2 – Management Supports User Engagement
- E.3 – Management Supports Work Transformation of IT Systems and Digital Platforms
- E.4 – Management Empowers User Committees to Guide IT Projects
- E.5 – Management Supports IT Leadership Roles across the HCO
- E.6 – IT Support Requirements
- E.7 – Project management

Table 14.5 assesses the role of HCO Management in supporting IT systems across the organization. This is the key to developing advanced IT systems that can assist in the implementation of an effective digital health strategy.

E.1 subcategory objectives assess whether HCO management considers IT integral to its business that can be used for competitive advantage.

E.2 subcategory objectives assess whether management is committed to ensuring effective user participation and training programs for improved system usability.

E.3 subcategory objectives assess management support of work transformation efforts in the effective design of IT systems and digital platforms.

E.4 subcategory objectives assess the number, type, authority, and responsibility of user committees.

E.5 subcategory objectives assess whether management assigns IT leaders throughout the HCO. In this scoring should be based on the provision of functions rather than separate positions.

E.6 subcategory objectives assess IT support requirements and capabilities.

E.7 subcategory objectives assess the PMO and their understanding of methodologies required for successful DT.

Table 14.5 Managing IT Systems

	Assessment Questionnaire: Managing IT Systems (Refer to Chapter 7)	Score
E.1	**Management Considers IT Integral to Business Strategy**	**1–4**
1	Involve CIOs in the development of HCOs strategic plan.	
2	Involve CIOs in changes to project priorities including additions of new projects.	
3	Ensure capital and operational funding are commensurate with IT requirements and expected outcomes.	
4	Empower functional committees to make decisions regarding the development and implementation of IT Roadmap.	
	Subtotal	
E.2	**Management Supports User Engagement**	**1–4**
1	Utilize functional prototypes during system design, to help providers, nurses, and other personnel visualize proposed system.	
2	Address functional committee recommendations prior to system implementation.	
3	Utilize pilots to identify and resolve system problems prior to house-wide implementation.	
4	Require proficiency assessment for users (including physicians) as part of training, prior to system access.	
5	Customize training programs to specialty workflows.	
	Subtotal	
E.3	**Work Transformation of IT Systems and Digital Platforms**	**1–4**
1	Involve IT in PI projects to assess the benefit of incorporating IT upgrades and associated costs.	
2	Adopt continuous PI to achieve, and maintain, the desired functional state.	
3	Adopt a "metrics culture" that links projects with quantitative benchmarks. PI is considered successful if desired benchmarks are achieved and maintained.	
4	Engage functional users in system analysis and design of projects.	
5	Develop a change management culture by successfully implementing PI projects of increasing scope and complexity.	

(Continued)

Table 14.5   (Continued)

	Assessment Questionnaire: Managing IT Systems (Refer to Chapter 7)	Score
6	Work with users and process redesign experts to customize information system, using vendor utilities and custom developments, to meet user requirements. System improvements are dictated by user requirements.	
7	Work with digital transformation teams to ensure that process design is efficient for users and patients while generating a longitudinal patient record and ensuring data security and privacy.	
8	Implement interoperability standards including APIs and other software programming techniques for seamless integration between internal systems, DHPs, and smart devices.	
9	Design effective UI systems and optimum user experience (UX) for care providers and patients.	
	Subtotal	
E.4	**Management Empowers User Committees to Guide IT Projects**	**1–4**
	NOTE: HCOs can implement fewer committees to represent desired functions. For example, a *clinical committee* can represent nursing, labs, pharmacy, radiology, and allied professionals.	
1	Empower *IT Executive Committee (ITEC)* to align the direction of IT with HCO mission. ITEC approves and oversees IT expenditures and benefit realization studies.	
2	Effectively utilize *IT Regulatory Committee (ITRC)* to understand regulatory guidance from CMS, TJC, AHRQ, state legislations, and other sources, related to HIT systems. ITRC serves as a fiscally responsible source for regulatory compliance. This Committee is chaired by Chief Compliance Officer.	
3	Empower *Provider IT Decision Council* to provide input in clinical projects such as EHRs, AI models, enhancements, training, and support. This Council is chaired by the Chief Medical Informatics Officer (CMIO).	
4	Empower *Clinical IT Decision Councils* to provide input for nursing, pharmacy, laboratories, imaging, and ambulatory systems. These Councils are chaired by functional experts. The nursing council is chaired by the Chief Nursing Informatics Officer (CNIO), if available.	
5	Empower *Data Governance Council* (DGC) to ensure a robust data governance strategy including data cleansing and other AI-related issues that require DGC review and approval.	

(Continued)

Table 14.5 (Continued)

	Assessment Questionnaire: Managing IT Systems (Refer to Chapter 7)	Score
6	Empower *Innovation Council* consisting of members from the Board of Directors and senior leadership team and led by the Chief Innovation Officer to investigate advanced technologies and ensure alignment with HCO-IT and functional users prior to implementation.	
7	Empower *Computer User Group (CUG)* to serve as a liaison between IT and user community on system bugs, functional problems, system enhancements, and updates.	
	Subtotal	
E.5	**Management Supports IT Leadership Roles across the HCO**	**1–4**
	NOTE: HCOs can combine these roles – for example, the DTO can manage digital technology, process improvement, and innovation requirements. Scoring of this subcategory should be based on the provision of the following functions regardless of whether the functions are supported through separate or combined roles.	
1	Support functions provided by Chief Information Officer (CIO), a member of the management team responsible for leveraging IT capabilities and collaborating with functional experts to generate IT systems that offer *business advantage*.	
2	Support functions provided by Chief Medical Information Officer (CMIO), who designs and implements systems that require significant physician engagement such as EHRs. CMIOs chair the *Provider IT Decision Council* and are involved in councils that address provider needs.	
3	Support functions provided by Chief Digital Transformation Officer (CDTO), responsible for HCO's digital transformation via the *Digital Transformation Office* (DTO). The DTO guides the development of hybrid care models and methodologies that advance the strategic mission of HCOs.	
4	Support functions provided by Chief Process Improvement Officer, responsible for PI efforts using LSS/PI tools, HFE, and innovative care models.	
5	Support functions provided by Chief Innovation Officer, responsible for investigating and implementing new technologies and leading the *Innovation Council*. The Chief Innovation Officer is responsible for the *Innovation Office* which comprises information systems and work redesign experts.	

(Continued)

Table 14.5 (Continued)

	Assessment Questionnaire: Managing IT Systems (Refer to Chapter 7)	Score
6	Support functions provided by Chief Privacy Officer (CPO), responsible for the ethical and legal use of information within HCOs. This position deals with the complexities of privacy within the evolving privacy framework of security breaches and operationalizing patient data including de-identification, transfer to third parties, and sale to vendors.	
7	Support functions provided by Chief Information Security Officer (CISO), responsible for driving cybersecurity design and implementation and communicating organizational risk management goals. Cybersecurity includes hardware and software solutions, policies & procedures, ongoing security updates, and user training.	
8	Support functions provided by Chief Technology Officer (CTO), responsible for ensuring efficient operation of management information systems (MIS) and supporting the CIO in fulfilling organizational goals and objectives.	
9	Support functions provided by Chief Data Officer (CDO), responsible for understanding and operationalizing big data in HCOs. The CDO understands key analytical outcomes such as PHM and CDS and uses reverse engineering to identify data requirements, data sources, and cleansing routines.	
10	Support functions provided by Chief Applications Officer (CAO), responsible for managing vendor-developed and in-house application systems. This position is key to implementing well-designed functional systems and is a prerequisite to digital transformation of HCOs.	
	Subtotal	
E.6	**IT Support Requirements**	**1–4**
1	Utilize SLAs (Service Level Agreements) to manage user support.	
2	Utilize metrics to manage software enhancements. Metrics should include time, cost, and desired outcomes (benefits) from software enhancements.	
3	Utilize metrics to manage hardware and network upgrades. Metrics should include time, cost, and desired outcomes (benefits) from hardware/network upgrades.	
	Subtotal	

(*Continued*)

Table 14.5   (Continued)

	Assessment Questionnaire: Managing IT Systems (Refer to Chapter 7)	Score
E.7	**Project Management**	1–4
1	Project Management Office (PMO) manages and oversees work transformation projects involving IT systems • PMO familiar with Agile methods, LSS, and human factors engineering techniques. • Utilize subject matter experts (SMEs) in projects. • Utilize metrics and desired benchmarks to assess project outcomes. • Understand scope and time commitments.	
2	Utilize project charter that is approved by key stakeholders prior to project initiation.	
3	Actively engage clinicians in system analysis and design through innovative methodologies such as boards, test systems, prototypes, and pilots.	
4	Utilize key performance indicators (KPIs) and benchmarks to measure project success. Where applicable, KPIs must track progress towards organizational CSFs.	
5	Regularly communicate with stakeholders including management, physicians, nurses, ancillaries, and allied health professionals.	
6	Utilize SDLC Framework in the context of HCOs. Manage project time, expense, and desired outcomes.	
7	Utilize Waterfall or Agile methodologies as appropriate. Have a working understanding of each methodology in healthcare organizations.	
8	Incorporate outcomes for key milestones in the project plan. Meeting intermediate milestones of time, cost, and desired KPIs can help successful project implementation.	
	Subtotal	

Usability of EHRs and IT Systems

Table 14.6 assesses the usability of EHRs and IT systems which includes the following subcategories:

- F.1 – Satisfaction Surveys
- F.2 – EHR Vendor Tools to Customize EHR Design and Navigation – *Vendor Controlled* (Pre-implementation)
- F.3 – EHR Vendor Support of AI Systems – *Vendor Controlled* (Pre-implementation)
- F.4 – Care Provider EHR Usability – *Vendor Controlled* (Post-implementation)
- F.5 – Care Provider EHR Usability – *HCO Controlled* (Pre-implementation)
- F.6 – Care Provider EHR Usability – *HCO Controlled* (Post-implementation)
- F.7 –Impact of External Parties on EHR Usability
- F.8 – Factors Impacting Patient Engagement

The F.1 subcategory and associated objectives are self-explanatory. We begin with subcategories F.2–F.7 which state that while designing EHR systems is the responsibility of EHR vendors, implementing these systems effectively is also the responsibility of HCOs and IT. In addition, EHR usability can be improved through pre- and post-implementation techniques. For example, F.2 assesses the design and flexibility of navigation tools and UI techniques to customize EHR navigation and workflows to meet specialists' requirements. These tools are developed by the EHR vendor prior to implementation in the HCO.

Similarly, F.3 assesses EHR vendor support of AI systems and associated tools, which are managed by the vendor regardless of implementation in an HCO environment. F.4 assesses promptness of vendor support to user-identified problems and prioritizing enhancement requests – post-system implementation.

F.5 assesses the effectiveness of factors that are HCO and HCO-IT controlled. For example, objective 7 requires a formal proficiency assessment of all users, including physicians, prior to using an information system. While physicians are willing to use internet-based training technologies, they are mostly unwilling to be assessed on their knowledge of navigating EHRs which are integral to patient care. Mistakes such as ordering incorrect medications can lead to dire consequences. Therefore, HCOs should work with physicians on mandating training and formal assessment prior to system access. Physician-desired improvements to functional and workflow design should be implemented as part of training and post-implementation (refer to F.6).

F.7 considers the impact of regulatory controls and payer documentation requirements on EHR usability and provider satisfaction. Finally, F.8 assesses the effectiveness by which the *digital front door* has been designed and implemented to influence patient engagement.

Table 14.6   Usability of EHRs and IT Systems

	Assessment Questionnaire: Usability of Healthcare Information Systems (Refer to Chapter 8)	Score
F.1	**Satisfaction Surveys** NOTE: score based on survey results	**1–4**
1	HCO utilizes provider satisfaction surveys and benchmarks (Arch Collaborative) to improve EHR usability.	
2	HCO utilizes patient satisfaction surveys (Press Ganey) to increase patient engagement in their health.	
	Subtotal	
	Care Provider EHR Usability – *Vendor Controlled* (Pre-implementation)	**1–4**
F.2	**EHR Vendor Tools to Customize EHR Design and Navigation**	
1	Screen flows, navigation requirements, and patient data conform to care provider specialties and preferences.	
2	Documentation, including flowsheets, is automated.	
3	Information is located efficiently and effectively.	
	Subtotal	
F.3	**EHR Vendor Support of AI Systems**	**1–4**
1	EHR vendor supports data interoperability with telehealth platforms, including complements such as RPMs, digital therapeutics, smart devices, and CRM systems for care provider decision-making. Patient information presented in EHR supports provider user interface needs. This can be enabled via external systems such as Apple Health.	
2	EHR vendor supports data and functional APIs to facilitate third-party extensions, such as CDS, speech recognition, and AI image recognition, to enhance system functionality.	

(Continued)

Table 14.6 (Continued)

	Assessment Questionnaire: Usability of Healthcare Information Systems (Refer to Chapter 8)	Score
3	EHR vendor supports any, or all, of the following AI tools – developed by EHR vendor, partners, or independent software vendors. Score for this objective should be based on the number of AI tools implemented and provider satisfaction. • Speech recognition system to reduce provider workload and improve turnaround time to complete patient records. • *Intelligent ambient solutions* to passively capture and create a detailed clinical note from multi-party conversations during onsite and virtual patient encounters and integrate in the patient's EHR. • Image AI algorithms to automate radiology reads for subsequent radiologist confirmation. • AI models scan free text systems to extract quality measures, treatments and their effectiveness, and medication errors. • CDS provides alerts and support care protocols for high-risk conditions such as predicting onset of sepsis and acute toxicities in patients receiving radiation therapy for head and neck cancers.	
4	EHR vendor supports tools for PHM and risk-based APMs.	
5	EHR operates as a care management system through intelligent assistance and controls. For example, EHR leverages evidence-based care plans that can be customized to support multiple chronic diseases. These care plans are used by care providers, across health systems, to manage patient care through alerts and reminders.	
6	EHR vendor validates AI tools on its platform for clinical applicability and absence of bias.	
	Subtotal	
F.4	**Care Provider EHR Usability – *Vendor Controlled*** (Post-implementation)	**1–4**
1	Post-implementation system problems are promptly communicated by vendor and resolved as promised.	
2	Vendor prioritizes, communicates, and implements enhancement requests as promised to users.	
	Subtotal	
F.5	**Care Provider EHR Usability – *HCO Controlled*** (Pre-implementation)	**1–4**
1	IT staff works with functional users to standardize the clinical note, patient assessment, and care plans.	

(Continued)

Table 14.6 (Continued)

	Assessment Questionnaire: Usability of Healthcare Information Systems (Refer to Chapter 8)	Score
2	IT team designs provider workflows prior to confirming integration specifications between AI models and EHRs.	
3	Project funding for implementing, training, enhancing, and supporting IT systems is commensurate with expected outcomes.	
4	IT generates quantifiable outcomes that measure EHR usability. The goal is to monitor EHR usability and ongoing improvements.	
5	IT generates EHR functional and operational workflows for care provider and support staff review, input, and approval.	
6	IT supports providers by creating specialty-specific EHR navigation, related workflows, and training.	
7	IT assesses user proficiency (including physicians) of upgraded EHR using standardized testing. User scores highlight the need for, and areas of, additional training.	
8	IT works with EHR vendor(s) to support data interoperability with telehealth platforms, including complements such as RPMs, digital therapeutics, smart devices, and CRM systems for care provider decision-making. Patient information resulting from distributed sub-systems is integrated in the EHR and supports physician UX.	
	Subtotal	
F.6	**Care Provider EHR Usability – *HCO Controlled*** (Post-implementation)	1–4
1	IT uses emails, newsletters, in person, teleconference, and phone to support post-implementation needs of physicians, nurses, and ancillaries. System problems, functional enhancements, and workflow improvements are actively communicated.	
2	IT establishes post-training consultation sessions to accommodate provider specialty and preferences in the EHR.	
	Subtotal	
F.7	**Impact of External Factors on EHR Usability**	1–4
1	HCO minimizes regulatory impact on provider documentation through standards, system, and workflow design.	
2	HCO minimizes impact of payer requirements on provider documentation through system and workflow design.	

(Continued)

Table 14.6 (Continued)

	Assessment Questionnaire: Usability of Healthcare Information Systems (Refer to Chapter 8)	Score
3	HCO minimizes impact of APM payer requirements on provider documentation through standards, system, and workflow design.	
	Subtotal	
F.8	**Factors Impacting Patient Engagement**	**1–4**
1	HCO utilizes a unified patient portal for the care continuum. This acts as the *digital front door*.	
2	HCO monitors active users of patient portal to meet patient engagement benchmarks.	
	NOTE: The *digital front door* provides patients access to the following functions and services.	
3	Access portal through the HCO website and mobile solution.	
4	Enter health data (PGHD) and social determinants of health (SDOH) through the portal.	
5	Enable patient consultation with providers through synchronous (telemedicine and phone call) and asynchronous (email and text) communication tools.	
6	Provide patients access to their EHI.	
7	Refill medications.	
8	Manage appointment scheduling.	
9	Provide consolidated bill payment.	
10	Provide email reminders for upcoming appointments, medication refills, proactive testing, and wellness programs.	
11	Support patient wellness programs, e.g., mental health applications.	
12	Support compliance with care provider orders, e.g., physical therapy portals provide videos to help patients comply with prescribed exercise routines.	
13	Support patient data exchange with Apple Health Record for patient review, input (PGHD), and provider review.	
	Subtotal	

Interoperability, Big Data, and AI Analytics

Table 14.7 assesses HCO sophistication related to data exchange, big data, and AI analytics. It comprises the following subcategories:

- G.1 – Standards
- G.2 – Data Exchange Levels and HIEs
- G.3 – Big Data and AI Analytics
- G.4 – Adopting AI Models

G.1 assesses the use of standards. HCOs that are using some of the coding systems and standards required by regulators and payers can score a 4/4 for objective 1. They do not need to use all standards included in objective 1. Consider objectives 7 and 8 that relate to USCDI v1 and v2 requirements. HCOs depend on their HIS vendors to implement these requirements for compliance. Therefore, HCOs can score their compliance while anticipating the availability of these elements in their HIS.

G.2 assesses HCO data exchange levels. For DT it is important to interoperate with other HCOs to access and aggregate patient data, along with the level of exchange. For example, exchanging patient data between organizations at HIMSS level 2 will alter staff workflow and negatively impact productivity, as compared to data exchanges at HIMSS level 3 (refer to objective 9).

Another example is objective 8 which assesses use cases offered by HIEs. Since these are a function of individual HIEs, it is helpful to review this list to determine if HCOs would like their HIE to offer select use cases. In addition to data exchange, most HIE use cases require storing patient data in their system, which suggests that HCOs must assess cybersecurity methodologies employed by HIEs. As long as HCOs are satisfied with the use cases offered by their HIE(s), they can score a 4/4 in this category.

G.3 assesses the organizational handling of big data and analytics and is another important component of DT. A key function that gets overlooked by HCO-IT and HIS vendors is the quality of data aggregated from different sources. Objective 5 assesses whether HCOs ensure data quality through standardization and cleansing algorithms. Without cleansing, analytical information becomes unreliable for clinical and business decisions. A key reason for biased and incorrect AI models is poor data quality.

G.4 addresses issues relating to adoption of AI models. While these models can be clinically and operationally helpful, it is important to ensure their applicability to provider patient population prior to use. The key issues to consider in AI models are objective, training data, and FDA compliance. Once these are approved by HCO providers, then AI models should be integrated in provider workflows prior to use.

Table 14.7 Interoperability, Big Data, and AI Analytics

	Assessment Questionnaire: Interoperability, Big Data, and AI Analytics (Refer to Chapter 9)	Score
G.1	**Standards**	**1–4**
1	Utilize coding systems for healthcare payment, treatment, and operations: HCPCS, CDT, NDC, CPT, LOINC, SNOMED-CT, and ICD-10.	
2	Utilize content standards to move key data sets across different organizational systems: HL7 v2, HL7 v3 – for messaging, Clinical Document Architecture (CDA) and Consolidated CDA (C-CDA) – for clinical documents and USCDI – standardized set of data classes and related elements.	
3	Utilize transport standards that define the format, document architecture, data elements, data linkage, and transfer methods: DICOM – medical image exchange, Direct Standard (XDR/XDM) – secure and direct health message exchange, Integrating the Healthcare Enterprise (IHE) – health data exchange, and National Council for Prescription Drug Program (NCPDP SCRIPT) – electronic prescription exchange.	
4	Utilize Fast Healthcare Interoperability Resources (FHIR) API supported data exchange.	
5	Utilize Sustainable Medical Applications Reusable Technologies (SMART) in conjunction with FHIR and define how third-party applications will be launched from the EHR and security protocols to exchange data with EHRs.	
6	Utilize identifier standards to uniquely identify patient records: Enterprise Master Patient Index (EMPI), to uniquely identify patients across HCOs, and Medical Record Index (MRI) to identify patient care history within an HCO.	
7	Compliance with USCDI v1 requirements (data classes and data elements).	
8	Compliance with USCDI v2 requirements (additional data classes and data elements).	
	Subtotal	
G.2	**Data Exchange Levels and HIEs**	**1–4**
	NOTE: Indicate Data Exchange Levels utilized by HCO. Since Levels 1, 2, and 3 progressively build on each other, HCOs that exchange data at Level 3 should also indicate data exchange at Levels 1, and 2. Level 4 data exchanges are generally conducted based on the exchange requirements of HIEs.	

(Continued)

Table 14.7 (Continued)

	Assessment Questionnaire: Interoperability, Big Data, and AI Analytics (Refer to Chapter 9)	Score
1	**Level 1:** Utilize Foundational data exchange level by conforming to basic connectivity requirements for exchanging organizational data sets with external systems.	
2	**Level 2:** Utilize Structural data exchange level by conforming to HL7 requirements for data exchange.	
3	**Level 3:** Utilize Semantic data exchange level by formatting data through standardized and coded data sets to enable the use of transmitted data by receiving systems.	
4	**Level 4:** Utilize organizational data exchange level by including framework for data governance, policy, agreements (privacy, security, and data sharing), and technological requirements to exchange data across organizations resulting in integrated workflows.	
5	HCO participates in local, state, or regional HIEs that support data exchange among participants. HIEs aggregate and analyze EHI for participant use.	
6	Use cases that can be leveraged from HCO's HIE/HIN (score based on HIE value adds) • Enable establishment of APMs such as MSSPs and ACOs. • Implement CMS Quality Payment Programs (QPP). • Implement payer-negotiated performance measures. • Support e-prescribing. • Utilize security and privacy services. • Support data aggregation and analytics. • Support PHM analytics. • Support collection and exchange of social determinants of health (SDOH) through public health and clinical data exchange. • Provide patient portals for access to clinical data and other value-add services. • Support alert systems for providers when their patients have been seen elsewhere within the network. • Use IHE-based brokering infrastructure to exchange FHIR payloads between members. • Support disaster recovery services.	
7	HCO participates in HIE that ensures security and privacy of patient EHI.	

(*Continued*)

Table 14.7   (Continued)

	Assessment Questionnaire: Interoperability, Big Data, and AI Analytics (Refer to Chapter 9)	Score
8	Information imported through HIEs does not negatively impact clinical staff productivity (score based on the following criteria): • Enable staff to retrieve select information from external systems. • Eliminate data duplication from external systems. • Effectively integrate information from external systems in the HCO-EHR.	
9	HCO participates, or plans on participating, in TEFCA through existing HIE/HIN.	
10	Implement onsite (hospital-based) medical devices, and communication systems through middleware to optimize care provider workflows.	
11	Utilize HIEs, or a secure VPN connection, to interoperate with telehealth platforms and smart wearables.	
	Subtotal	
G.3	**Big Data and AI Analytics**	**1–4**
1	Generate clinical alerts and notifications to improve patient care,	
2	Utilize descriptive analytics for quality, and administrative decision-making in HCOs.	
3	Utilize predictive analytics for operational and administrative decision-making in HCOs.	
4	Generate large digital data sets using telehealth and other digital platforms.	
5	Ensure data quality through standardization and cleansing routines. Utilize algorithms to make data quality acceptable for clinical and business analytics.	
6	Utilize AI Analytics to support PHM and value-based care.	
7	Utilize AI Analytics to support *precision* or *personal* medicine.	
	Subtotal	
G.4	**Adopting AI Models**	**1–4**
	NOTE: HCOs should assign scores to the following objectives based on existing AI models or their understanding of those they may be considering.	
1	AI model training data is well-defined, reflects desired outcomes of the ML model, and avoids inherent biases.	

(*Continued*)

Table 14.7   (Continued)

	Assessment Questionnaire: Interoperability, Big Data, and AI Analytics (Refer to Chapter 9)	Score
2	AI model training data is de-identified and secured to protect the privacy and security of big data.	
3	AI models are designed in compliance with radiologist workflows to assess concurrent findings in a modality.	
4	AI models are available through EHR vendors, cloud vendors, and AI marketplaces. Selected models integrate with HCO EHRs and support provider workflows.	
5	Providers can determine the absence of bias and test AI model(s) for applicability to their patients.	
7	HCO uses FDA guidelines to determine whether CDS detects life-threatening diseases such as stroke or sepsis and generates an alert to notify a care provider. In this instance, the software is treated as a device and subject to FDA approval.	
8	HCO use FDA guidelines to determine whether CDS meets the four criteria to classify as a non-device. If it does, then ensure FDA guidelines (criteria 4) are followed for non-device software: • Plain language descriptions of the software purpose, medical input, underlying algorithm. • Patient-specific information and other knowns/unknowns for consideration.	
	Subtotal	

Security, Privacy, and Technical Considerations

Table 14.8 assesses important considerations related to successful DT efforts. It includes the following subcategories:

- H.1 – Cybersecurity Risk Management: Governmental Resources
- H.2 – Frameworks
- H.3 – Considerations for Cybersecurity Program
- H.4 – Cybersecurity Guidelines
- H.5 – Intrusion Detection
- H.6 – System Response
- H.7 – System Recovery
- H.8 – Ethical Privacy Program
- H.9 – Technical Considerations: Security and Privacy Controls

H.1 assesses HCO awareness of and use of governmental resources that offer cybersecurity advisement and assessment services.

H.2 assesses HCO awareness and use of cybersecurity frameworks. While understanding the structure and requirement of frameworks can be arduous, they are excellent resources for comprehensive and standards-driven cybersecurity compliance.

It is important to consider certain factors for cybersecurity. These considerations are assessed in H.3. Consider objective 3 in which the CISO should preferably *not* report to the CIO to design acceptable compromises. However, most HCOs design their organization structures for CISOs to report to CIOs since they are both "technical" roles. However, these roles have very important yet competing priorities. For example, security considerations that require changing passwords every three months become untenable for providers. This forces busy providers to "save" their passwords in public places for easy access. While frequently changing complex passwords is recommended best practice, implementation by providers may lead to increased cyber exposure. This and other factors that proactively prepare HCOs while balancing cybersecurity practices with system usability are covered in H.4.

H.5–H.7 assess HCO preparedness for detecting, responding, and recovering from cyber attacks. Employee training and compliance with established procedures to detect cyber intrusions efficiently and effectively is assessed in H.5. Once an intrusion has occurred, it is important to shut off sensitive areas as soon as possible. System detection and response functions are best implemented through continuous monitoring and automation. HCOs are well advised to look into SIEMs and MSSPs for protection. Finally, to ensure that cybercriminals who demand ransomware cannot withhold patient EHRs with effect, system backups and restores must be carefully configured, implemented, and continuously evaluated for integrity.

H.8 offers guidelines for implementing an ethical privacy program. These guidelines support privacy framework methodologies which consider the impact on patient privacy due to cyber breaches and operational decisions. For example, selling patient data to payers and marketers for monetary gain without a clear understanding of how data privacy will be handled by these entities.

H.9 assesses technical considerations for security and privacy controls. These considerations span the gamut of data documentation, storage, and transfer. In fact, well-designed technical considerations such as cloud services, VDI, and DaaS protect HCO networks improve user workflows and save costs. In addition, appropriately segmenting networks becomes an effective strategy to protect sensitive patient information from cyberattacks.

Table 14.8   Security, Privacy, and Technical Considerations

	Assessment Questionnaire: Security, Privacy, and Technical Considerations (Refer to Chapter 10)	Score
H.1	**Cybersecurity Risk Management: Governmental Resources**	**1–4**
1	Utilize services offered by the Cybersecurity & Infrastructure Security Agency (CISA) and AHA's Cybersecurity and Risk Advisory Services.	
2	Utilize governmental resources for impending cyberthreats and advancements in risk management strategies.	
3	Inform local FBI offices and CISA of cyberthreats or cyberattacks.	
	Subtotal	
H.2	**Frameworks**	**1–4**
1	Utilize cybersecurity framework that incorporates organizational risk management (e.g., NIST or HITRUST).	
2	Utilize a privacy framework that considers privacy breaches in relation to system, product, or service operations with data, in addition to cybersecurity. Data may exist in digital, paper, or voice format. (e.g., NIST)	
3	Obtain cybersecurity certification by utilizing Framework that incorporates a comprehensive risk management program. (e.g., HITRUST)	
	Subtotal	
H.3	**Considerations for Cybersecurity Program**	**1–4**
1	Integrate HCO cybersecurity risk management practices with the organizational risk management strategy.	
2	Design cybersecurity procedures that minimize user workflow "friction" and increase user compliance. It is important to reduce the impact on system usability due to security mandates.	
3	The CISO does not report to the CIO. This is advisable to avoid conflicts in system design and security. For example, while the CIO's goal is to improve system usability, the CISO's goal is to ensure system security even if it negatively impacts system usability.	
4	Utilize certified security personnel (in-house staff or external consultants) to design and establish the cybersecurity program.	
5	Manage third-party cybersecurity risk management preparedness through an ongoing review process.	

(Continued)

Table 14.8 (Continued)

	Assessment Questionnaire: Security, Privacy, and Technical Considerations (Refer to Chapter 10)	Score
6	Design cybersecurity risk strategy as a component of HCO risk management program.	
7	Purchase cyber insurance policy to protect HCO against liability, expenses, and loss of revenue.	
	Subtotal	
H.4	**Cybersecurity Guidelines**	**1–4**
1	Require strong passwords including automatic lockouts after three attempts.	
2	Require periodic change of passwords (PWs). Ensure that periodic PW changes do not increase PW exposures and sharing.	
3	Provide care givers proxy access to the patient portal.	
4	Enable MFA on systems that are vulnerable to cyberattacks or can compromise ePHI.	
5	Use VPN to send and receive emails to encrypt data in motion.	
6	Protect HCO through firewalls and anti-malware software that are kept up to date.	
7	Implement security patches that address known vulnerabilities in vendor application systems as soon as available. Refer to CISA for known exploited vulnerabilities.	
8	Implement controls outlined in CISA's guidance related to cloud services.	
9	Implement an annual cybersecurity training program that includes phishing emails and social engineering techniques used by hackers to trick users into undesirable actions. Training programs must include formal assessment of system users.	
10	Disable all nonessential ports and protocols across the HCO.	
	Subtotal	
H.5	**Intrusion Detection**	**1–4**
1	Implement an IDS by training cybersecurity IT experts to identify and assess unusual network behavior. Program IDS to generate alarms upon encountering a suspicious event.	

(*Continued*)

Table 14.8 (Continued)

	Assessment Questionnaire: Security, Privacy, and Technical Considerations (Refer to Chapter 10)	Score
2	Utilize Security Incident and Event Management (SIEM) systems which use advanced analytics on security logs, events, and data files to detect anomalies and threats.	
3	Utilize Managed Security Service Provider (MSSP) if HCOs do not possess in-house expertise. MSSP can provide firewall management, intrusion detection, VPN management, vulnerability scanning, and anti-malware services.	
	Subtotal	
H.6	**System Response**	**1–4**
1	Utilize automated IDS to shut off sensitive part of HCOs network upon detection of adverse events.	
2	Train IT staff to disconnect infected areas of the network for IDS that require a manual response.	
	Subtotal	
H.7	**System Recovery**	**1–4**
1	Backups are tested regularly to ensure integrity. They include data, application executables, and images of preconfigured OS and associated software applications.	
2	Backups employ a parallel hardware configuration and are kept in a separate offline location that can be linked back to the HCO. Cloud systems, preferably, are used for backups of patient data.	
3	Use a comprehensive business continuity plan that considers different severities of cyberattacks including system unavailability due to ransomware. Downtime procedures include test exercises to ensure that every member of the crisis response team understands their roles and responsibilities and backup communication systems.	
	Subtotal	
H.8	**Ethical Privacy Program**	**1–4**
1	Ensure compliance with Information Blocking requirements by providing access to USCDI and EHI.	
2	Utilize a Privacy Framework that incorporates controls to account for security and operational considerations related to patient privacy.	
3	Privacy Officer reports to the Board – Audit and Compliance Committee.	

(Continued)

Table 14.8 (Continued)

	Assessment Questionnaire: Security, Privacy, and Technical Considerations (Refer to Chapter 10)	Score
4	Ensure that collection of patient data is necessary but not excessive and follows HIPAA's 'minimum necessary' rule.	
5	Ensure that patient data retention follows policies defined by the healthcare entity and federal organizations.	
6	Ensure that the Notice of Privacy Practices is followed closely.	
7	Investigate breach of privacy complaints using pre-approved standards. Findings are reported to the Privacy Officer regardless of the responsible party.	
8	Report breach findings to the patient including privacy violations, resolution status (if found), or a statement that the complaint was unfounded.	
9	Empower employees to report their discovery regarding privacy violations.	
10	Implement a comprehensive audit program with proactive reviews of attempted or actual privacy violations. This may require integrating audit logs from multiple systems.	
11	Document how aggregate patient data is used and/or sold to third parties and for what purpose. Conduct audits to ensure data is being used as per the original agreement.	
12	Ensure the workforce is knowledgeable regarding HIPAA Privacy fundamentals and ethical privacy policies implemented by the HCO.	
	Subtotal	
H.9	**Technical Considerations: Security and Privacy Controls**	**1–4**
	NOTE: cloud providers and client devices.	
1	Utilize cloud for mission-critical applications • Public, private, or community cloud type.	
2	Utilize cloud computing for data aggregation and analytics • Public, private, or community, cloud type.	
3	IT assesses security preparedness of cloud providers by gaining access to tools and protocols used by cloud service providers.	
4	IT utilizes a combination of thick and thin clients to support a variety of applications. Data security is considered in these decisions.	

(Continued)

Table 14.8 (Continued)

	Assessment Questionnaire: Security, Privacy, and Technical Considerations (Refer to Chapter 10)	Score
5	IT utilizes desktop virtualization such as desktop as a service (DaaS) and virtual desktop infrastructure (VDI) to support thin client configurations.	
	NOTE: segmenting HCO network architecture.	1–4
6	Segregate IoT devices, client devices, databases, servers, and medical devices on different network segments. Network segmentation is based on importance of each device type and sensitivity of EHI stored.	
7	Restrict access to third parties since they may act as a gateway to mission-critical systems and ePHI data.	
8	Balance the needs of legitimate users with additional security layers to prevent cyberattacks.	
9	Constantly monitor network performance to close gaps or vulnerabilities in network infrastructure.	
10	Regularly audit and update network segments to accommodate new users and business needs.	
	Subtotal	

Work Transformation Assessment

Work Transformation Methodologies

Table 14.9 includes work transformation methodologies that include the following subcategories:

- I.1 – Triggers for LSS Projects
- I.2 – LSS Tools and Methodologies
- I.3 – Human Factors Engineering (HFE) Methodologies.

We consider work transformation as the "glue" that brings technologies and users together for effective digital health. In digital transformation, users include care providers and patients.

I.1 represents the various triggers in healthcare to initiate LSS projects. In order to score this subcategory, HCOs should consider the different rationale they have used for initiating LSS projects. A high subtotal indicates organizational awareness of LSS methodologies that work best to resolve different problems.

I.2 represents different LSS tools, techniques, and methodologies used by HCOs. In general, organizations that score well in I.1 should get an acceptable score in I.2. A key to implementing LSS tools is the DMAIC methodology, which is structured and data-centered. This methodology is effective for PI projects and is closely associated with agile principles. In addition, as objective 9 indicates, there are certain LSS tools that are used mainly as support for other tools. Therefore, if HCOs have used either of these tools for objective 9, they can score a 4/4.

I.3 represents HFE tools and techniques to design and implement systems. Healthcare is different from most industries in that workflows are not only different by care providers, but they also change with situations. Therefore, workflow design becomes challenging and is best accomplished using HFE tools and techniques.

DT results in distributed care models that comprise multi-disciplinary teams utilizing multiple modalities. This requires functional and information integration for care coordination which, in turn, is designed using UI design principles and design thinking to generate high usability and user experience. Design thinking is an iterative approach that uses rapid prototyping and agile methodologies. While these methods may be new for HCOs, they should research them to determine applicability to their digital health journey.

Table 14.9 Work Transformation Methods

	Assessment Questionnaire: Work Transformation Methods (Refer to Chapters 11, 12)	Score
I.1	**Triggers for Lean Six Sigma (LSS) Projects**	1–4
	NOTE: identify the projects that have been successfully completed. Projects are considered successful if they meet pre-determined benchmarks (refer to Chapter 11). Assign a score of 1–4 depending on project success.	
1	Improve turnaround time for IT to resolve issues called into the support desk.	
2	Reduce wait/idle time for patients.	
3	Eliminate wait/idle time and non-value-add tasks for clinical personnel.	
4	Improve utilization of diagnostic equipment.	
5	Minimize inventory – disposable supplies, instruments, equipment, and medications.	
6	Eliminate medication errors via alerts, notifications, rules, and clinical decision support.	
7	Decrease movement of patients, supplies, and equipment through process, spatial, and IT optimization.	
8	Improve EHR usability, for providers, and nurses.	
9	Improve usability of clinical and ancillary systems, for ancillary and allied health professionals.	
10	Improve usability of financial/administrative systems and operational processes, for financial and administrative personnel.	
11	Implement a new, or upgraded, HIS that impacts key areas of the HCO.	
	Subtotal	
I.2	**LSS Tools and Methodologies**	1–4
1	HCO utilizes LSS/DMAIC, a structured and data-centered methodology for PI efforts.	
	NOTE: HCO has experience with the following LSS tools to conduct projects of varying scope and complexity (refer to Chapter 12). Scores should reflect a working understanding of each tool.	
2	HCO uses process flowcharts.	

(Continued)

Table 14.9 (Continued)

	Assessment Questionnaire: Work Transformation Methods (Refer to Chapters 11, 12)	Score
3	HCO uses Value Stream Mapping (VSM).	
4	HCO uses Root Cause Analysis (RCA).	
5	HCO uses A3 thinking (based on Deming's PDCA principles).	
6	HCO uses Plan-Do-Check-Act (PDCA).	
7	HCO uses Kaizen Events (rapid improvement events).	
8	HCO uses Failure Mode and Effects Analysis (FMEA).	
9	HCO uses 5S, Poka Yoke, Kanban.	
	Subtotal	
I.3	**Human Factors Engineering (HFE) Methodologies**	**1–4**
	IT utilizes human factors engineering tools to optimize IT systems (refer to Chapter 8).	
1	IT emphasizes *User interface* (UI) design principles for EHRs and other IT systems.	
2	IT utilizes *Design Thinking*, to encourage rapid prototyping and agile methodologies.	
3	IT understands *User experience* (UX) design principles to optimize system usability.	
	Subtotal	

Developing a Change Management Culture

Table 14.10 assesses whether HCOs have cultivated a culture that effectively deals with functional disruptions. It is necessary to assess for this category prior to initiating DT efforts since they result in significant process disruptions which, if not handled appropriately by staff and management, will result in failure. This category consists of three subcategories:

- J.1 – Process Improvement Levels
- J.2 – Digital Transformation Levels
- J.3 – Transforming Organizational Culture

J.1 assesses HCO implementing successful PI efforts of different scope and complexity. Successful PI efforts must, over time, maintain integrity of revised processes, and desired outcomes. However, as HCOs discover, PI efforts are better classified as CPI (continuous process improvements) which require ongoing monitoring of metrics and continuous improvements. Without ongoing efforts, these systems revert to their original state, or worse. Prior to scoring these objectives, it is important for HCOs to reassess LSS projects to see if they are achieving desired outcomes – post-implementation. If not, then these projects cannot be considered successful.

It is important to assess the success of cross-functional PI efforts. It is recommended that HCOs conduct *cross-functional PI projects* of different scope and complexities. These projects are classified as *Low, Medium*, and *High* impact based on the scope and depth of process changes implemented and sustained.

J.2 assesses HCO efforts regarding DT projects. *HCOs that are assessing their readiness to initiate DT efforts may wish to remove this subcategory from their customized framework.* HCOs should employ a phased approach for digital health transitions. A pilot phase serves as proof of concept which can be expanded to develop the startup phase followed by growth and the mature phases. All phases should help to operationalize the HCO digital health vision.

J.3 assesses HCO preparedness to successfully transform organizational culture to participate in, and implement, sustainable process changes, and disruptions. The keys to successfully transform organizations are management commitment, involvement of functional users, quantifiable metrics that represent progress towards desired goals and objectives, and ongoing monitoring and improvement of redesigned efforts.

We end this chapter by offering a guide for HCO DT efforts. The following steps form a compendium of requirements for DT.

Table 14.10 Developing a Change Management Culture

	Assessment Questionnaire: Cultivating Culture of Change Management in HCOs (Refer to Chapter 11)	Score
J.1	**Process Improvement Levels**	1–4
	NOTE: This subcategory should be scored by HCOs that have implemented, or are considering implementing, PI initiatives.	
1	Conduct *functional PI projects* in individual departments to improve operational efficiency and effectiveness. Improvements in support department functions can impact the entire HCO. Post-implementation PI efforts must continue to sustain or improve project outcomes.	
	NOTE: Conduct *cross-functional PI projects* – of different scope and complexities. A majority of HCO processes fall under this category. These projects are classified as *Low, Medium,* and *High* impact based on the scope and depth of process changes implemented and sustained over time. PIs must be monitored for ongoing sustainability, or improvements, post-implementation.	
2	*Low-impact* cross-functional projects engage fewer departments in their joint operations – *for example, reduce patient wait times for scheduled ambulatory visits.*	
3	*Medium-impact* cross-functional projects engage several departments. The impact of these projects on organizational culture is defined by the scope and complexity of involved processes – *for example, consider the processes involved in patient TAT in ERs. These processes can include ancillaries, supply areas, patient transport, availability of consultants, and ER departmental operations.*	
4	*High-impact* cross-functional projects engage most clinical departments in HCOs that impact patient outcome, patient, and provider satisfaction. Successful completion of these projects will influence organizational culture to accept operational changes – *for example, consider the processes involved in the following scenario: patient arrives via ambulance at the ER, emergency surgery, admitted to an ICU, transferred to acute care unit, case management, and discharged including discharge instructions.*	
5	Conduct *organization-wide PIs* to optimize patient care services including direct care, indirect care, and support processes, offered by the HCO. Organization-wide PI efforts are effective in transitioning organizational culture towards change management. PIs must be monitored for ongoing sustainability, or improvements, post-implementation.	
	Subtotal	

(Continued)

Table 14.10   (Continued)

	Assessment Questionnaire: Cultivating Culture of Change Management in HCOs (Refer to Chapter 11)	Score
J.2	**Digital Transformation Phases**	1–4
	NOTE: This subcategory should be scored by HCOs that have implemented, or are considering implementing, DT. HCOs that are considering DT initiatives should score based on their understanding of phases and their alignment with business objectives.	
1	*Pilot Phase:* incorporates DT project(s) designed to address key operational problems and roadblocks that significantly impact patient care. Successful outcomes from pilot project(s) form the foundation for implementing a multi-phase digital transformation approach.	
2	*Startup Phase:* derived by expanding the pilot phase. The startup phase utilizes work transformation methods to embed advanced digital technologies in revised care models. This phase supports a transition towards value-based models, and digitally transform HCO care models using telehealth and supporting DHPs. This phase can be used to construct key service offerings for patients via a *digital front door.*	
3	*Growth Phase:* further operationalizes the HCO digital health strategy using technical and process complexities that integrate virtual, onsite, clinic, and home care. It supports a comprehensive transition to value-based models. DHPs selected in these efforts support data and functions APIs to encourage innovation in AI analytics, software, hardware, and services. This phase drives innovative service offerings for patients to form a comprehensive digital front door.	
4	*Mature Phase:* completes operationalization the HCO digital health strategy using technical and process complexities that integrate virtual, onsite, clinic, and home care. This phase continuously evolves the use of digital technology and enables the generation of innovative care models. In addition to supporting the HCO digital health goals and objectives, this phase standardizes digital offerings to support external entities.	
	Subtotal	
J.3	**Transforming Organizational Culture**	1–4
1	HCO Board of Directors and senior leadership actively support a culture of LSS efforts by engaging with rank-and-fine employees and managers who have undergone previous PIs.	

(Continued)

Table 14.10   (Continued)

	Assessment Questionnaire: Cultivating Culture of Change Management in HCOs (Refer to Chapter 11)	Score
2	Management at all levels supports LSS and ongoing PI efforts. It supports transparent user communication and ongoing outcomes measurement to monitor progress towards desired outcomes and develop remediation strategies.	
3	HCO PI and DT efforts rely on active involvement of functional users. Key users approve redesigned systems prior to implementation.	
4	HCO supports post-implementation review and continuous PI efforts.	
5	LSS/PI projects are metric driven to monitor progress towards desired outcomes which are driven by benchmarks. Metrics and outcomes are established prior to system analysis and design and include the following traits: (a) quantifiable, (b) ratio-based (e.g., output/time, patient satisfaction) (c) readily available data to generate metric results, (d) ongoing monitoring to measure progress.	
6	LSS tools and techniques are adapted to the complexities and variations in healthcare processes. Information systems are considered in the design and implementation of work transformation efforts.	
7	"Change Management" Culture: the HCO culture has adapted to process and functional disruptions resulting from work transformation efforts. Key components of change management are *management/IT commitment* and a *metrics-driven* culture.	
	Subtotal	

Steps for Digital Transformation

While culture, people, legacy, and technology (in-house systems and DHPs) are crucial to the DT of HCOs – successful transformation efforts are primarily dependent on the support of senior leadership.

Well-designed and implemented PI projects transform the HCO culture to effectively transition through process changes and disruptions. Therefore, HCO work transformation efforts should be evolutionary – conducted with increasing levels of complexity. As change levels become disruptive, HCOs should utilize "agile" techniques to permit users to design a prototype and test and iterate system change prior to implementation.

The assumption in this book has been that HCOs will utilize vendor-developed HIS, DHPs, and telehealth systems. The goal of these efforts should include an omnichannel patient experience that improves access and engagement. Most importantly, HCO leadership must understand best practices for managing the complexities generated as a result of work models that transcend physical care to virtual and at-home care while increasing reliance on automated systems to monitor, collect, and present patient data.

The order in which these steps are accomplished should be decided by HCOs.

1. Leadership, including the Board of Directors, senior executives, mid-level managers, and line managers, supports digital health and DT initiatives. This includes understanding and mitigating risks associated with such efforts.
2. Leadership attends training sessions on increasing patient access and engagement through hybrid configurations that meet the digital health vision.
3. Leadership participates in training sessions on DHPs that include telehealth platforms, CRM vendor partners, AI models, DTx, RPMs, and smart wearables that best meet their strategic vision. They must understand the strengths, weaknesses, and governance protocols of each DHP and how best to select, configure, and implement them.
4. Leadership creates a DT office (CDO) led by the CDTO (Chief DT Officer) with in-depth working knowledge of the HCO culture, hybrid care models, functional workflows, work transformation methodologies, and DHPs.
5. Leadership, through a digital transformation steering committee (DTSC), defines a comprehensive digital health strategy that documents future goals and objectives and incorporates advanced digital technologies. This document should include scope, complexity, and desired outcomes, including critical success factors (CSFs), and key performance indicators (KPIs) to achieve organizational goals and objectives.
6. DTSC (includes CDTO) conducts an HCO DT readiness assessment using the Assessment Framework offered in this chapter.
7. DTSC identifies interaction(s) that should be restructured (provision of patient care for the desired service is an interaction). Identify functions and work processes associated with these interaction(s). Identify barriers that limit the ability of interactions to be efficient and effective. Devise methods to remove or circumvent the barriers using digital systems.
8. DTSC supports pilot(s) to address key operational requirements and serve as proof of concepts. Expanding the scope of successfully

implemented pilot projects is a good way to transition HCOs to a broader scope of DT projects.

9. Leadership, IT department, employees, and physicians embrace a culture that strives for continuous PI. DT efforts should be attempted once HCOs have successfully implemented *high-impact PI efforts.*

10. Leadership, in conjunction with IT Management, creates a project team with the appropriate skills to manage and lead the DT effort. This should include representatives from the following areas: PMO, functional areas, legal guidance, LSS, IT, and HFE. Ensure that project leadership, and team, understands existing workflows, desired outcomes, and potential of digital technologies to disrupt existing care models.

11. Train project teams on DHPs and their workflow disruption potential using multi-disciplinary teams and care coordination in hybrid configuration using LSS and other PI methods. Project teams must understand the impact of potential DHP M&As on meeting the strategic vision of their HCO.

12. Implement DHPs based on strategic requirements and level of technical complexity. Ensure that these systems can meet the current and future needs of the HCO.

13. Generate metrics and best practice benchmarks. In DTs, monitoring performance around metrics is critical to determine if the transformation is working as planned. A note of caution: HCOs should be careful not to rely on metrics that incorporate high "noise factors" – essentially metrics that do not measure progress towards desired goals. A rule of thumb is to monitor five to seven metrics that can evaluate progress towards critical success factors.

14. Utilize project management techniques that work best for the transformation effort under consideration. For example, the agile framework should be considered for managing DT projects.

15. Evaluate the technological sophistication of the IT team to ensure they can assist with designing, developing, and implementing DHPs to meet desired project outcomes. The cybersecurity program should be able to manage decentralized systems including data sets.

16. Evaluate previous work transformation efforts (PIs or DTs) for areas of potential improvement. Adapt best practices from work transformation efforts in comparable organizations.

Epilogue

The healthcare system is highly fragmented with patient care provided by a myriad of hospitals, ambulatory clinics, labs, imaging centers, pharmacies, and practitioners. These businesses coordinate their contributions culminating in the care of patients. The coordination system has continued to evolve, from the pre-information system phase to the information system phase, and is transitioning to the AI-enabled digital health platform phase.

The pre-information system was paper-based and required manual intervention to coordinate fragmented services. Physician orders and documentation were written on paper and transmitted to ancillaries, pharmacies, and care providers either manually or via fax. Paper medical records were used in provider organizations to manage the care process and comply with regulatory and payer requirements.

The information system phase culminated in electronic health records that improved care coordination via interfaces and emails. This system also improved checks and balances on the patient record which became easier to access. On the other hand, providers continued to write paper orders that were entered into the information system by nurses, pharmacists, allied health professionals, and clerks. The HITECH meaningful use program incentivized healthcare providers to enter orders and documentation directly in EHRs. The physician order entry system was further enabled by vendor-developed clinical rules that leveraged electronic health information to reduce the probability of medication errors. While provider usability of computer systems remains a problem, this phase further enabled coordination among providers, payers, and regulators.

The health system is currently transitioning to the AI-enabled DHP phase. The technology enablers in this phase are further decentralizing EHI through nontraditional providers of care that service select parts of the care continuum and patients that use mobile health apps such as fitness devices for patient wellness and wearable devices for early diagnosis and treatment of diseases. The decentralized EHI generated during this phase results in large data sets that must be coordinated through interoperability, data aggregation, and analytics and leveraged by AI-enabled clinical decision support and intelligent EHRs.

AI-enabled devices will play an increasingly important role since they continuously monitor and improve patient treatment using machine learning models. Existing digital therapeutics and DHPs that utilize machine learning treatment models will become an essential part of chronic condition management for diseases such as COPD, asthma, diabetes, heart disease, and cancer. In these situations, provider intervention can be facilitated through alerts that lead to change in care. In addition, provider use of clinical decision support models to diagnose and recommend treatments will be mandatory.

To continue the transition to digital health, this phase must align patient health goals with reimbursement models that reorient the provision of care by healthcare entities. This is the reason US healthcare should transition to capitated value-based care models to incentivize population health management and patient engagement. In these care models, the goal of healthcare businesses will align with patient engagement and wellness efforts and keep them away from expensive treatments often diagnosed during later stages.

Finally, transitioning chronic disease management to home care models can significantly reduce the cost of care while improving patient outcomes and satisfaction. After all, there is no place like home.

Index

Printed in the United States
by Baker & Taylor Publisher Services